INCLUSIVE LEADERSHIP IN HIGHER EDUCATION

Inclusive Leadership in Higher Education examines leadership efforts that move beyond simple diversity programs in the journey toward the institutional transformation necessary to create inclusive educational environments. Chapter contributors from higher education institutions across the globe share how leadership is developed and implemented at all levels to create more inclusive organizational cultures. Diverse chapters address the forces and factors associated with organizational change while examining leadership theory, policy, and practices. This important volume provides a comparative perspective, highlighting common themes across a range of institutional and cultural contexts to help leaders promote an organizational mind-set and culture of inclusion and inclusiveness.

Lorraine Stefani is President of the International Higher Education Teaching and Learning Association (HETL) and Professor of Higher Education Strategic Engagement in the Faculty of Education and Social Work at the University of Auckland, New Zealand.

Patrick Blessinger is Chief Research Scientist for the International Higher Education Teaching and Learning Association (HETL) and Adjunct Associate Professor of Education at St John's University, USA.

INCLUSIVE LEADERSHIP IN HIGHER EDUCATION

International Perspectives and Approaches

Edited by Lorraine Stefani and Patrick Blessinger

Routledge
Taylor & Francis Group

NEW YORK AND LONDON

First published 2018
by Routledge
711 Third Avenue, New York, NY 10017

and by Routledge
2 Park Square, Milton Park, Abingdon, Oxon OX14 4RN

Routledge is an imprint of the Taylor & Francis Group, an informa business

© 2018 Taylor & Francis

Library of Congress Cataloging in Publication Data
A catalog record for this book has been requested

ISBN: 978-1-138-20143-9 (hbk)
ISBN: 978-1-138-20144-6 (pbk)
ISBN: 978-1-315-46609-5 (ebk)

Typeset in Bembo
by Taylor & Francis Books

CONTENTS

TABLES

FOREWORD

Leadership cannot just go along to get along. Leadership must meet the moral challenge of the day

Jesse Jackson

It has been very difficult to understand the rapid changes the world has been experiencing over the last couple of years in terms of stretching our political and social fabric to areas we would never have thought imaginable. We live in a time of uncertainty despite the incredible progress we've made in basic human rights for all, including what many in our modern societies believe is critical to a bright and prosperous future – the right to an education that is directed to the full development of the human personality and to the strengthening of respect for human rights and fundamental freedoms. It is within this context that Lorraine Stefani and Patrick Blessinger have brought together a diverse collection of relevant and timely research from leading scholars across the globe on a topic that is more important today than ever – inclusive leadership in higher education. After reading through the following chapters, I'm certain that I've found a definitive resource that encompasses much of the challenges and opportunities each and every institution of higher learning currently faces, and by the sign of our times, will face for a long time ahead.

This book is more than a collection of theories, research, and arguments for who should be leading our institutions of higher learning and the many reasons why this is critical to everyone's future throughout the world, even for those who may not value the benefits, both seen and unseen, of higher education towards a just and humane world. In many ways, the reader is asked to reflect on what it means to be a leader, what leadership means to the variety of constituencies that make up an organization or community, how leadership can be effective to the health and well-being of the individuals within and beyond, and what qualities make a great leader. But even more so, these chapters start a conversation about the meaning and significance for leadership that is inclusive, that represents diverse thinking and being, and how difficult it is to truly ensure that all voices are heard equally with respect and compassion. For institutions of higher learning, both public and private, do not function outside of the societies from which they reside, despite a tradition and nature of independence of thought and actions. Rather, as many would agree, higher education seeks to answer some of the world's most challenging issues while helping us to make sense of what it means to be human. And to do that, we must also challenge the notion that only individuals from a certain set of expectations, experiences, and background are entitled to lead, regardless of the level of authority or responsibility within the organization.

I believe that Stefani's and Blessinger's book is very timely for higher education overall as it seeks to articulate some of the most salient issues that leaders throughout these organizations are increasingly needing to address every day. Whether it is the curriculum that is being taught; the style and approach to teaching; both the traditionally prepared and the underserved/underrepresented student; the demographic of the faculty, staff, and administrators; or even the style, presence, or approach to working with others, today's higher education leaders have to be responsive to the needs of a diverse group of stakeholders in an environment where the cost of attendance and completion of a degree continues to grow beyond the reach of more and more people. And while for many years, these issues were never seriously considered because of traditional notions of what higher education should be, along with hierarchical and cultural biases, today's students, their parents, and their communities are much more open and demanding that higher education delivers on its promise of being a basic human right that ultimately helps these individuals, their families, and their communities grow and prosper.

I hope that the reader will find, just as I did, that the interrogation of the literature is extensive and refreshing. The chapter authors open our eyes to a variety of questions about what leadership has looked like traditionally, what is possible in terms of diversity and inclusiveness, and the challenges and opportunities higher education organizations and individuals face to become more broad-based and balanced. To start, we have to ask ourselves the following: What, exactly, do we mean by inclusive leadership? Why is it so critical to the sustainability of our higher education institutions? And does it make much difference when addressing our world's problems, let alone ensuring that our graduates (provided that our traditionally underrepresented students are retained) are able to find opportunities that reward them personally and professionally after they complete their education?

As the reader will soon discover, these chapters enable us to see leadership in a different light, taking us on a journey of what is possible. Stefani and Blessinger have chosen inclusive leaders, teachers, and researchers to write about their own experiences as well as those who have been able to rise through the ranks to serve in a variety of leadership positions throughout higher education. We can begin to understand those issues that are both unique to the sector and common to many organizations, and learn what qualities and competencies are desired by those leaders or potential leaders to be successful. What was most insightful to me, and contrary to what some leadership researchers insist is not much of a factor, is how important it is that local customs, cultures, and expectations of leadership influence who is supported, promoted, or viewed as effective. Inclusion is relative to place, time, and space. In an example from one of the chapters, it is pointed out that the emphasis for inclusion in North America is diversity, while in Western Europe and Asia, the focus is on women, and not on other minority groups. I can't help but think how the latter may change over time in Western Europe given the current refugee crisis and the freedom of movement within the borders of EU countries. It stands to reason based on social justice principles that significant populations of students will want to see more representation in their higher education faculty, staff, and administrators. In a chapter from South Africa, recent events demonstrate what can happen when those voices are not heard and addressed with genuine concern and sincerity.

One of the measures of a good book is whether it generates more questions than answers. I think that what the authors of each of these chapters have done is give us great beginnings from a global perspective on the kinds of dialogue that our higher education institutions must be having if they are to continue to respond appropriately and consciously to important issues. No longer can these organizations remain as ivory towers with silos that compartmentalize knowledge and actions that only the lucky few can access and experience. The authors force us to think big, to question who should be leading and for what reasons, and to consider seriously that the old manners in which individuals govern are outdated and out of touch with what is expected.

As recent political events throughout the world have shown, we are at a critical juncture in how people believe they should be led. Should we continue to look for leaders through a lens where only the few who have traditionally been chosen based on a narrow view of leadership are the only ones qualified? Or should we broaden the scope to consider other factors that are desired of our leaders, like bringing together and valuing a variety of perspectives and experiences that invariably lead to better and more collaborative decisions and actions? The notion that great leaders are ones who makes decisions on their own, that they alone are responsible for the success of all, is old and tired and unrealistic.

I believe that the chapters that Lorraine Stefani and Patrick Blessinger have gathered together here take us on a path forward that is hopeful, exciting, and insightful. Leadership is a journey, one that is best lived when including others, even those you may not agree with but who have earned your respect based on their commitment to the values that you hold dearly. To be an inclusive leader in higher education is to celebrate and inspire those we serve, to provide a teaching and learning environment that is welcoming and challenging, and to create a safe space to nurture the human spirit. No matter where you are on this leadership journey, the ideas and information provided here will serve you well as you find that path to overcome the moral challenges of our day.

Corey Gin
Director for the Leadership and Employee Enrichment Program (LEEP)
California State University, East Bay

ACKNOWLEDGMENTS

We would like to thank all of our colleagues who gave up their time willingly and unconditionally to contribute to this timely volume on the critical issue of inclusive leadership in higher education. Taken together, the chapters give us both a sense of hope that slowly but surely the issues of diversity and inclusion are being taken seriously around the world, and a sense of challenge that we are still on a journey to promote inclusion as a core value of higher education.

We would also like to give special thanks to Heather Jarrow (our Routledge editor) who gave so much time and encouragement to us during the early drafts of the book proposal right through to the publication of the book.

I would like to thank the Faculty of Education and Social Work at the University of Auckland for its contribution of time and funding for this important writing project.

I would also like to thank my partner Fran Devaney for her endless patience with my academic career.

Lorraine Stefani

PREFACE

The Urgent Matter of Inclusive Leadership in Higher Education

At the time this book was in preparation and authors from many different parts of the world were carrying out research and interrogating their own understandings of inclusive leadership, there was a great deal of turmoil in different parts of the world. In the USA, several universities were coping with demonstrations over racial injustice on campus, and the actions, or inactions, of college and university leaders were called into question (e.g., Jaschik, 2016). The US presidential campaign was under way. In South Africa, university protests which turned violent were taking place which, although ostensibly about prohibitively high tuition fees, actually had their roots in apartheid and colonialism (e.g., Hall, 2016). Issues of race, identity, fees and unemployment were provoking unrest across the world. Britain was showing its worst side with increased violence and xenophobia after the shock result of the Brexit referendum and the British government was suggesting clampdowns on international students coming to UK universities (e.g., Karabell, 2016). The Middle East was in a state of extreme turbulence with the shocking wars in Syria and the Yemen (e.g., Bew, 2015; Almasmari and Dewan, 2016).

Readers may ask what all of the above has to do with a book on inclusive leadership in higher education – is it not all a step removed? The answer to the question in essence sums up the reason for, and the need to offer, this book in the first place.

The US presidential election campaign of 2016 provided some shocking insights into how some people claiming the mantle of leader and leadership see fit to behave in what we are supposed to believe is the world's greatest democracy! The abuse that has been hurled at women, the disabled, the poor, Mexicans, Muslims, African-Americans, the parents of a soldier killed in Iraq who just happened to be Muslim, has known no bounds. We can argue that it is just politics but, if that is so, there can be little wonder there is such unease and unrest around the globe in this, the 21st century. What one of the candidates for the presidency, Donald J. Trump, showed the world is that many leaders in the United States of America condone and even encourage misogyny and sexism, racism, and other oppressive behaviors. Many thousands of people in the USA support Donald Trump, voted in as the next President of the USA on November 8, 2016, ostensibly because they are tired of the 'establishment' and feel left behind. Donald Trump told them what they wanted to hear. We can without doubt feel some empathy, or even sympathy, with the sentiments of those who are feeling left behind, the working poor, the disenfranchised, all suffering the effects of the appalling inequities occurring in rich countries (e.g., Arnade, 2016). However, what is much more difficult to comprehend is the weight of support for Donald Trump from Republican Party grandees, the Senators. Most of the Republican Party Senators are white, middle-class and overwhelmingly male. By standing by their man, these grandees of the Grand Old Party, as the Republican Party is known, essentially condoned the abuse and the discriminatory remarks. What this shows is just how far removed we are from the noble idea of inclusive societies.

If the constant negative rhetoric being reported about anyone who is 'not like us' in whatever geopolitical region or nation we care to observe is what current and potential university students are seeing and hearing all the time, what impression is it making on them? Is the seemingly acceptable abusive and discriminatory rhetoric we are hearing from all around us the new normal? Is this the conception of leadership our students will embrace? Are inclusion and inclusive leadership out-dated terms belonging to a narrative that never really got off the ground? Such a challenge being put before us from some of the world's self-proclaimed great democracies creates an urgency not to lose the narrative of inclusion and inclusive leadership but to strengthen it through example and education. Higher education must encompass critical thinking, emotional intelligence and cultural awareness, and indeed be an instrument for progress towards social equity. It is a place and a space to strengthen both the narrative and the actuality of inclusion and inclusive leadership. In these troubled times renewed focus on inclusion, leadership and higher education is critical and hence the *raison d'être* for this book. The chapter authors who contributed to this book were chosen, not only for their scholarly reputations and contributions, but also for their commitment and standing within their own communities of practice regarding their significant efforts to be role models of inclusive leadership in higher education.

A Brief Overview of Chapters

In chapter 1 the editors examine the current landscape of higher education with respect to diversity, inclusion and human rights for education. They also provide extensive insights into the concepts of inclusion and leadership and the multiple adjectives that are in vogue to describe leadership; terms such as 'authentic', 'servant', and 'transformational'. The intention of the chapter is to introduce much of the terminology that comes through the following chapters and to set the scene for the wide range of interpretations and nuances of the key terms of reference of the book. The chapter ends with a plea for educators to make inclusive leadership a core value of our universities.

Three chapters address the issue of women in leadership in very different ways. Gender politics in higher education is perhaps the most widely researched aspect of inclusion. While clearly there have been changes over the decades and we now see the gender balance shifting at professorial level, the figures we can gather still show appalling levels of imbalance. It is heartening therefore to lead this trio of chapters with an optimistic narrative from Cathy Sandeen and colleagues (chapter 2) providing insights into how a highly diverse group of women developed their leadership skills, how they supported and promoted inclusion and inclusive environments as a matter of course – not as an add-on to their individual roles as college and university presidents, but as part of normal practice. It is highly apt that they include in the title 'women making a difference'.

We see the other side of the coin of this positive narrative in Hayes Tang's interrogation of the literature relating to women in leadership in universities in East Asian countries (chapter 3). Clearly there has been little focus on the idea of inclusive leadership in East Asian countries such as the People's Republic of China, Japan, Hong Kong, South Korea and Taiwan, and certainly little or no attempt to break down the 'old boys' network' culture and the societal expectation that women's role is taking care of the family. Hayes Tang ends his chapter by suggesting a more humanistic approach to recruitment, retention and reward for a more powerful and healthier development of East Asia's intellectual capital within the academic professions.

In chapter 4, Kirsten Locke not only provides us with a comprehensive introduction to the concept of intersectionality, she also gives extensive insights into research on inclusive leadership using intersectionality as the paradigm. She does this by means of a case study approach, exploring the experiences of three women in leadership positions in a Danish university and examining the barriers women experience in attaining formal named leadership positions. Locke also argues for an extension of the scope of intersectionality to include the particular aspects of organizational culture that create additional barriers for women entering into leadership roles. Interestingly, while Locke essentially dissects the concept of intersectionality for the reader, four other chapter authors touch on this paradigm: Cathy Sandeen and colleagues (chapter 2), Eqbal Darandari (chapter 7), Enakshi Sengupta (chapter 8) and Santamaría and Santamaría (chapter 11). With the overall increase in recognition of its potency as a significant paradigm and four different chapter authors either giving a full explanation or touching on its importance in terms of researching leadership, intersectionality emerges in this book as a key to further researching the idea of inclusion and inclusive leadership.

In her chapter Cathy Gunn (chapter 5) takes us on a different journey, that of building a culture of distributed/distributive leadership. Gunn reminds us that the university is a highly complex organization and that leadership within such complexity is a collective capacity. This immediately takes us away from that well-worn path of the 'heroic leader' narrative and into a context that in itself allows for the development of a much more inclusive approach to building leadership capability and capacity. Using teaching and learning as the vehicle for action learning, Cathy provides three case studies of inclusive leadership projects intended to engender a culture and ethos of inclusive leadership. The positive argument for distributed leadership is that many more people from across a department, faculty or institution can, and do, take on leadership roles and responsibilities for different aspects of academia. The mission critical issue is that development and support are promoted and provided to enable individuals to understand the meaning of leadership and being a leader.

This latter point is affirmed by Fiona Denney in her chapter on inclusive leadership in UK universities (chapter 6). Denney describes a project she led, funded by the Leadership Foundation for Higher Education, whereby eighteen academics from five different universities were interviewed and asked probing questions about their experience as leaders. What Denney found through this research was that preparation for leadership in many universities is entirely inadequate for the challenging roles many are expected to take on. This chapter dovetails with that of Cathy Gunn because of the issue of preparing people for leadership roles. Promoting and supporting distributed/distributive leadership emerges as potentially a significant enabler in building inclusive leadership cultures in higher education – but only if attention is paid to preparing academic staff in a meaningful way to take on leadership roles.

Another interesting issue that Fiona Denney raises in her chapter is that of the set of inclusive leadership competencies drawn up by the UK Employers Network for Equality and Inclusion. ENEI commissioned a report entitled *Inclusive Leadership... driving performance through diversity!* (Bucks New University, & ENEI, 2016). The competencies essential to inclusive leadership include: individual consideration (showing respect for all); inspirational motivation (being encouraging and uplifting); intellectual stimulation (providing appropriate challenges); unqualified acceptance (diversity and inclusion); empathy, listening and persuasion. The full complement is presented in the chapter. Eqbal Darandari from King Saud University in Saudi Arabia also cites the work of ENEI and in her chapter she provides insights into the ways in which working environments can be measured for inclusion and how leaders can be appraised for their inclusiveness using tools such as those provided by ENEI.

In the minds of some, Saudi Arabia would not necessarily be a country we would look to and hope to find an inclusive ethos in higher education. However, Eqbal Darandari (chapter 7) gives us an interesting insight into the range of interventions made at King Saud University to support inclusive leadership. She makes the case strongly that the idea of inclusion is not only context-dependent but also time-, space- and place-dependent. Saudi Arabia has undergone many changes especially regarding the workforce. It is not so long ago that key positions in universities and in industries were held by non-Saudis but, over the years, there have been strenuous efforts to build capacity within the Saudi population itself. The figures Darandari provides on the gender balance relating to staff and students in higher education are also interesting. Using King Saud University, the top-performing university in Saudi Arabia, as a case study, she provides an honest overview of the 'tough waves' that have been, and are still being, navigated to promote and support inclusive leadership in a challenging conservative environment.

In chapter 8, Enakshi Sengupta introduces us to unexplored territory regarding inclusion and inclusive leadership. The universities from which she has drawn case studies of inclusive leadership are the American Universities of Central Asia, Kurdistan and Iraq, Sulaimani. Most readers will know of these regions primarily because of the past and current wars and geo-political conflicts. We do not often think about the challenges faced by universities in these regions. As Eqbal Darandari opines in chapter 7, context, time, space and place are critical factors when we consider inclusion and inclusive leadership. In addition to the issues of leadership in the three universities in Sengupta's chapter, she writes eloquently about the issue of 'exceptionality'. Some students attending the universities she is writing about have disabilities, are orphaned as a consequence of wars or are the children of martyrs of the wars. Special funding and scholarships are available for many of these students. However, as is the case in many different situations and scenarios, there are people who feel that greater privileges are afforded to students from challenging circumstances. We might consider this to be a zero sum game mentality – when some people gain, others must lose. It is situations like this that make the idea of inclusive leadership difficult to theorize. The world is complex and complicated and becoming more so in the 21st century.

We are taken into different territory again through chapters 9 and 10 from Brenda Leibowitz and Mandla Makhanya respectively. When this book was conceived, it would not have been possible to predict the level of outrage that has erupted into violent protest at universities in South Africa. A theme which comes through in these chapters, which are very different from one another, is that the wounds of the apartheid era in South Africa are still very raw and true healing is a long way off. In her chapter, Brenda Leibowitz from the University of Johannesburg, one of the universities that has faced terrifying riots as seen by outsiders, makes a truly humbling point when she asks the question: 'What can South Africa teach the world in regard to inclusive leadership?' Reading her chapter and that of Mandla Makhanya we are reminded that it is only just over two decades since the apartheid era ended and Nelson Mandela became the leader of the nation after the multi-racial democratic elections of 1994 (Waldmeir, 1998). Some of the students currently rioting did not live through the apartheid years yet they see themselves being subjected to non-inclusive curricula and being differentiated along racial and socio-economic lines. An interesting comment from one of Leibowitz's interviewees is that "an inclusive university is not an autonomous entity but an institution that can be owned and perceived as relevant to the wider community" and one feels that this must be recognized and understood in order to keep moving forward towards a united country and a more inclusive society. Brenda and her interviewees also consider inclusion and inclusive leadership to be relational and that past and future, space and place need to be given full consideration before generalities about inclusive leadership can possibly be made.

Mandla Makhanya (chapter 10) brings in another dimension when he writes about 'decoloniality' as a key driver in the current unrest. Mandla gives us a contextual overview of the university of which he is the current Vice-Chancellor, Unisa, the University of South Africa which is described as a "mega open and distance learning institution". Mandla sees the unrest, which has spread widely, as being the result of frustration amongst the student population regarding their sense of belonging in higher education due to the slow pace of transforming and decolonizing the higher education learning spaces and places. Mandla also presents a series of initiatives that he and his team have implemented to support this much needed transformation. He likens the idea of inclusive leadership to servant leadership (Greenleaf, 1977). As with his colleague Brenda Leibowitz, Mandla Makhanya in his authenticity humbles the reader.

In a further push to widen the scope of our understandings of inclusion and inclusive leadership, Santamaría and Santamaría examine the idea of culturally sustaining leadership. In a first in this book, Lorri and Andrés Santamaría (chapter 11) bring in the issue of the Lesbian, Gay, Bisexual, Transgender, Queer, Questioning and Intersex (LGBTQI) community and leadership. Drawing on their own extensive research which they have carried out on the topic of culturally sustaining leadership, Santamaría and Santamaría argue that it takes grit and gravitas to examine our practices in all aspects of academia and to identify our own potential prejudices regarding the diversity with which we must all engage in the wider society and in higher education. They argue persuasively that this is a moral imperative toward social justice in the face of inequity. What is interesting are the subtleties within their text which hint at the inequities the authors themselves have faced and continue to face in their careers.

In the penultimate chapter (chapter 12), John Anchan provides a poignant reminder in an echo of a comment made by Brenda Leibowitz (chapter 9) that a university is not an autonomous space, rather it is an entity that should be fully engaged with the community of which it is part. Anchan is paying particular attention to the injustices of the past directed towards the indigenous community of a particular region in Canada. Anchan argues that inclusive leadership is not something we add on as an extra, but that it is a mindset that must pervade the entire institution and that members of the local community should not be seen as 'apart' from the university, but rather that their views, their input, their engagement and their leadership is a privilege for the university and enriches the student and staff experience.

Concluding Comments

At the beginning of the journey to publish this book, the editors believed it could be possible to offer a theory of inclusive leadership. The breadth and depth of the chapters proved us wrong. The scope of inclusion and inclusive leadership would appear to mitigate against the imposition of a theory intended to fit all interpretations of the term. However, some critical points arise that provide pathways forward in our research and practice as leaders in higher education:

- Intersectionality as a research paradigm would take us beyond the 'norm' in the current research and literature on leadership which has tended to be based on the experience and understanding of predominantly white, middle-class Americans.
- In complex organizations such as universities and other institutions of higher education, leadership needs to be interpreted in terms of collective capacity – achieved through meaningful distributed leadership. This offers a platform for the development of a culture of inclusive leadership.
- There needs to be adequate preparation for leadership, whatever the level of responsibility, as opposed to assumptions being made regarding skills not necessarily related to leadership.
- There are tools that offer the potential to measure the inclusivity of organizations and well-defined characteristics we may seek in future leaders.
- Inclusion and inclusive leadership are relational, context-, time-, space- and place-dependent, and we must also consider past history and future aspirations when we consider the interpretation of the terms.

The final chapter of the book revisits the terms of reference in the light of the chapters received from international scholars and poses the question: Where to from here? Despite the many encouraging and heartening chapters in this book, we also see how far we still have to travel before we can truly proclaim higher education to be a place of inclusive leadership. We hope this book provides encouragement and inspiration for everyone concerned with inclusive leadership in higher education.

References

Almasmari, H. and Dewan, A., 2016. Yemen: The 'forgotten war' cloaked in the shadow of Syria. *CNN News*, October 6, 2016. Available at: <http://edition.cnn.com/2016/10/06/middleeast/yemen-conflict/> [Accessed October 25, 2016].

Arnade, C., 2016. What do Donald Trump supporters really want? Respect. *The Guardian*, July 30, 2016. Available at: <https://www.theguardian.com/us-news/2016/jul/30/what-do-donald-trump-voters-want-respect> [Accessed October 25, 2016].

Bew, J., 2015. The Syrian tragedy and the crumbling world order. *New Statesman*, [online] September 15, 2015. Available at: <http://www.newstatesman.com/world/middle-east/2015/09/syrian-tragedy-and-crumbling-world-order> [Accessed October 25, 2016].

Bucks New University, & ENEI, (2016). *Inclusive Leadership...driving performance through diversity!* Retrieved from https://www.cipd.co.uk/binaries/inclusive-leadership_2016-driving-performance-through-diversity.pdf [Accessed 12 June 2017].

Greenleaf, R.K., 1977. *Servant leadership: A journey into the nature of legitimate power and greatness.* New Jersey, USA: Paulist Press.

Hall, M., 2016. South Africa's student protests have lessons for all universities. *The Guardian*, 3 March, 2016. Available at: <https://www.theguardian.com/higher-education-network/2016/mar/03/south-africas-student-protests-have-lessons-for-all-universities>   [Accessed October 25, 2016].

Jaschik, S., 2016. Epidemic of racist incidents. *Inside Higher Education*, 26 September, 2016. Available at: <https://www.insidehighered.com/news/2016/09/26/campuses-see-flurry-racist-incidents-and-protests-against-racism> [Accessed October 25, 2016].

Karabell, S., 2016. Brexit: How xenophobia has hijacked the UK. *Forbes: Leadership*, February 21, 2016. Available at: <http://www.forbes.com/sites/shelliekarabell/2016/02/21/brexit-how-xenophobia-has-hijacked-the-uk/#2560715d7e8e> [Accessed October 25, 2016].

Waldmeir, P., (1998) *The anatomy of a miracle – The end of apartheid and the birth of new South Africa.* USA and London: Rutgers University Press.

1

INCLUSIVE LEADERSHIP IN HIGHER EDUCATION

Inclusion as a Core Institutional Value

Patrick Blessinger and Lorraine Stefani

Introduction

Although much has been written on the topics of diversity, inclusion, leadership, and higher education, there remains a dearth of literature on the intersection of these topics. A central aim of this chapter is to explore how education leaders can use leadership to create an organizational culture and mindset that respects and values all forms of diversity and identities, and that helps prepare administrators, faculty, and students to live and work in an increasingly pluralistic and globalized world.

To address these issues, the current higher education landscape is examined with respect to diversity, inclusion, and human rights for education. The chapter also focuses on the fundamental purpose and aims of leadership and how leadership can be developed at all levels within higher education institutions to create more inclusive organizational cultures. The forces and factors (e.g., exogenous and endogenous forces, planned and reactive, incremental and transformative) associated with organizational change from a leadership perspective will be touched on briefly.

The analysis presented in this chapter is indebted to the work of the following educational scholars: Altbach, Reisberg, & Rumbley, 2009; Barnett, 2012; Basit & Tomlinson, 2014; Beiter, 2006; Beitz, 2009; Blessinger & Anchan, 2015; Brighthouse & McAvoy, 2009; Burke, 2012; Curren, 2009; de Wit, 2013; Dewey, 1916; Freire, 1970; Karmel, 2009; Kezar, 2009; Kovbasyuk & Blessinger, 2013; Marginson & Sawir, 2011; McCowan, 2013; McMillan, 2010; Noddings, 2013; Palfreyman & Tapper, 2009; Smith, 2014; Trow, 1974; Vygotsky, 1989; and Woods, 2011.

The Need for Inclusive Leadership

The argument presented in this chapter is that creating an inclusive higher education community is an essential ingredient in helping to achieve social equality and is an important element of meaningful lifelong learning. A chief aim of inclusion is to eliminate negative attitudes and beliefs associated with race, ethnicity, sex, gender, sexual orientation, lifestyle, socio-economic class, age, language, religion, disability, and their intersections, since these identities are not mutually exclusive of each other. Also, identities may be visible or invisible and the interrelationships among the different identities may manifest themselves in unforeseen ways. This intersectionality of identities is often multi-layered and complex. For instance, people may belong to different groups and may experience both prejudice and privilege at the same time (Cole, 2009; Smith, 2014; Symington, 2004).

Negative attitudes relating to difference may be the result of hegemony, elitism, supremacism, or any attitude that privileges one group over another. For instance, these attitudes may be reflected in curricula that are solely centered on authors that are all from the same ethnicity or gender. The premise of this chapter is that it takes effective leadership at all levels to change policies and practices needed to create a more inclusive organizational culture and mindset that reflects both the reality of multiple identities and the increasing levels of diversity in society

Current Higher Education Leadership Models

The interest in leadership goes back thousands of years because of its usefulness and application in every sphere of life (e.g., political, military, business, religious, educational) (McCaffery, 2004). The formal study of leadership is not a new phenomenon either. Research on leadership has evolved from the trait approach to leadership in the 1800s to modern theories and styles of leadership which include, among others, the following: authentic leadership, contingency leadership, consensus leadership, democratic leadership, distributive leadership, intellectual leadership, moral leadership, servant leadership, transformational leadership, and values-based leadership. The multiple theories and styles may also be categorized using different criteria (e.g., trait, behavior, contingency, power) (Amanchukwu, Stanley, & Ololube, 2015). The general trend in leadership research and theory development has been towards an interdisciplinary approach to better understand leadership from multiple perspectives and disciplinary lenses.

Despite its long history and the many theories and styles on leadership, there is no single universally accepted definition of leadership (Mello, 1999). However, the common theme running through leadership theories and styles is the ability to influence others. Thus, the following definition of leadership is used: *leadership is the ability to influence others to achieve a goal* (Northouse, 2007). This definition implies several important aspects of leadership: 1) leadership is influence oriented *(ability to influence)* – leader actions and decisions enable the group to act; 2) leadership is relationship oriented *(others)* – it is a social relationship between leader and followers; and 3) leadership is future oriented *(to achieve a goal)* – it focuses on the group reaching a goal(s).

Using this definition, leadership is based on the following assumptions: 1) leadership can be learned and developed over time; 2) leadership can be employed using different styles of leadership together with different decision-making styles; 3) various contextual factors (e.g., political, economic, socio-cultural, nature of goals sought, and the type, size, mission, etc. of the organization) influence the type(s) of leadership used; and 4) various factors influence the quality and effectiveness of the leader (e.g., position within organizational structure, communication with followers, interactions among different personalities, decision-making styles) (Amanchukwu, Stanley, & Ololube, 2015).

In addition, Kouzes and Posner (2012) find the following practices to exist in effective leaders: 1) they model the way; 2) they inspire a shared vision; 3) they challenge the process; 4) they enable others to act; and 5) they encourage the heart. Regardless of the factors involved, leadership effectiveness is ultimately judged on the effectiveness of the leader in working with and through others to achieve the goal(s).

Thus, common themes that characterize effective leaders include: being future oriented (i.e., leaders inspire a shared vision), enabling others to act (i.e., leaders establish the direction and lead the way), and being trustworthy and credible (i.e., leaders operate ethically and with integrity). These characteristics are also indicative of a transformational orientation to leadership. A study by Bateh and Heyliger (2014), found that a transformational leadership style led to increased job satisfaction among faculty whereas a passive/avoidant leadership style led to decreased job satisfaction among faculty. One important aspect of transformational leadership is its focus on continually improving the quality of the relationship between leaders and followers and fostering self-realization in their followers (Bass and Riggio, 2006; Li & Hung, 2009).

Challenges of Traditional Leadership Models

The inclusion agenda naturally involves leadership because inclusion impacts every aspect of the institution and requires leadership at all levels in order to make it successful. Educational leadership can be an effective means to create a more inclusive institutional culture at all levels of the organization. It is important educational leaders examine the different conceptions of leadership (as discussed in the previous section) that may be useful in highly distributed organizations like higher education institutions.

Given the nature of higher education institutions and the particular challenge of making inclusion a high priority, inclusive leadership is grounded in the following leadership styles: democratic leadership, distributive leadership, and transformational leadership.

Democratic leadership focuses on meeting the needs and interests of the group through shared decision-making and participation. It emphasizes the principles of equity, equality, and inclusion. Democratic leadership can create highly productive work groups and as a leadership approach it fits well with an organization comprising a highly skilled, professional, and autonomous workforce (Martindale, 2011).

Distributive leadership is suitable for complex institutions (e.g., universities, hospitals, research facilities) where the tasks performed involve people from different functions and levels within the institutions. It emphasizes the principles of community, collaboration, and collective action. Distributed leadership can create highly productive work groups with high morale because it views leadership as a social process that is shared by both leaders and followers. As with the similar democratic leadership, it tends to work better in work groups that are highly skilled, professional, and autonomous (Spillane & Diamond, 2007).

Transformational leadership is aimed at creating positive change in individuals, groups, institutions, and other social settings. It emphasizes the principles of change, empowerment, and community. Transformational leadership is intended to increase capacity and capabilities at all levels. It tends to work better in organizations that are mature, structured, and professionalized. To create effective change, transformational leaders must create a high degree of respect and rapport with followers, be a model of integrity and moral leadership, and create a shared sense of belonging through an inspiring vision. Transformational leaders inspire followers to see beyond their own self-interests in order to work for the greater good (Bass, 1990).

Higher education institutions that operate within democratic societies have a responsibility to uphold basic democratic principles and human rights. Since inclusion is a basic democratic principle and education is a human right, then leadership that is oriented around these features provides a promising approach to leadership within higher education institutions, especially given the distributed nature of leadership in such institutions. An inclusive theory of leadership holds that **inclusive leadership** as a leadership style, with its emphasis on participation, community, empowerment, and respect for different identities, can provide an effective way to build an inclusive university culture.

Diversity and Inclusion in Higher Education

The concept of diversity is grounded in the premise that having diversity in a workplace or any group provides positive benefits overall since it has the potential to draw on different strengths, viewpoints, talents, etc. Inclusion is based on the principle of equal and equitable treatment for all which is a matter of social justice. Equal opportunity laws seek to ensure that no student is disadvantaged with regards to access to higher education. As such, inclusion agendas seek to protect basic human rights and, more specifically regarding higher education, they seek to create student populations that are more socially representative by increasing access opportunities from all segments of society. Diversity and inclusion are complementary and they reinforce each other. In short, *inclusion is a set of practices that help create more diverse environments.*

Moving beyond Access

While much progress has been made over the last several decades in this area, more work still remains to move beyond widening participation programs (albeit very important) and move towards creating more inclusive institutions in every aspect and at every level in higher education. For instance, an institution may be highly diverse in terms of student demographics but it may not be diverse in terms of its faculty, staff, and leadership. In addition, it may not be diverse in terms of its curriculum or its teaching and learning methods. Diversity must be defined by more than demographics, albeit student access for historically underrepresented groups is a natural starting point. Democratization of higher education has initially and naturally centered on access issues (that is, more equality or equity of access opportunities) and participation issues (that is, greater engagement in the teaching–learning process). Issues receiving less focus, until recently, have been completion issues, that is, students achieving expected learning outcomes upon graduation and life success issues such as achieving career and personal goals. In addition to these critical issues that apply to the student body, diversity and inclusion must also address other groups such as faculty, staff, and leadership as well as teaching, learning, curricula, research, and community engagement issues.

In addition to creating more diverse institutions that are representative of the broader society and the communities they are embedded in, institutions should also be actively engaged in creating and sustaining inclusive practices that respect and engage different identities and viewpoints (related to race, ethnicity, sex, gender, sexual orientation, socio-economic class, caste, age, language, religion, disability, and their intersections) in its teaching, learning, curricula, etc. Without inclusion, one can be part of the student or faculty body but one may still feel marginalized or excluded. Inclusion moves beyond what the law requires to create a more humane approach to education where all identities and viewpoints are respected and embraced, not just tolerated. Since complexities and tensions can arise around environments with multiple identities, the strategies needed to create more inclusive and pluralistic learning communities need more discussion at all levels (Smith, 2014, 2009; Chin & Sanchez-Hucles, 2007; Gutman, 2003; Maher & Tetrault, 2007).

A growing number of higher education institutions now seek to move beyond relatively simple widening access programs and move towards more multifaceted approaches of integrating inclusion into all aspects of the educational experience. For instance, this could involve creating a learning environment that better enables all students and faculty to develop more fully, not just cognitively but also socially, psychologically, and professionally. Ultimately, issues dealing with diversity, inclusion, identity, power, justice, rights, and agency are deeply connected to the strength, health, and longevity of a democratic society, and as such, inclusion is a major imperative for educational leaders.

Exemplars

A concrete example of this movement is the UK Higher Education Academy (HEA) program (Wray, 2013) that aims to develop a more inclusive culture in higher education. HEA defines an inclusive teaching and learning culture as one that "enables all students to develop academically, professionally and personally to fulfill their potential." In addition to the HEA report, a good overview of the issues introduced above is presented by Blessinger & Anchan (2015), Smith (2014), Basit & Tomlinson (2014), Woods (2011), and Burke (2012) among others.

The HEA report discusses the following practices by some UK higher education institutions which, although not specifically highlighting leadership in higher education, will nevertheless require effective leadership across the institution if successful implementation is to be achieved:

- University of Edinburgh: The aim is the design and delivery of curricula that are inclusive of all students, enabling them to participate fully to achieve their full potential.
- University of Exeter: It is only through engagement with an inclusive learning and teaching environment that such a culture can develop.
- University of the West of Scotland: The project had three broad aims: 1) to embed the vision for an inclusive culture into the new University of the West of Scotland's (UWS) learning, teaching, and assessment strategy; 2) to explore the gap between existing UWS policy/strategy in inclusion and current practices; and 3) to identify ways to bridge this gap.

The diverse chapters in this volume offer a range of approaches being taken towards embedding inclusion into universities. Many of them also highlight the challenges of doing so.

The Inclusive University

Inclusion in higher education moves beyond celebrating diversity and towards the integration of inclusion into all policies, structures, and activities associated with the educational experience. Ideally, inclusion involves developing an inclusive culture and mindset that is reflected in the institution's mission, vision, and shared values statements (Meacham & Barrett, 2003). This inclusive mindset is then diffused throughout the institution and infused within the teaching–learning process, the research process, and through institutional–community engagement and partnerships. It involves honoring individual and group identities with those identities reflected in the overall institutional identity. This type of university can be aptly described as the inclusive university.

The nature of democratic societies puts them in a position to move away from a closed and exclusivist higher education paradigm based on power and privilege claims and towards an open and inclusive paradigm based on rights and justice claims. Democratically oriented societies have been gradually moving away from exclusivist higher education systems and towards more inclusive higher education systems. This represents a major paradigm shift which is reflected in the more diverse student populations we are seeing in many countries. The clearest evidence of this shift is the huge increase in demand for higher education around the world. Given the fact that inclusive practices are more in alignment with democratic principles, it is no surprise that this shift is occurring to a greater extent in democratic societies (Blessinger & Anchan, 2015).

Exclusivity is characterized by power and privilege claims and is most commonly exemplified as a closed system whereas inclusivity is characterized by the needs of society and the individual, by democratic ideals, and by diversity in all its forms. Inclusivity therefore seeks to remove unnecessary and arbitrary barriers to entry (i.e., creating an open system). It is within this context that this chapter seeks to examine and better understand how inclusive leadership can be used to create more inclusive institutions.

The Changing Higher Education Landscape

In recent history, higher education has been experiencing tremendous growth worldwide. The increased demand for educational services has brought with it the imperative for change in order to respond to the needs of new students, faculty, and other stakeholders. This section describes the major factors driving this demand. Hence, change is, by and large, an adaptive process to the changing environment of the higher education landscape.

Pressure for Change

The increasing focus on diversity and inclusion in higher education has been driven, to a large degree, by multiple factors such as increased pluralism, transnational immigration flows and globalization, internationalization of higher education, calls to remedy past discrimination and oppression against disenfranchised and minority groups, and the accompanying appreciation for and sensitivity to human rights and democratic principles. When the negative impacts of social problems are high, people are more compelled to act in ways at both the individual and social levels that bring about resolution to the problems.

Because of these and other factors, diversity and inclusion in higher education have evolved over the last several generations as a result of both bottom-up social movements (e.g., human rights movements, women's rights movements, indigenous rights movements) and top-down political actions (e.g., United Nations Human Rights Declaration, United States Civil Rights Act). In response to the pressures for change and to the view of many that education is uniquely positioned to solve a significant number of society's problems, the missions of educational institutions have, by and large, evolved to take on a growing set of responsibilities. Within this context, higher education can now be viewed as a multi-purpose enterprise that is the result of political, social, and economic macro factors as well as personal, group, and institutional micro factors.

The ultimate aim of these bottom-up and top-down efforts is to create a more fair and just society. Although these trends have been occurring worldwide, they tend to be most noticeable in highly pluralistic countries such as the United States and Canada, many countries across Europe, other OECD countries and democratic nations. The more pluralistic or democratic a country, the greater the demand for equal and equitable treatment for all groups, especially minority groups who may feel that their needs and concerns have not been fully met.

Institutional Inertia

However, pressure to change is often met with organizational inertia which can result in a slow pace of change. Inertia is defined as *resistance to change*, whether intentional or unintentional, and it is an inherent feature of all institutions due to their stable structures. Thus, within any institution, there is a built-in tension between adaptation and stability (i.e., between change and resistance to change). Nevertheless, pressure to change does occur in order to address certain political, social, and economic problems that exist within society, new laws are created to try to remedy those problems, and in turn, institutional policies and practices arise in response to those laws, creating a *virtuous cycle of social development*.

This cycle tends to be most pronounced in democratic societies which base their social way of life and their political governance on democratic principles. As such, inclusive leadership is grounded in democratic principles to guide its actions and inclusive leadership involves several interrelated and interdependent factors such as human rights, democracy, identity, agency, power, pluralism, ethics, access, policy, and justice.

Human Rights in Higher Education

Many societies place great faith in education, as systems of formal learning, to solve some of today's pressing social and economic problems. Education is often seen as the basic foundation for social, economic, and personal development. Education is taken to mean all levels and types of education, including basic education (primary and secondary) and tertiary education (further and higher). Education at all levels is increasingly viewed as a universal human right. But what does a universal human right to education really mean? In short, it means that education is so important to the continual development of social reproduction (Bourdieu & Passeron, 1977), it yields so many positive benefits at the micro and macro levels (Hanushek & Woessmann, 2007), and is such a defining feature of what it means to be human, to deny people the opportunity to learn throughout the course of their lives (lifelong and lifewide learning) would be an injustice to the individual and would have deleterious effects for society (Spring, 2000; Vandenberg, 1990).

McCowan (2013) put it this way: "A universal right to HE does not, therefore, require, or even encourage, all people to attend university. It may be that only a small proportion of the population will opt for it" (p. 126).

Key Theories

Much research has been conducted and several theories have been developed over the past several decades to confirm the benefits (at both the social and individual levels) derived from education. Chiefly among these theories are human capital theory (Becker, 1993; Schultz 1961), modernization theory (Inkeles & Smith, 1975; McClelland, 1961; Rostow, 1960), and dependency theory (Frank, 1967; Santos, 1970). More recently, according to McCowan (2013), the ideas of post-structuralism and post-colonialism have provided alternative views to the politico-economic oriented theories of laissez faire (i.e., *Wealth of Nations*) and central planning (i.e., *Das Kapital*). In addition, globalization provides another macro oriented theory to help explain the phenomenon of rapidly expanding education throughout the world.

Another view, the human rights view, is that education is important not just because of the socio-economic benefits it yields, but because it is a basic human right for all. Thus, a discussion on inclusion and diversity should also start with a discussion on human rights since human rights is the broad construct from which diversity and inclusion issues emerge. As noted by Chapman (2007), the human rights movement has been an ongoing global movement aimed at improving the rights of all people irrespective of their political, social, or economic context. Human rights are opposed to systems and practices that weaken the humane treatment of people, such as racism, sexism, and elitism. These three major forms of prejudicial behaviors can lead to other forms of prejudice such as bigotry, ageism, classism, rankism, cronyism, and supremacism. When human rights become codified in law, they are called civil rights and they represent a major milestone in the evolution of human society. Human history shows that in the absence of human rights protections and a humane rule of law, abuse, and mistreatment of people becomes, unfortunately, too common.

McCowan (2013) defines a human right as a *justified claim on others*. They are justified because they serve to safeguard the most basic facets of humanity (e.g., life, freedom, well-being, dignity, security). As such, they are the highest priority claims on others to treat people humanely. A human right is non-conditional and is not dependent on any other justification other than the principle of humane treatment. This defining characteristic distinguishes it from other theories. A human rights approach views humans as moral agents rather than simply as beneficiaries, however great those benefits (e.g., social, cultural, economic) may be. By framing education as a human right, education becomes a requirement for justice and an obligation to be met.

Rights may be defined as either positive rights (rights that require an action) or negative rights (rights that require an inaction). From this perspective, the right to education can be viewed as a positive right because it requires a proactive action on the part of others (the duty bearers) to bring it into existence. Most constitutions, as in the US Bill of Rights for instance, tend to focus on negative rights (e.g., freedom of speech, freedom of religion) whereas positive rights (e.g., education, social security) are often protected by legislative laws or judicial decisions. The right to education is a complex matter because, as with all rights, it must deal with questions such as: who is/are the duty bearer(s) (e.g., governments, leaders, students, faculty, parents, communities) and what are their specific responsibilities? McCowan (2013) argues that laws protecting the right to education are essential but the "law does not contain the answer to the question of whether there is a valid claim that all people have a right to education, and what that right corresponds to" (p. 16). Thus, concerning the right to education, the ultimate equation is a moral one, not a legal one. In other words, it is the normative argument of moral reasoning that ultimately provides the justification and foundation for the legal protection of rights.

The Link between Human Rights and Inclusive Leadership in Higher Education

The current racial unrest in universities particularly in the USA and in South Africa, while shocking perhaps to onlookers, is not really surprising. Higher education cannot be separated from the imperatives of inclusive democracy and there is a critical link between education and politics. There is a renewed sense of urgency to consider the significance of universities as formal spheres of learning that can and should provide citizens with the kinds of critical capacities, modes of literacies, knowledge, and skills to read the world critically and participate in shaping and governing it (Giroux, 2011). The discontent we are seeing in the student body in universities in many countries surely challenges us to consider new discourses given that identity, citizenship, and agency are organized through pedagogical relations and practices. In universities in South Africa icons of colonialism and white supremacy are coming under attack. The issues of the predominantly 'white' nature of the curriculum more than two decades post-apartheid are causing rage among the black student population. Racial taunts and 'exclusive' practices in universities in the USA are leading to challenges across racial divides on the issue of freedom of speech.

These challenges are not intractable but they surely pose questions for the leadership in higher education institutions. Leaders need to apply their critical thinking to establish or re-establish the university as a truly democratic space that encourages inclusive dialogue and debate. This means that leaders need to recognize talent from all sectors of the student body, they must encourage learning and teaching strategies that are transformational, not just transactional. On the one hand it may seem a daunting task to create an inclusive culture in universities, but given that diversity of the student population is often one of the key points lauded and applauded in university advertising material, it is imperative if these diversity statements are to have any meaning in that the reality matches the rhetoric.

Conclusion

Based on the current literature on diversity and inclusion, and on the emerging trends in building inclusive educational environments, this chapter has attempted to move beyond an interpretation of inclusion as simply an access or hiring issue and beyond conflating diversity with inclusion. Rather, it has examined inclusion from a human rights and educational leadership perspective. The argument being made is that building a culture and mindset of inclusion is imperative in order to create a meaningful learning environment that embraces and values diversity. This chapter has purposely avoided being overly prescriptive or formulaic about how institutions should create more inclusive organizational cultures. Specific strategies for inclusion are important but educational leaders are in the best position to determine how to develop strategies that best fit the context of their particular organization. Given the growing importance of higher education to the well-being of society and democracy, it is important that educational leaders recognize inclusion as a core institutional value.

References

Altbach, P. G., Reisberg, L., & Rumbley, L. E. (2009). *Trends in global higher education: Tracking an academic revolution*. Paris: UNESCO.

Amanchukwu, R. N., Stanley, G. J., & Ololube, N. P. (2015). A review of leadership theories, principles and styles and their relevance to educational management. *Management*, 5(1), pp. 6–14.

Barnett, R. (2012). *The future university: Ideas and possibilities*. London: Routledge.

Basit, T. N. & Tomlinson, S. (2014). *Social inclusion and higher education*. Bristol, UK: Policy Press.

Bass, B. M. (1990). From transactional to transformational leadership: Learning to share the vision. *Organizational Dynamics*, 18(3), pp. 19–31.

Bass, B. M. & Riggio, R. (2006). *Transformational leadership*. Mahwah, NJ: Erlbaum.

Bateh, J. & Heyliger, W. (2014). Academic administrator leadership styles and the impact of faculty job satisfaction, *Journal of Leadership Education*, 13(3), pp. 34–49.

Becker, G. S. (1993). *Human capital: A theoretical and empirical analysis, with special reference to education*. Chicago: University of Chicago Press.

Beiter, K. (2006). *The protection of the right to education by international law*. Leiden: Martinus Nijhoff.

Beitz, C. (2009). *The Idea of human rights*. Oxford, UK: Oxford University Press.

Blessinger, P. & Anchan, J. P. (eds) (2015). *Democratizing higher education: International comparative perspectives.* New York: Routledge.
Bourdieu, P. & Passeron, J. (1977). *Reproduction in education, society, and culture.* London: Sage.
Brighthouse, H. & McAvoy, P. (2009). Privilege, wellbeing, and participation in higher education. In: Raley, Y. and Preyer, G. (eds), *Philosophy of education in the era of globalization.* New York: Routledge, pp. 165–180.
Burke, P. J. (2012). *The right to higher education: Beyond widening participation.* New York: Routledge.
Chapman, A. (2007). *Human rights: A very short introduction.* Oxford, UK: Oxford University Press.
Chin, J. L. & Sanchez-Hucles, J. V. (2007). Diversity and leadership. *American Psychologist,* 62(6), pp. 608–609.
Cole, E. R. (2009). Intersectionality and research in psychology. *American Psychologist,* 64 (3), pp. 170–180.
Curren, R. (2009). Education as a social right in a diverse society. *Journal of Philosophy of Education,* 43(1), pp. 45–56.
Dewey, J. (1916). *Democracy and education: An introduction to the philosophy of education.* New York: Macmillan.
de Wit, H. (ed.). (2013). *An introduction to higher education internationalisation.* Milan: Universita Cattolica University Press Vita e Pensiero, Centre for Higher Education Internationalisation (CHEI), UCSC.
Frank, A. G. (1967). *Capitalism and underdevelopment in Latin America.* New York: Monthly Review Press.
Freire, P. (1970). *Pedagogy of the oppressed,* New York: Continuum.
Giroux, H. (2011) *On critical pedagogy.* New York: Bloomsbury.
Gutman, A. (2003). *Identity in democracy.* Princeton, NJ: Princeton University Press.
Hanushek, E. & Woessmann, L. (2007). *Education quality and economic growth.* Washington, D.C.: World Bank.
Inkeles, A. & Smith, D. H. (1975). *Becoming modern: Individual change in six developing countries.* Cambridge, MA: Harvard University Press.
Karmel, J. (2009). *The right to education.* Saarbrücken: VDM Publishing.
Kezar, A. (2009). *Rethinking leadership in a complex, multicultural, and global environment.* Sterling, VA: Stylus Press.
Kouzes, J. M., & Posner, B. Z. (2012). *The leadership challenge.* San Francisco, CA: Jossey-Bass.
Kovbasyuk, O. & Blessinger, P. (eds) (2013). *Meaning-centered education: International perspectives and explorations in higher education.* New York: Routledge.
Li, C-K. & Hung, C-H. (2009). The influence of transformational leadership on workplace relationships and job performance. *Social Behavior and Personality,* 37(8), pp. 1129–1142.
McCaffery, P. (2004). *The higher education manager's handbook: Effective leadership and management in universities and colleges.* New York: Routledge.
McClelland, D. C. (1961). *The achieving society.* New York: Van Nostrand.
McCowan, T. (2013). *Education as a human right: Principles for a universal entitlement to learning.* New York: Bloomsbury Publishing.
McMillan, L. K. (2010). What's in a right? Two variations for interpreting the right to education. *International Review of Education,* 56, pp. 5–6.
Maher, F. A. & Tetrault, M. K. T. (2007). *Privilege and diversity in the academy.* New York: Routledge.

Marginson, S. & Sawir, E. (2011). *Ideas for intercultural education*. New York: Palgrave Macmillan.

Martindale, N. (2011). Leadership styles: How to handle the different personas. *Strategic Communication Management*, 15(8), pp. 32–35.

Meacham, J. & Barrett, C. (2003). Commitment to diversity in institutional mission statements. *Diversity Digest*, 7(1–2), pp. 6–9.

Mello, J. A. (1999). Reframing leadership pedagogy through model and theory building. *Career Development International*, 4, pp. 163–169.

Noddings, N. (2013). *Education and democracy in the 21st century*. New York: Teachers College Press.

Northouse, P. G. (2007). *Leadership: Theory and practice*. Thousand Oaks, CA: Sage

Palfreyman, D. & Tapper, T. (2009). *Structuring mass higher education: The role of elite institutions*. New York: Routledge.

Rostow, W. W. (1960). *The stages of economic growth: A non-communist manifesto*. Cambridge, UK: Cambridge University Press.

Santos, T. D. (1970). The structure of dependence. *American Economic Review*, 60(2), pp. 231–236.

Schultz, T. W. (1961). Investment in human capital. *American Economic Review*, 51(1), pp. 1–16.

Smith, D. G. (2009). *Diversity's promise for higher education: Making it work*. Baltimore: Johns Hopkins University Press.

Smith, D. G. (ed.) (2014). *Diversity and inclusion in higher education: Emerging perspectives on institutional transformation*. New York: Routledge.

Spillane, J. P. & Diamond, J. B. (2007). *Distributed leadership in practice*. New York: Teachers College, Columbia University.

Spring, J. (2000). *The universal right to education: Justification, definition, and guidelines*. New Jersey: Lawrence Erlbaum.

Symington, A. (2004). Intersectionality: A tool for gender and economic justice. Women's rights and economic change. *Association for Women in Development*, No. 9.

Trow, M. (1974). Problems in the transition from elite to mass higher education, in OECD (ed.) *Policies for Higher Education*. Paris: OECD, pp. 51–101.

Vandenberg, D. (1990). *Education as a human right: A theory of curriculum and pedagogy*. New York: Teachers College Press.

Vygotsky, L. S. (1989). *Pedagogical psychology*. Moscow: Nauka.

Woods, P. A. (2011). *Transforming education policy: Shaping a democratic future*. Bristol, UK: Policy Press.

Wray, M. (2013). Developing an inclusive culture in higher education: Final report. York, UK: Higher Education Academy. Retrieved from <https://www.heacademy.ac.uk/sites/default/files/inclusive_culture_report_0.pdf> (Accessed 3 March 2017).

2

LEADERSHIP CHALLENGES FOR WOMEN COLLEGE AND UNIVERSITY PRESIDENTS

Personal Perspectives from Women Making a Difference

Cathy Sandeen, Christine K. Cavanaugh and Deborah Ford

For the past decade, higher education in the United States has experienced enormous challenges. Attention to the issues of affordability, access, attainment, and accountability has exploded on the public agenda. National presidential candidates regularly tout their higher education policy agendas, whereas in the past, such policies would rarely be mentioned. More and more struggling colleges have shuttered their doors mainly due to declining enrollments and fiscal challenges, regulation at all levels has proliferated, racial conflicts sadly occur on a regular basis, and academic freedom and free speech have been challenged. The list goes on.

All but a handful of elite colleges and universities have fewer and fewer resources, the result of reductions in state funding or pressure to keep tuition fees low. At the same time, we in higher education are being called upon to provide quality postsecondary degrees and credentials to more Americans than we have ever attempted in our history. We need stellar academic leadership, we need it now, and we need to be able to tap into the full range of talent within our colleges and universities to provide this leadership.

It is within this context that we explore the challenges and leadership approaches of women who hold positions as chief executives of US colleges and universities. We do so by allowing these women to voice their own perspectives. This chapter is based on in-depth interviews with 21 female college or university presidents or chancellors. This study is exploratory and qualitative and builds on previous work. (In addition, two of the authors are sitting chancellors and the third is an executive coach to presidents and chancellors.) The wealth of data and experience on which to draw was extensive.

The goal was to dig deeper into the professional and personal lives of women presidents and chancellors and understand how they experience and navigate their own environments to create impact. The opportunity to glean their discernment process, the personal meanings they derive, and what they view as their impact provides much deeper insights into the leadership characteristics and behaviors than do traditional trait assessment approaches. Despite significant differences in background, many common themes emerged that will inform revising and rethinking leadership development programs as well as how best to foster an adequate talent pipeline, and perhaps most importantly, will inspire other women to seek top leadership positions in our colleges and universities.

Relevant Research

The following section provides a brief overview of key research on women in higher education leadership relevant to our work with special focus on demographic trends, gender/race/class, gender expectations, and women's leadership styles.

Demographic Trends

There continues to be a gap in the number of women leaders in president and chancellor positions in higher education despite the fact there are more women graduating and entering into the teaching profession within American colleges and universities (American Council of Education (ACE), 2012; AAUW, 2016). The 2015 National Center for Education Statistics (NCES) reported that women began eclipsing men in terms of degree attainment beginning in 2000 and 14 years later, 37 percent of women between 25 and 29 years had earned a bachelor's degree, compared to men at 31 percent. With 76 percent of K-12 teachers and 48 percent of college faculty positions in the US filled by women, women are well represented in education careers (NCES, 2015). Based on these data, it might not be unreasonable to expect that now or in the near future, 50 percent of all college and university leaders will be women.

However, women remain underrepresented as tenured faculty (AAUW, 2016). These trends create pipeline and access shortage for institutions seeking diverse applicant pools as well as women who aspire to leadership positions. As of 2011 – the most current statistics available – only 26 percent of college presidencies were held by women (ACE, 2012). This demonstrates a slight positive growth trend from just under 20 percent in 1998 and 23 percent in 2006. Over this same period, the largest gains for women serving as presidents has occurred at two-year institutions where 33 percent of presidents are women. Still, women held only 22 percent of the presidential positions at four-year institutions, both public and private (ACE, 2012).

Gender/Race/Class

Another body of work focuses on possible reasons for the slower-than-desirable progress in women attaining leadership roles in higher education. For example, Gamez-Vargas (2011) found that many universities still seem to hold a 'patriarchal role expectation'. *The Chronicle of Higher Education* noted that men still outnumber women among the newly appointed deans, provosts, and presidents (Hammond, 2015).

In response to these issues, in 2016 the American Association of University Women (AAUW) conducted a meta study of research on women and leadership in higher education and identified five main reasons for women's lack of progress: (1) fewer women in the pipeline as potential applicants; (2) persistent sex discrimination; (3) caregiving responsibilities; (4) lack of effective networking and mentors; and (5) stereotypes and bias. Confronting and eliminating these reasons are necessary steps for assuring that future generations of women will have equal access to leadership opportunities.

Research on generational differences among women leaders also has begun to emerge. For example, one researcher found that more senior women leaders indicated that they were not as 'troubled' by the work–family life balance as were younger women college presidents (Hertneky, 2010). In general, these older women college presidents did not have the same children or family commitments as their younger counterparts (Song & Hartley, 2012). This and other findings indicated differences and expectations based not only on age, generation, and gender, but on racial and ethnic lines depending on family commitments and social norms.

Intersectionality was originally used as a framework to explore how the socially and culturally constructed categories of gender, race, and class interact to shape experiences (Crenshaw, 1989; Guy-Sheftall, 2009; Oikelome, 2016). In this initial framing, measurement of the experiences of intersectionality resulted in an 'additive' approach. Race is seen as an overlapping factor with other variables such as generation; for example, "black women education administrators are found to have a notably different leadership style if they were born before or after the civil rights movement" (Kezar & Lester, 2008, p. 63). Patricia Arrendondo (2011) expanded this approach by discussing ethnicity and other ways of identifying, to express the role conflicts facing Latinas with intersecting identities of ethnic and racial heritage, sexual orientation, class, and occupation. Arrendondo argued that the term is also applicable to women of color who are higher education leaders as they also negotiate social norms and demographic categories.

AAUW (2016) further expanded on the relationships among gender, race, and class by pointing out that race, ethnicity, age, income, health, and sexual orientation all affect women's leadership experiences. They indicated, for example, that women of color experience and confront ethnic and racial discrimination differently than do white women, and differently again from men of their same ethnic or racial group (AAUW, 2016).

Gender Expectations

Another group of researchers focus on the different and harsher standards female presidents face compared with their male counterparts. For example, Hertneky (2010) and Jablonski (1996) explored the role of physical appearance and women leaders' abilities to cultivate a managerial yet sufficiently feminine persona, making sure not to 'overdo' one or the other. Moran (1992) described how being a manager had been traditionally seen as a 'masculine' trait and inappropriate for women.

For many women college presidents, leadership seems to stress 'female' characteristics like 'being a colleague', and fostering a community of cooperation and interdependence. Many sources emphasized that the most distinguishing characteristics of women college presidents' leadership is their preference for a more 'democratic or participative style' (Moran, 1992).

Leadership Styles

Kezar (2014) observed that women's leadership styles and behaviors differ from traditional ideas about leadership including "hierarchy, acting alone, often through top-down power and influence strategies" (p. 117). More recent notions of good leadership tend to stress "collaboration, with leaders acting collectively in concert with others" (p. 117).

This theme of leadership through collective action and inclusivity threads its way among other writing. According to Wolverton, Bower, and Hyle (2008), "Leadership is about relationships; working with people, getting people to work with you, you simply cannot do it all" (p. 97). Nan Keohane (2012), former president of Wellesley College and Duke University, reflected on the complexity of relationships between leaders and followers and the challenges of democratic leadership: "The ends we seek through governance encompass the coherence, aspirations, stability, moral character, and creative vision of our communities, and the protection of the rights and liberties of individuals" (pp. 7–8).

While not exhaustive, this literature review touches on some of the major issues and themes of women's leadership in higher education and sets the scene for analyzing these interview data. Are elements of more collective and inclusive leadership styles and gender concerns reflected in in-depth conversations with a diverse range of women presidents?

Approach

This research incorporates discussions and notes (Women's Voices, 2014) from the Legacy Conference held in Racine, Wisconsin, November 2014. Thirty women higher education leaders convened to re-engage in a conversation started in the late 1980s and captured in Astin and Leland's (1991) seminal text, *Women of Vision, Women of Influence*. The goal of the Legacy Conference was to reflect upon and articulate the impact of women presidents and chancellors from the late 1980s to the present.

Following the conference, from 2014–2016, a series of in-depth, relatively unstructured interviews were conducted with experienced women presidents and chancellors to further examine the question of the impact of women's leadership in higher education. In addition, data collected between 2010 and 2011 from interviews with eight additional female presidents or chancellors, was contributed by one of the authors.

In total, 21 women of diverse backgrounds and from various types of institutions were interviewed,[1] each having served in the capacity as the executive leader of an American college or university during the last 25 years. Interviewees identified as either white (16) or as a woman of color (5). At the time of their interview, 12 were currently sitting presidents and 9 were retired; 6 were serving in their second presidency; 4 were serving as a system head or association leader; 11 were from public institutions; and 10 were from private/religious institutions. The accumulated leadership experience of the women totaled well over 150 years serving in the role as a president or chancellor.

Interviews spanned 60–90 minutes each and were relatively unstructured and wide-ranging.[2] Though a group of consistent questions were used across interviews, no preconceived framework was applied in conducting the interviews themselves. Interviews were transcribed or carefully noted. Interview data were analyzed for similarities and key themes.

For our analytical framework, we turned to a recent edited volume, *Women and Leadership in Higher Education* by Longman and Madsen (2014), which provided a comprehensive and current overview of the women's leadership issues. The nine chapters in Parts III and IV of Longman and Madsen's work focus on leadership experiences, characteristics, and qualifications of women presidents and chancellors, many written by women presidents and chancellors themselves. Across these chapters, a range of knowledge, qualities, experiences, and leadership characteristics emerged, including:

- consultative/democratic/participative, team leadership, collaboration, relational inclusiveness, multiple perspectives, empowerment, development and learning, ethics, integrity, common purpose (Kezar, 2014, pp. 117–34);
- adversity and resilience (Diehl, 2014 pp. 135–52);
- authenticity, care and relationships, gender socialization (Gardiner, 2014, pp. 152–68);
- gender role expectations, public conflicts, sports/athletics (Bucklin, 2014, pp. 169–85); securing legitimacy, managing authenticity, emotional intelligence, overcoming deficits (Bornstein, 2014, pp. 189–96);
- athletics and academic medicine (Hart, 2014, pp. 197–204);
- multiple constituents (Penney, 2014, pp. 205–12);
- crisis management (Garcia, 2014, pp. 213–18);
- groundedness (Holbrook, 2014, pp. 219–225).

Rather than generating our own list of characteristics as a framework to organize and analyze our interview data, we derived our categories from the extensive list cited above. We found that many of the categories overlapped and could be distilled to the following major categories of leadership characteristics, qualities, and behaviors:

- collaboration/teamwork/participatory style;
- relational inclusiveness; vision/common purpose;
- securing legitimacy/overcoming deficits; resilience;
- authenticity/integrity/self-awareness;
- gender role expectations.

Our interview data were analyzed and characterized according to these categories in the sections below.

Findings

Collaboration/Teamwork/Participatory Style

> I was recruited as a change agent, but I knew I needed to take some time. At the beginning, I needed to give people what they wanted: recognition and listening. Then we began discussing strategic planning in a broad-based, organic, consultative, bottom-up way before a more formal process.

We did see evidence that women do express having a collaborative leadership style and that they seek win-win strategies when making decisions. Women presidents advocate for the needs of their campus, lead with a focus on developing individuals and teams, and see the benefits of being inclusive. Comments supporting this view were prevalent and were embedded throughout interview data. On teamwork, one president shared, "It's important to develop a senior team. The previous administration had been a 'hub and spoke' approach where the president worked separately with each vice president. I am changing it to a true team concept." Broad inclusivity was reflected in a comment about leading the strategic planning initiative: "We included 100 faculty, staff, and students who participated on committees. The process took eight months. Now we're in the end of the fourth year and are doing an update of the plan. This is change in a structured way." One president reflected on the importance of honesty and transparency: "A strong leader will talk about what is not going well in addition to what is going well."

Another woman commented on the importance of women leaders bringing voice to social issues. She believed this was an important part of her success as a president and that by leveraging the resources of the campus community she could give back and address broader societal issues. One respondent commented, "women show greater sensitivity and awareness to marginalized groups of employees and students." Another shared, "I try to foster dialogue: the shared exploration leading to mutual understanding."

Another president emphasized the need for modeling and maintaining civility: "At the core of this is respect for others' point of view. I demonstrate this through the following: listen to others; ask for others' thoughts, ask domineering participants to avoid monopolizing the conversation." She further pointed out, "We live in a world where conflict and dogmatism prevail as a norm. We all perform better in an environment where dialogue and civility exist."

These women presidents acknowledged the difficulty of leading change and the importance of both understanding the culture of an institution and communicating openly and often. One commented, "The pace of change needs to be acceptable to the culture of the institution. It can't be too fast or it will grind to a halt. There are so many areas where work is needed, you can't change everything at once." Another reflected: "We need to be agents of change, but realize that change is incremental. Be patient."

Relational Inclusiveness

> The president needs outstanding communication skills and needs to demonstrate that you are listening.

Closely related to collaborative style was an intentional focus on individual relationships as a prerequisite for effective leadership. The women in this study believed they were successful as a result of being collaborative and building relationships. As one explained, "You need to pay attention to the interpersonal dimension." And another: "One of my most important individual traits is what I call 'high-touch', getting to know people personally."

Similarly, another stressed, "the single most important job as president is human development, meaning supporting growth in talent and moving at a rate that promotes the talent around you." Building relationships helps to broaden a base of support for the leaders and one leader noted, "Work continuously to build and maintain your base while being deliberate and intentional." One respondent talked about the importance of having good interpersonal skills and honing the ability to deal with the "sane and the crazy." Another commented, "you need to be a part of the entire campus community, even when things may not be of interest. You realize that you cannot stand in a corner and just observe when you are the president." Being present and being engaged are factors contributing to the success for women leaders.

Several presidents directly addressed the importance of building relationships with faculty in particular: "It's important to be able to move the faculty and it's very important that faculty get to know you as a person." Another reiterated and expanded on this theme, "It's important to get faculty to know you as a person. Realize the president will make decisions that do not please everyone. There will be more trust if the campus community knows me as a person."

Other respondents articulated specific proactive strategies to get to know faculty personally. One shared, "I worked to build relationships with faculty – lots of individual conversations, small group conversation and monthly faculty lunches with a group of 12 mixed faculty and no agenda." Another noted, "When I began my presidency, I asked to meet with each faculty member, approximately 100, for 30 minutes in their offices. It was important that I went to their offices, both as a gesture and to see their offices – what was important to them. I asked about their favorite class to teach, their scholarship, and about [name of institution]." Another described her strategies: "You need to get to know faculty personally and pay attention to them. Acknowledge them. Follow their scholarship. Read [campus name] newsletters and comment on accomplishments of faculty. Send short emails and hand written notes. You need to really like faculty. Don't lump them into one category."

In a more general sense, one interviewee noted: "The leader sets the tone. There are critical consequences of the leader's tone. You need a consistency of approach." All the women believed having greater sensitivity and awareness served them well as they led their diverse campus communities and improved success for students and employees of color.

Vision/Common Purpose

Don't just be a 'do-er,' you need to be a visionary and strategic as well.

The women presidents in this study all commented on the importance of building a shared vision on campus and working with constituents towards a common purpose with focus and determination. They had a crystal clear understanding of their respective institutions' missions and remained in alignment with their missions while moving their campus forward.

Such alignment was reflected in this comment: "I strive to balance the covenant of tradition with the covenant of change [because] there is wisdom in the status quo." Another added her take on the relationship between past and future: "Tradition may not move us forward in these times; we need to be flexible and nontraditional." One interviewee articulated a specific formula: "Vision + thought leadership + direction + support = intended outcomes on deadline."

Strategy and focus were additional strong themes: "You need to set priorities always, but especially in turbulent times. Effective leaders pursue a limited number of strategic goals and do so with discipline and focus, knowing the mission of the institution." The imperative to change was also apparent: "I need to be able to transform the institution in some way. Know what is central to keep, what reflects the core values of the institutions, but still keeps the college moving ahead." Another was reminded of the importance of aligning vision and mission, "You need to be very centered in terms of vision and mission. Ask, why are you doing something? You need to push for change, but not from above. Always remember the legacy of the institution."

The role of vision and strategy emerged even when discussing the day-to-day details of dealing with a budget cut: "I am not in favor of across the board budget cuts. You can only do that so often. It's like trimming a tree. You cut back more than you want to ensure that future growth is healthy. You need to make cuts strategically, according to vision, and as humanely as possible." Communication and relationship building were interwoven with strategy and vision for many interviewees: "The president needs to have clear values, consistency, express candor about changing course, be transparent."

Securing Legitimacy/Overcoming Deficits

You just learn every day.

Several of the women presidents noted the importance of taking time to understand what you do not know and close any gaps that are discovered. These women demonstrated commitment to continuous personal and professional development, consistent with Bornstein's (2014) suggestion that women presidents "seek out mentors, training programs, and opportunities to gain knowledge and experience with elements of the presidency that may be unfamiliar [e.g., fundraising, budgeting, public speaking, working with a board]" (p. 194).

Many of the women interviewed made an honest and detailed inventory of experiential gaps and sought out professional and personal development opportunities. For example, one interviewee systematically and intentionally filled out her own portfolio prior to seeking her first presidency: "Leading one function as a vice president does not give you the exposure you need so as provost I asked for other assignments like student affairs projects, university task forces, serving as faculty rep for athletics, working on budgets, international projects, and accreditation." Another observed that being a dean of a large school provided good preparation in business and finance, academic affairs, facilities, strategic planning, fundraising, accountability, enrollment, and quality, but that "gaps included student life, athletics, and working with a board." Another felt her background as a vice president for student affairs allowed her to learn about "what goes on outside of class," but acknowledged a need for "knowing crisis management."

The need for additional development may not be apparent until the new president steps into the position. One interviewee admitted that when she became a president she was surprised by the amount of time needed to care for and support the governing board, estimating she spent 40–50 percent of her time on board relations and governance. Another woman began her presidency by asking the board that hired her, "What is untouchable and where are the minefields that will get me or the university in trouble?"

A number of presidents participated in formal higher education leadership development programs: "I went to the AASCU President Bootcamp where they reminded us to cover all the stakeholder bases at all times and know the dynamics of all the groups and try to maintain balance." Others employed coaches and networks: "Executive coaches help a lot and presidents are willing to help other presidents." Similarly, "You need a trusted partner or a trusted confidant, a neutral third-party to discuss things with. An executive coach can help."

Resilience

> Nourish your intellectual self. You need to have a way to 'clear your head' and maintain centeredness.

Resilience took two forms within our interview data: dealing with challenge and adversity and nurturing the self. The women presidents were open in sharing some of their biggest surprises, admitted mistakes, or unexpected issues encountered during their presidencies. For example, one reflected on mistakes made while moving forward to dis-establishing a failing professional school: "I could have communicated better so I apologized and admitted mistakes. The main thing I learned [through this experience] was tell what you think, listen, and follow through on actions." Another felt she damaged the trust of her faculty at a time when she eliminated an expensive inter-term January session. She admitted: "The change was not communicated properly. It was discussed, but not enough. It caused a faculty revolt." What did she do in response? "I admitted the mistake and apologized and I also protected the new dean of faculty who became the focus of criticism."

Another described a number of major change initiatives, including revising the curriculum, using debt for the first time for a capital project, and changing the composition of the board. Through these experiences she admitted her biggest mistake was "thinking that facts alone will win an argument, it's really all about people and how they feel."

Almost all of the interviewees revealed how lonely leadership can be as a president. All of the women noted the importance of being present and visible on campus and in the community. Some wrestled with being seen as a role or title and not as a person. One observed that you "cannot brainstorm out loud" because statements might be construed as decisions and innocent comments made in informal social situations are often misinterpreted or taken out of context.

One interviewee shared how she allowed her presidency to be all-consuming but could not address it or change her behavior while serving as president. She is now retired and acknowledged that she is "taking better care of herself and is focusing on important family relationships." All of the women talked about being more intentional to reflect on their work and lives and mentoring the next generation of leaders. The women interviewed did not have regrets over how they spent their time but acknowledged that the demands of the position controlled much of their lives. Taking care of self and investing in relationships were high priorities for both retired and sitting presidents.

Many interviewees shared practical advice for other women leaders: "Protect and manage your own calendar. Make time for exercise. Seek an 'integrated life' where you fit in personal and professional activities. Forget the idea of balance. Balance is a myth." Another admitted: "I needed to determine when I could get work done. For example, I work at home one morning per week, thinking, reflecting, and writing speeches. I try to lead an integrated life. For example, I'll take part of an afternoon to get my nails done if I'm going to be working all weekend."

Authenticity/Integrity/Self-awareness

> Lead as you are and do not try to be someone you are not.

The concept of 'authentic leadership' versus charismatic or transformational leadership has emerged within popular management/leadership literature (George, 2004). At its essence, the ability to be open and transparent is a hallmark of authenticity. Authentic leaders are honest with themselves and others and lead through self-awareness, openness, and show a willingness to consider opposing viewpoints (AAUW, 2016).

Embedded in, and woven throughout previous sections is the tendency of interviewees to exhibit a high level of self-awareness about their own levels of experience and their role as a chief executive. They expressed the importance of having a "clear sense of knowing yourself" and "not taking self too seriously."

Continuing on previous observations, 'awareness' encompassed acknowledgement of the highly public context of a college or university presidency. One president illustrated this awareness: "The leader is always under observation. Responses are public, not personal, always." Another observed: "You are now a public person – your life is not your own and you live in a glass house and you are always being watched"; "Related to this is the powerful influence of the statement, 'the president said …' and how this is used with and without your knowledge." They noted, as presidents, you are 'on' all of the time. One woman shared: "It is a 24/7 job. You are under a microscope."

One respondent who rose through the ranks at one single institution and came to understand that the "president sets the tone for the entire campus." Still another developed awareness of the position and her responsibility: "my biggest surprise was realizing 'the buck stops here', that I needed to step up and make decisions at some point." And another: "To be a good leader, it's beyond skills. It's a temperament. You need to be a credible academic leader, not operations only. You need mental toughness and agility. You need to enthusiastically embrace what the day will be – whatever the day brings." And another, "You need to get energy from being around people no matter how tired you are. You need to enjoy people. You will get a second wind."

Gender Role Expectations

> Gender is neutral in terms of good leadership.

Besides admitting women's unique challenges with work–life balance, our interviewees did not automatically blame their gender for their challenges. If they encountered barriers commonly associated with gender, they often reported having an attitude of "enjoying the challenge" or ignoring the barrier and simply moving on with their responsibilities. This was not about being reticent or not speaking out when injustices were presented. These women tended not to 'dwell' on potentially gender-focused situations. Some of the women college presidents did not seem to be concerned or acknowledge gender issues at all. Others alternated between ignoring their gender or using gender traits to their advantage as reflected in this statement: "I respect competency more than anything else ... Calling out differences as a woman is a negative, for example stressing empathy, etc. I believe it is a negative. Don't call it out." [At the same time], "I can take a maternal approach, saying 'I care for you,' for example reaching out, making phone calls and hospital visits. Make difference work for you. But my staff think I'm difficult. I may be too direct for my own good. I'm too direct for [name of her state]."

One woman admitted surprise that stereotypes for gender and race do not diminish as one moves up the ranks on campus. Another interviewee noted, "You need to overcome gender bias, for example, an informal, personable style may be interpreted as not tough enough to make decisions. And we need to overcome obstacles of limiting our expectations and limiting our choices." Some interviewees did bring to the surface difference in women's leadership styles. For example: "I had experience as a woman in a man's discipline. Women are better at fostering group activities and at listening. Earlier in my career I learned to listen, to delegate to best performers, to use influence rather than authority, and learned to take the other person's point of view."

Gender did emerge in terms of seeking out a professional network. Several respondents valued the growing network of women presidents and felt as if women were finally reaching critical mass at professional meetings. This growing network provides more resources for women leaders and more opportunities to share perspectives. One woman shared, "This role can be lonely and going to the [public restroom] was a place for life and work conversations with other women." Another shared, "women are respected more for their contributions as leaders and there is more recognition that women can be among today's leaders."

Even though respondents have more women as colleagues today than when they started their presidencies, they believe strongly that they need to promote and mentor more women who aspire to leadership roles in higher education, especially the presidency.

Summary and Conclusion

Our interview data reaffirm previous interview-based studies of leadership traits, qualities, and strategies of women who lead institutions of higher learning. Because of the depth of our interviews and the number of women who participated, our chapter provides additional richness to the existing body of knowledge. Our interviewees exhibited strong leadership traits – they are leaders who identify a focused vision, build high-performing teams, foster positive interpersonal relationships, communicate thoughtfully and strategically, and focus on their own continual learning. These women leaders were well aware of the role gender (as well as race and class) played in informing their leadership and how it may have affected their careers, but they did not seem to dwell on or amplify their gender within their professional spheres, except for seeking out other women for advice and mentoring. Given that these women appear to be successful and thriving in a time of challenge, what might we do to encourage more women to seek leadership positions?

Many of our interviewees identified structured leadership programs as important in their careers. A number of programs have emerged in an effort to prepare women for and encourage them into high-level leadership roles and to build a support network for existing and future women leaders. These efforts include the National Center for Institutional Diversity (NCID) at the University of Michigan, the American Council of Education Fellows Program, the HERS Institute (Bryn Mawr, Denver, and Wellesley), and AASCU's Millennial Leadership Initiative just to name a few. All are examples of in-depth, longer-term, cohort-based leadership development programs that focus on preparing, enhancing, and advancing those who want to move into leadership positions in higher education, especially those from historically underrepresented groups. The American Council of Education sponsors an initiative 'Moving the Needle' started in 2014, that seeks to promote strategies to increase the number of women in senior leadership positions in higher education through programs, research, and resources.

These programs provide important opportunities for women to envision themselves as leaders (Ballenger, 2010; Hertneky, 2010). Perry and DeLeonardo 2011, p. 2) noted that when a woman is reluctant to take on the college president leadership role, it can be because "the path is not obvious or welcoming to them" and/or they are not actively promoting themselves. Some women college presidents report that they had a personal calling to the presidency and were inspired by initial encouragement from others (Tunheim and Goldschmidt, 2013). Women can more easily envision themselves as the leader when they have powerful female mentors, role models, and specific tactics guiding the way.

The authors hope one practical application of this chapter is to show the human side of women leaders and encourage other women to take up this important work. Many of these interviewees commented on the joy and inspiration derived from their positions, as challenging as they are. To this point the interviewees observed: "It's a labor of love at some point. It's not a paycheck. It's not a status symbol"; "It's not a glamorous job; it's relentless, but it's a wonderful career"; "It's always about the students; you get to see the lives you change."

Notes

1 Interviewees' type of institution and region: Private, East Private, Mid Atlantic; Private, Midwest; Private, Midwest; Private, Midwest; Private, West; Private, West; Private, West; Private, West; Private Religious, Mid Atlantic; Regional Public, East; Regional Public, Mid Atlantic; Regional Public, New England; Regional Public, South; Regional Public, West; Regional Public, West; Regional Public, West; Regional Public, West; Research Private, Mid Atlantic; Research, North Central; System, North Central

2   Range of questions used in unstructured interviews: What general skill set is needed in a college/university presidency? What techniques do you employ to remain connected with your faculty? What techniques do you employ to remain connected with your students? How would you describe the culture at your institution and how did you come to know it? What are some of the general challenges of a college/university presidency? What advice would you give to a new president? What are the current big issues in your institution? What surprised you when you became president? What are the most important aspects of leadership? Can you address the issue of communication and communication style in your role of president? Please describe your path to the presidency. What role has strategic planning played during your presidency? Did you encounter any challenges working with your board? What is the high point of your job as president? Please describe a mistake you have made and how you recovered from it. Can you address the issue of women as leaders? Which other presidents do you look up to? What question would you like to ask other presidents? Describe some of the impacts you have seen as a result of having more women in positions of president. In your opinion, what are some of the secrets to success for women presidents in today's world?

References

American Association of University Women (AAUW), 2016. *Barriers and bias: The status of women in leadership.* Washington, DC: AAUW.

American Council on Education (ACE), 2012. *The American college president 2012.* Washington, DC: American Council on Education.

Arredondo, P., 2011. The 'borderlands' experience for women of color as higher education leaders. In: Martin, J. L., ed. *Women as leaders in education: Succeeding despite inequity, discrimination, and other challenges.* Westport, CT: Praeger, pp. 275–298.

Astin, H. S. and Leland, C., 1991. *Women of influence, women of vision: A cross-generational study of leaders and social change.* San Francisco, CA: Jossey-Bass.

Ballenger, J., 2010. Women's access to higher education leadership: Cultural and structural barriers. *Forum on Public Policy: Women and Careers*, 5. Available at: <http://forumonpublicpolicy.com/vol2010no5/archivevol2010no5/ballengerJordan.pdf> [Accessed 10 August, 2016].

Bornstein, R., 2014. Leadership legitimacy, managed authenticity, and emotional stability: Keys to a successful presidency. In: Longman, K. A. and Madsen, S. R., eds. *Women and leadership in higher education.* Charlotte, NC: Information Age Publishing, pp. 189–196.

Bucklin, M. L., 2014. Madame president: Gender's impact in the presidential suite. In: Longman, K. A. and Madsen, S. R., eds. *Women and leadership in higher education.* Charlotte, NC: Information Age Publishing, pp. 169–185.

Crenshaw, K., 1989. Demarginalizing the intersection of race and sex: A black feminist critique of antidiscrimination doctrine, feminist theory and antiracial politics. *University of Chicago Legal Forum*, 1(8). Available at: <http://chicagounbound.uchicago.edu/cgi/viewcontent.cgi?article=1052&context=uclf> [Accessed 8 August, 2016].

Diehl, A. B., 2014. Approaches of women leaders in higher education: Navigating adversity, barriers, and obstacles. In: Longman, K. A. and Madsen, S. R., eds. *Women and leadership in higher education.* Charlotte, NC: Information Age Publishing, pp. 135–152.

Gamez-Vargas, J., 2011. A professor's life after becoming the university presidential partner. *International Journal of Leadership in Education: Theory and Practice*, 14, pp. 423–442.

Garcia, J., 2014. No te dejes: Giving voice to issues that choose you. In: Longman, K. A. and Madsen, S. R., eds. *Women and leadership in higher education.* Charlotte, NC: Information Age Publishing, pp. 213–218.

Gardiner, R. A., 2014. Women leaders, authenticity, and higher education: Convictions and contradictions. In: Longman, K. A. and Madsen, S. R., eds. *Women and leadership in higher education*. Charlotte, NC: Information Age Publishing, pp. 153–168.

George, B., 2004. *Authentic leadership: Rediscovering the secrets of creating lasting value*. San Francisco: Jossey-Bass.

Guy-Sheftall, B., 2009. Black feminist studies: The case of Anna Julia Cooper. *African American Review*, 43(1), pp. 11–15.

Hammond, R., ed. 2015. Almanac of higher education 2015. *Chronicle of Higher Education*, 61(43).

Hart, A. W., 2014. Docs, jocks and other wildlife: The challenge and potential for women leaders in the 21st century public research university. In: Longman, K. A. and Madsen, S. R., eds. *Women and leadership in higher education*. Charlotte, NC: Information Age Publishing, pp. 197–204.

Hertneky, R. P., 2010. The role of balance in women's leadership self-identity. *Advancing Women in Leadership Journal*, 30(14). Available at: <http://www.advancingwomen.com/awl/Vol30_2010/Hertneky_Balance_vol_30_No_14_9_21_10.pdf> [Accessed 15 July, 2016].

Holbrook, K., 2014. Grounded. In: Longman, K. A. and Madsen, S. R., eds. *Women and leadership in higher education*. Charlotte, NC: Information Age Publishing, pp. 219–225.

Jablonski, M., 1996. The leadership challenge for women college presidents. *Initiatives*, 57(4), pp. 1–10.

Keohane, N. O., 2012. *Thinking about leadership*. Princeton, NJ: Princeton University Press.

Kezar, A., 2014. Women's contributions to leadership and the road ahead. In: Longman, K. A. and Madsen, S. R., eds. *Women and leadership in higher education*. Charlotte, NC: Information Age Publishing, pp. 117–134.

Kezar, A. and Lester, J., 2008. Leadership in a world of divided feminism. *Journal of Women in Higher Education*, 1(1), pp. 51–75.

Longman, K. A. and Madsen, S. R., eds. 2014. *Women and leadership in higher education*. Charlotte, NC: Information Age Publishing.

Moran, B. B., 1992. Gender differences in leadership. *Library Trends* 40(3), pp. 475–491.

National Center for Education Statistics (NCES), 2015. Education attainment of young adults (Report). Available at: <https://nces.ed.gov/programs/coe/pdf/coe_caa.pdf> [Accessed 15 July, 2016].

Oikelome, G., 2016. Pathway to the presidency: The perceived impact of race, gender, and other identity structures on the journey: Experiences of white and African American women college presidents. PhD. Immaculata University.

Penney, S. H., 2014. Twenty-first century presidents must work with multiple stakeholders and be agents of change. In: Longman, K. A. and Madsen, S. R., eds. *Women and leadership in higher education*. Charlotte, NC: Information Age Publishing, pp. 205–212.

Perry, M. E. and DeLeonardo, M. C., 2011. Rising voices: Women's leadership in Jesuit higher education. *Conversations on Jesuit Higher Education*, 41(18).

Song, W. and Hartley, H. V. III., 2012. *A study of presidents of independent colleges and universities*. Washington, DC: Council of Independent Colleges.

Tunheim, K. A. and Goldschmidt, A. N., 2013. Exploring the role of calling in the professional journeys of college presidents. *Journal of Leadership, Accountability, and Ethics*, 10(4), pp. 30–39.

Wolverton, M., Bower, B. L. and Hyle, A. E., 2008. *Women at the top: What women university and college presidents say about effective leadership*. Sterling, VA: Stylus Publishing.

Women's voices on influence and vision: A legacy conference, 2014. *Agenda*. Available at: <http://www.johnsonfdn.org/conference/womens-voices-influence-and-vision-legacy-conference> [Accessed 15 July, 2016].

3

WOMEN AND INTELLECTUAL LEADERSHIP IN EAST ASIA'S ACADEMIC PROFESSIONS

A Review of the Literature

Hei-hang Hayes Tang

Introduction

In general terms we see in the academic professions a serious absence of women academic role models (Luke, 1998; Siann and Callaghan, 2001; Baker, 2010; Macfarlane, 2011; Howe-Walsh and Turnbull, 2014) and a lack of self-efficacy for advancement to senior and leadership positions (Ely, 1994; Savigny, 2014). Given that a dominance of masculine patterns of communication, leadership and performance-driven culture is observed in academia (White, 2003), alternative kinds of mentoring, guidance and personal encouragement by senior female professors can be highly beneficial to their junior women fellows. Research findings by Lam (2006) reveal that women academics consider it more ideal to be mentored by senior colleagues of the same gender. Had there been more senior professors with similar gendered experiences, aspirations and subjectivities to their own, junior women academics perceive that they might have found it easier to "model success" (Lam, 2006, p. 153).

The under-representation of women in senior levels of the academic hierarchy, especially in the fields of science, engineering and technology (Siann and Callaghan, 2001), implies an insufficiency of mentorship. There is a shortage of mentorship designed for junior women academics (Fu, 2015) and training for female academic managers (Luke, 1998). The reality of female under-representation at the higher academic ranks and in most journal editorial boards (Morley, 2014) signals to junior academic women the cultural and structural impediments to career success, which affects their self-efficacy about academic advancement, and perceived competence about attaining more senior positions (Savigny, 2014). Many women academics thus aspire more to 'catch up' with their research progress and performance than to 'ambitiously' seek to attain a leadership position

(Chen, 2008; Özkanlı *et al.*, 2009). This is especially the case for women academics who already are assigned heavy loads of administrative responsibilities (Luke, 1998, p. 48). Therefore, concerns regarding time commitment for managerial tasks, work–life/family balance and personal health keep a considerable number of junior female scholars from aspiring to take up greater intellectual roles in the academy (Acker, 2014). More problematically, the predominance of males and the subtle prevalence of a masculinist culture in senior management does not encourage female academics to expend their energies in tackling existing access impediments to intellectual leadership (White, 2003; Chen and Hune, 2011). It is argued that self-confidence, ambition, aggression, as well as quests for productivity, competitiveness and strategic planning are masculine traits in nature (Madera, Hebl and Martin, 2009), whereas the feminine attribute of caring is considered as "a form of negative equity" in higher education leadership (Morley, 2013, p. 123).

This chapter will provide an in-depth literature review of articles addressing gender inequities in academia in Hong Kong, Japan, the People's Republic of China, South Korea and Taiwan. The key focus will be on impediments to women's representation at leadership level in higher education. Little research to date has been carried out on the wider issues of inclusive learning environments or inclusive leadership in higher education in East Asia.

Impediments to Women's Representation in Academic Professions

Arguably, academia is an area where male culture and norms are practiced, favored and maintained (for example, Husu and Morley, 2000; Harley, 2003; Aiston and Jung, 2015). Impediments to access and success in senior and leadership positions lie in the bonding culture among the academics leading the academy. More often than not, males dominate those leadership positions and even today their networks form something of an 'old boys' network' (Luke, 1998; Fu, 2015; Aiston, 2011). In subtle ways, the old boys' network takes shape, not merely in the form of formal mentorship relationships, but in informal ways too. More accessible to male academics than their female colleagues (Nikunen, 2012), the informal networks offer sites for male academics to acquire more social capital in the form of insider information, collaboration opportunities and collegial/mentoring support with a view to advancing their scholarly career (De Welde and Laursen, 2011). Academics who can focus their time and energy on the socializing endeavors around the old boys' networks can become better informed of the rules of the game in the neoliberal academy, including research collaboration and publication strategies, as well as the assessment criteria for tenure and promotion. This career-related information is especially important given the reality that the assessment criteria for appraisal, contract renewal, tenure and promotion is often insufficiently transparent, and women junior academics are less well-informed of the rules of the game of the academy (Chen, 2008). Males are more likely to benefit from the social capital derived from their networks

(Bagilhole and Goode, 2001). Because culturally, men are less likely than women to devote themselves to family and household responsibilities (Savigny, 2014), they can commit more time to social networking after office hours. In such a scenario, gender bias can happen in human resources decisions, particularly when the assessment and appraisal processes remain confidential (Morley, 2013). Structurally and culturally, women academics and their career advancement cannot benefit fully from the norms and practices of the academic policies which lack inclusivity (Howe-Walsh and Turnbull, 2014).

The structural and cultural impediments for women academics to fully commit to career advancement also lie outside the academy, namely in the significant struggles they encounter in negotiating and striking work–family balance (Bailyn 2003; Probert, 2005; Özkanlı et al., 2009; Neale and Özkanlı, 2010; Beddoes and Pawley, 2014). Luke (2002), for example, particularly notes how Asian culture espouses a definite concept of femininity, insisting that women's roles and conduct in public life be framed by a configuration of cultural expectations, namely women as submissive and well-behaved wives/mothers/homemakers with restrained and quiet conduct in public life (p. 60). Citing Bhalalusesa (1998), Raddon (2002) and Beddoes and Pawley (2014), Aiston and Jung (2015) argue that the cultural expectations and discourse of becoming a 'good mother' conflict with the devotion required to be a successful academic (p. 210). It is not yet a key issue for university leaders to enable women faculty to become both 'successful academics' and 'good mothers' (Raddon, 2002). In the meantime, there is a gender difference in the time allocation for research/teaching and (hence) research productivity. Female academics in general focus more on teaching, pastoral care and administrative work for quality assurance (for example Hughes, et al., 2007).

A Snapshot of East Asia's Academic Professions

In East Asian higher education contexts, it was once culturally expected that the leaders would be male academics (Luke, 1998; Kloot, 2004). In psycho-cultural terms, female academics internalize the impediments, barriers and biased treatment which they both encounter and perceive. Such internalization in women's psyche impedes their aspirations and actions toward leadership advancement (Heilman, 2001; Cubillo and Brown, 2003; Eagly and Carli, 2007). The gender stereotypes in intellectual leadership (Nguyen, 2013) shape the interactions and practices taking place in higher education management. In the article 'I got to where I am by my own strength: Women in Hong Kong higher education management', Luke (1998) interviewed female academics who engaged in Hong Kong intellectual leadership. Given their minority status, they often feel isolated, pressured and not trusted. Usually when a woman colleague serves as the first and only female member of a committee, the other members – who are all males – respond by querying the words and deeds, as well as ability and trustworthiness of the female member of the team. The predominantly male committee plays the role of gatekeeper to ensure the competence of the 'new' member joining the leadership team. In the worst and most problematic cases, male gatekeepers perceive that females are less competent in engaging in management roles (Schein, 2007). Self-confidence is therefore seen by women academics as of importance for their success in the academy (Lam, 2006, p. 154).

Brief examples of inequities for women in East Asian countries include the fact that in Hong Kong, female academics at senior ranks spend 10 percent more of their professional time on teaching than males, and junior female academics spend 17 percent more time. In the case of Japan, senior women professors devote 41 percent more of their time to teaching than their male counterparts. This gendered disparity in understanding a meaningful academic life may partly explain why Hong Kong and Japanese female academics have the lowest research productivity (Aiston and Jung, 2015, p. 215). Although the different orientations for teaching and research can be considered the result of individual preference and professional judgement, research productivity and portfolio are the key indicator/ 'currency' of scholarly achievement in the 'prestige economy' in global higher education (Morley, 2014; Aiston and Jung, 2015). The following sections review and articulate the empirical studies which examine the cases of Hong Kong, Japan, the People's Republic of China, South Korea and Taiwan.

Portraits of the Profession: Representation and Intellectual Leadership of Women Academics in East Asia

Hong Kong

Hong Kong is one of the 'higher' education systems, well known for its concentrated presence of world-class universities. Hong Kong higher learning institutions, especially research-intensive universities, have been entrepreneurial in positioning themselves in world-class ranking systems in the age of globalizing academic capitalism (see, for example, Tang, 2014). Aiston (2014) regards the academic profession as a 'greedy' profession, demanding time commitment around the clock. When '24/7 dedication' is the norm for productive and successful academics, female colleagues, who are culturally expected to be more responsible for family commitments, encounter structural limitations to devoting time and energy in a focused manner (Aiston, 2011). Professional commitments can be inconveniently interrupted by everyday household affairs.

Hong Kong women academics perceive that marriage and children are the most significant "career impediment" and the issues they need to take into account when making career choices (Luke, 1998. p. 43). All interviewees in the doctoral study on Hong Kong senior women academics by Lam (2006) reveal that tensions between their familial and professional roles pose barriers in their career advancement. In the case of marriage with professional couples in Hong Kong, usually the wife makes greater concessions (for example, following the husband's job relocation) when "dual career conflicts" arise (Luke, 1998. p. 47). Prolific female academics need to negotiate a 'double-day' to fulfill both professional and family responsibilities (Aiston, 2014). In this way, marriage and family may encroach on the professional aspirations of Hong Kong female academics. Lam (2006) suggests that finding the 'right' husband who supports his wife's scholarly achievements is vital to the career success of women in academia.

In her article, 'Leading the academy or being led? Hong Kong women academics', Aiston (2014) argues that the academic profession is essentially gendered in the way that it rewards the competencies and skills which are supposedly masculine, whereas women academics who make their academic life with those attributes are considered and appraised as 'unfeminine'. More importantly, male academics assume the role of gatekeeper in academic leadership, forming elite male circles, directing university decision-making processes and individual scholars' career progression (p. 59). The subjectivities of 'woman' and 'academic' are essentially incompatible (Krefting, 2003), virtually placing female academics outside the core of intellectual leadership. The minority of senior women academics usually encounter difficult collegial relationships with male colleagues simply due to their different career goals, aspirations and life goals (Lam, 2006, p. 150).

In the survey carried out by Aiston (2014), the results show that women academics receive more funding internally from their own department/institution than external/public funding. Rather, male academics tend to indicate they are recipients of public research funding. But more problematically, despite the fact that, in open application for prestigious grants where males and females attain a similar standard on scholarly merits, the final scoring of 'excellent' is more likely to be distributed to male applicants than their female counterparts (the majority of whom are labelled 'good') (Benschop and Brouns, 2003; Aiston, 2014). In the case of Hong Kong, the government-sponsored grant 'General Research Fund' (GRF) is the most prestigious public grant in the higher education system. However, applications are not anonymized, and Aiston (2014) argues that such non-anonymity in the selection processes makes gender bias a knotty issue (p. 66). This impediment to obtaining prestigious research grants poses a significant obstacle to career advancement and access to intellectual leadership. Lam (2006) claims, debatably, even though there is more liberal access to academic achievement and scholarly success, some female academics prefer confining themselves to family commitments, sustaining a happy marriage, raising children well and supporting a husband in career success (p. 155)!

In the academic profession in Hong Kong, only 20 percent of senior professorial positions are taken up by women academics (Aiston, 2014). Alongside an increased participation in higher education by female students across Hong Kong universities in recent decades, there is a slight rise in female presence in junior academic positions (Lam, 2006; Postiglione and Tang, 2008). There are currently no female presidents (vice-chancellors) in Hong Kong universities. The Education University of Hong Kong (formerly the Hong Kong Institute of Education) had its first and only female president from 1997 to 2002, but Aiston (2014) observes that the institution saw a decline in the representation of women academics in senior professorial positions (p. 61).The institution has made attempts in the past decade to re-name and re-orientate from a teachers' college serving the local teaching profession to a University of Education aspiring to become a world-class institution for the Asian region. The convergence of managerial and leadership styles of the top-tier Hong Kong universities (which are predominantly public institutions accountable to society and taxpayers) engaging in the neo-liberal pursuits of research productivity and world-class status may explain, in part, this shift in gender (im)balance in the senior academic positions of the Hong Kong Institute of Education/Education University of Hong Kong. Nevertheless, across the board, female academics have been under-represented in senior academic positions in Hong Kong universities (Lam, 2006, p. 4).

Japan

Family, alongside government and the corporate sector, constitute the key pillars of social institutions making up modern Japanese society. In the Japanese state/family ideology, men are embedded in career (for example in the once-permanent salary-men work appointments with large corporations) whereas women are embedded in family. The gendered division of labor for the social institutions of family, government and corporate is imperative for the national project of modernizing Japan as Asia's economic and cultural power house. Submission to such gendered division of labor is the way for 'archetypal' Japanese citizens (Mackie, 2002) to play out their Japanese national spirit and patriotic loyalty. Alternative suggestions to the archetypically national discourse, for instance, advocating for women's leadership, invites Japanese men's resistance, and women's resignation (Usui, Rose and Kageyama, 2003, p. 96). In the everyday life of Japanese women, the notion of 'good wife, good mother' creates a moral cognition of 'correctness' and inhibits their aspirations and actions in seeking a career that leads to leadership positions. Cultural factors impede Japanese working women's progress to institutional and national leadership.

In the case of academia in Japan, there was, however, a significant increase in numbers of female academics at the turn of the 21st century. Citing the School Basic Survey published by Japan's Ministry of Education, Culture, Sports, Science and Technology (MEXT), Kimoto (2015) reported that representation of women academics rose from 9.4 percent of Japan's academic profession in 1992 to 17.4 percent in 2007. However, many more females than males are in lecturer positions (p. 91) which are lower in status, power and prestige in the Japanese academic hierarchy.

In the disciplines and fields of science, female scientists are significantly under-represented (Kano, 1988; 2007; Kimoto, 2015). In her article 'Japanese women in science and technology', Kuwahara (2001) discovered that women scientists and engineers constituted only 10 percent of the scientific workforce. For the purpose of maximizing the potential of scientists in Japan, Homma, Motohashi and Oht-subo (2013) examine ways to promote equal participation for women scientists through leadership development. They find that a minimal number of women scientists are in visible leadership roles (p. 530). Despite the fact that women attempt to act as agents of change for redefining the relationship between family and workplace, female presence in leadership roles remains insignificant (Usui, Rose and Kageyama, 2003).

Academics are expected to commit about 70 hours per week to research on top of other academic tasks, and Japanese women scientists always encounter challenges in balancing professional and domestic responsibilities (Homma, Motohashi and Ohtsubo, 2013). They also face difficulties re-entering academia after having children. Interestingly, research findings by Homma, Motohashi and Ohtsubo (2013) discovered that 70 percent of women scientists' spouses work in similar fields whereas half of the spouses of male researchers are full-time house-wives. For married scholars, professional work in academia requires particular coordination, negotiation and support from their spouse, especially for 'dual career' couples, to work out the strategies and decisions regarding time manage-ment, geographic work location and shared domestic responsibilities. Due to these factors, the gap in research productivity for Japanese women academics is dramatic (Aiston and Jung, 2015, p. 209) and hence female colleagues in the Japanese academic profession are devoting 41 percent more of their time to teaching compared with their male counterparts. Along with Hong Kong female peers, Japanese women academics attain the lowest research productivity amongst East Asian academics (Aiston and Jung, 2015, p. 215). The disadvantaged position of Japanese women academics signifies a great loss of potential productivity for Japanese society.

The People's Republic of China

Not unlike their counterparts in other East Asian academic professions, women academics in Chinese research universities encounter or perceive role conflicts between domestic and professional lives, negative experiences of gender stereo-types, gender-based discrimination and lack of access to professional networks (Zhang, 2010, p. 736). In a culturally implicit manner, there is general favoritism for boys within mainland Chinese culture. For instance, opportunities for advanced training or study abroad are more likely given to male academics than females. Talented women applicants are overlooked when academic appoint-ments are considered (Zhang, 2000, p. 22). This elusive cultural practice is espe-cially perceived by Chinese academic women and they consider it a critical impediment to their academic success (Rhoads and Gu, 2012, p. 741). In the masculine managerial culture, the male leaders discuss management issues and make human resource decisions in their own circles. In a selection committee for new staff, they highlight concerns about the possibility of a female applicant getting married and having children as legitimate, and make discriminatory recruitment decisions. Rhoads and Gu (2012) explain that is part of the reason for women's under-representation in mainland China's academic professions.

Gaskell, Eichler, Pan, Xu and Zhang (2004) argue that, given the uniqueness of modern China's political history, the status of women has been an important agenda throughout the modernizing period of the People's Republic of China. Female academics make up more than 30 percent of the PRC academic profession, alongside the increased participation of female students in higher education (p. 512). The People's Republic advances the scientific and technological development of the country through strategic development of Chinese higher education. Having said that, Zhang (2000) observed the segregation of women's representation across the academic hierarchy and maintained that "their number at different levels clearly forms into the shape of a pyramid" (p. 17) in that the higher the position's rank, the fewer the number of women academics. The paper presents the cases of five Chinese universities for training teachers (known as 'normal universities') which show the shape of a pyramid with female academics taking up about 10 percent of full professorial roles, approximately 20 percent of associate professorships, nearly 35 percent of lecturer positions and almost half of other auxiliary posts. This distribution mirrors that of other Chinese universities (see, for example, Fan, 1999), with the exception that gender balance is more likely among the lecturer and auxiliary posts in Chinese normal universities/institutions for teacher training (Zhang, 2000, p. 512).

One specific problem of gender discrimination in Chinese academia is gender-biased retirement policies (Zhang, 2000; Rhoads and Gu, 2012). By the rules in mainland China's academic profession, the retirement age for female academics is 55 (for professors the retirement age is 60), five years earlier than for Chinese male academics. According to Zhang (2000), women academics in their 50s have accumulated substantial experience in the profession and can be productive given their maturity in scholarly work (p. 22). However, they are forced to leave the academic profession. The potential for full career development for Chinese women academics is therefore restrained and Zhang (2000) argues that they are "deprived of five years of effective competition" (p. 22).

Apart from the gender disparity in career opportunity, Chinese academic women also perceive social prejudice and discrimination which are prevalent in a subtle manner throughout their academic lives (Rhoads and Gu, 2012). More often than not, female academics in mainland China are assigned less important tasks and have access to less significant social networks (for instance those that are not related to research and funding). This is especially the case when Chinese universities are more oriented to scientific research and consider teaching of secondary importance (see, for example, Zhang, 2000). As a result, the decision-making positions are less accessible to women. In her study on the job-related stress of women academics in Chinese research universities, Zhang (2010, p. 744) reports an interviewee who revealed:

... you can't really find any clues suggesting that males and females are treated differently. But when it comes to funding and research, you can see the clear difference between men and women; you will find female professors doing a lot of basic work to connect with the students but not getting the same opportunities to connect with the government or the administration.

cultural matters affect the building of social networks and accumulation of social capital. Another study of Chinese women academics by Rhoads and Gu (2012) highlights that, "Men have their own way of networking and we are left out" (p. 745). Meanwhile Zhang (2000) confirms that female academics in mainland China encounter obstacles in building networks, due to their career status and lack of intellectual resources. Shortage of female role models and mentors situates Chinese academic women in a disadvantageous position (p. 171). Another respondent in the research by Rhoads and Gu (2012) claimed that she aspired to take on leadership roles but not to be involved in the "dirty politics" (p. 745). The respondent seems to imply that dirty politics as such is more masculine in nature.

Given the dual role of family and professional duties, Chinese academic women experience greater stress levels than their male counterparts who are expected to concentrate only on career development. Female academics in China will only have satisfactory lives when they can manage both their domestic and academic responsibilities well. Otherwise, be it research productivity, intellectual advancement or pace of progress in job performance, Chinese women academics will be stressed and exhausted (Rhoads and Gu, 2012, p. 168). Zhang (2000, p.25) summarizes that women in the Chinese academic profession generally encounter unfairness in personal loads, opportunity structure and effective competition (for example, time off due to pregnancy and child care). Apart from addressing the lack of university policies for maternity leave, the Chinese academic profession can become more friendly to academics of both genders (and retain talent for the profession) by understanding a meaningful academic life from female perspectives. Rhoads and Gu (2012) suggest that Chinese female academics – shaped by the gender traits and structural disadvantages which they face – see a balanced life as more valuable than focused professional success, treasure processes more than outcomes, take evaluation from others more seriously and have greater demand for self-efficacy (p. 170). In the Chinese tradition, women's ability is held in low regard and the case is made that males outperform females in many aspects (Zhang, 2000, p. 24). Chinese academic women may have overly low self-esteem which leads to them having a subordinate position in the academic profession.

South Korea

As with other East Asian higher education institutions, feminization of the professoriate has occurred within South Korea in recent decades. Pang (1993) cited data from South Korea's National Institute of Educational Evaluation and reported the rise of female representation since the 1980s, namely from 15 percent in 1980 to nearly 20 percent in 1990. Meanwhile, the case of South Korea shares the general pattern that women are less well represented further up the academic hierarchy. In their article, 'Trailblazing women in academia: Representation of women in senior faculty and the gender gap in junior faculty's salaries in higher educational institutions', Lee and Won (2014) confirmed the trend that female academics are less likely to be tenured or promoted than their male colleagues (p. 331).

Professional careers are not the destinations young Korean women are encouraged to aspire to or pursue (Pang, 1993). Traditional gendered views in Korea mean that Korean women who manage to participate in the academic profession experience great discomfort in their positions (Koh, 1987, p. 2). Family socialization embodying less traditional emphases on gender stereotyping is helping girls to excel in intellectual development. However, the 'discomfort' originates from the deep-seated masculine organizational culture in Korean institutions, including universities. Korean female academics do not always find it easy to establish collegial relationships with men. According to academic researches, males view academic women as less successful and 'less appropriate' (Shin, 1981; Yu-Tull, 1983; Pang, 1993). In a problematic way, female academic staff in South Korean universities are seen as 'women' not as academic peers or colleagues (Min and Huh, 1998; Kim, Yoon and McLean, 2010). Whilst Korean male academics are ambitious and aggressive in seeking status, power and prestige for their career advancement, women are excluded from their old boys' networks with a 'chilly climate' towards female academics (Riger, et al. 1997; Kim, Yoon and McLean, 2010). Korean academic women are less likely to be invited to, or considered for, leadership positions (Koo, 2007). Women academics have difficultly being heard in any academic discussion/decision-making processes, as women's representation is hardly a critical mass in the South Korean academic profession.

Significantly, one aspect of discrimination against Korean academic women is in tenure and promotion (Lee and Won, 2014). Using the traditional role of Korean women in the domestic domain as justification, academic men do not encourage the access of females into the core positions of the Korean academy. Korean male academics consider males more appropriate than females in the professoriate because of traditional expectations of women as wives and mothers (Johnsrud, 1995, pp. 26, 32).

From the perspective of Korean women academics, they consider the professoriate a prestigious profession but their foremost concern is their domestic responsibilities. Their family commitment is no weaker than that of their full-time housewife counterparts (Pang, 1993). It is a general phenomenon in Korean society that, notwithstanding the rising numbers of women involved in paid employment, Korean females are still expected to play dual roles (Johnsrud, 1995). Based on the structural impediments and cultural expectations/constraints, some Korean female academics do not aspire to senior administrative positions

(Shin, 1981). In a subjective and comparative light, Korean academic women perceive that they are less competitive than women faculty in America in the face of gender-related issues in the academic professions (Shin, 1981; Cheong, 1982; Pang, 1993).

Taiwan

Taiwan has a marginally better representation of women academics among the East Asian cases (Chen, 2008, p. 332). The presence of women university presidents is not totally rare, with more than 5 percent of females among over 100 Taiwanese university presidents (Chen, 2011). In the article 'Managerialism and its impact on female academics in Taiwan', Chen (2008) reported that most women academics perceive overload in teaching duties and administration tasks, and encounter the challenge of focusing mainly on research and publications. They are generally not well-informed of the criteria for promotion but research and grant application records are increasingly essential for academic promotion (Peng, 2006). Performance indicators, for example the number of publications in journals in the Social Science Citation Index, have become an imperative indicator in the academic life of Taiwanese academics (Chou, 2014).

Lack of guidance and mentorship, as in other East Asian cases, adds force to the disadvantaged position of female academics in Taiwan. The ever-increasing managerial culture of Taiwanese universities invites the resistance of some women academics, including their reluctance to align their own research agenda with the strategic planning of their universities or funding agencies (Chen, 2008). A vicious cycle is then formed and affects Taiwanese academic women in such a way that they are too occupied with teaching and administration to be competitive in research productivity, and don't have the time and resources to win major research grants. Without major research grants, they are ineligible to apply for senior posts. These circumstances explain the empirical research that finds under-representation of women in the senior ranks of the university organizational structures (Hung, 2004; Chen, 2008). More importantly, Chen (2008) discovers there is less likelihood of female academics serving in leadership positions in institutions with greater prestige and privilege (p. 333). Another aspect of segregation observed is that more women academics can be found in private universities, in comparison with their public counterparts.

Towards Inclusivity of Intellectual Leadership in East Asia's Academic Professions?

The critical literature review in this chapter examines key empirical research into women's representation and intellectual leadership in East Asia's academic professions. The review concludes that there is significant similarity across the case studies – from Hong Kong, Japanese, Chinese, South Korean and Taiwanese universities – in terms of women's under-representation and impediments to access intellectual leadership roles. The traditional Confucian culture concerning the gendered division of labor for maintaining a good and harmonious society still gains currency in the cultural practices of everyday life among most academics and their families.

Despite the feminization of Asian workforces, wives and mothers are still expected to hold total responsibility for domestic affairs. Gender stereotypes and bias make women academics bear dual responsibilities. Female academics enjoy less of the efficiency of academic time use than men, including for research and publication commitments which are predominant indicators for attaining status, power and prestige in the race for world-class university status. The absence of a critical mass of women in leadership positions reinforces the masculinist culture in higher education governance and management, hence the formulation of policies is less likely to democratically embrace women's perspectives and concerns. Illiberal access to male-dominated old boys' networks and shortage of gender-sensitive mentorship restrain female academics from becoming full members of the academy. The vicious cycle impedes career mobility for academic women in East Asia. In turn, female academics internalize the difficulties, barriers and biased treatments which they experience. Justifiably, the predominance of masculinist culture in mainstream intellectual leadership does not attract women academics to overcoming the prevailing hurdles of access to intellectual leadership in East Asia.

Yet, the academic literature meanwhile reveals some variations and diversity regarding inclusivity of intellectual leadership across East Asia's academic professions. For example in the case of Hong Kong, domestic responsibilities possibly affect academic women the least, in comparison to their counterparts in East Asia. This is because, among working professional families/couples, employment of full-time, live-in domestic helpers/maids is commonplace (Aiston, 2014, p. 64). This aspect of impediment to career advancement can be largely alleviated. Other than that, the ethos of the Hong Kong workplace, given its relatively better gender equality, attracts many more talented young women to the private sector than to academia (Luke, 1998, p. 40), as they can gain better salaried jobs, better work–family balance and better promotion prospects. Fu (2015) claims that the Hong Kong higher education sector falls behind the Hong Kong business sector regarding gender-conscious and family-friendly initiatives in supporting women's career lives (p. 82). In Japan, the opening of more casual job positions allows more Japanese female academics to enter the academic workforce, but they remain in non-permanent work status. This poses a problem for the long-term, healthy development of Japanese academia (Normile, 2001a). Meanwhile, the organizational hierarchy of Japanese research groups, where full professors possess "near-absolute power" (Normile, 2001b, p. 817), is where junior Japanese academic women encounter academic harassment and discrimination in subtle forms which, in turn, keep women from career progression. Regarding mainland China's academic profession, alongside discriminatory employment practices and retirement policies, Rhoads and Gu (2012) suggest that one merit of the Chinese system is that it ideologically (if not always in practice) treats female and male academics as 'all comrades in arms' and they are necessarily equals. They report one case among their interviewees where a male academic leader considered the family and professional conditions of women and allowed her occasional career arrangements. In that case, a Chinese woman academic with children was promoted to associate professor and her extra family responsibilities were recognized, notwithstanding her less-than-stellar research record (p. 746). In the case of South Korea, female academics comply with the cultural norms and structural reality in their academic profession. Researching job satisfaction of women faculty at Seoul's universities, Pang (1993) finds that Korean academic women are not particularly satisfied or dissatisfied with the promotion opportunities available to them. They also do not perceive a significant difference of workload as compared with their male colleagues. But they admit that greater time commitment is needed for performance in research work and special projects.

Results from empirical research into women academics show consistently that family support, self-efficacy and determination appear to be the prerequisites for women's success in academe. Usui, Rose and Kageyama (2003) offer recommendations for attaining a gender-friendly collegial environment for Japanese higher education institutions, including offering organizational support to facilitate women's intellectual leadership and legitimizing women's leadership through embracing feminine values and perspectives in discussions and decisions on intellectual leadership. Doing so can enable the scholarship of women academics to be fairly assessed and their authority asserted. Increasing the number of females in senior positions can establish much-needed role models to help mentor junior generations of women academic professionals (p. 532). These ideas are transferable across East Asia and could help promote a 'pipeline' of women academics prepared to enter into senior leadership roles and, over time, provide the much-needed role modelling for young women entering into intellectual leadership in the East Asian academic professions.

Unsurprisingly female academics across East Asia are keener advocates of equality, diversity and inclusiveness, than male academic leaders (Fu, 2015, pp. 79–80). Without empowering and capitalizing on women's talents and skills (Nguyen, 2013, p. 135), there will be ongoing loss of potential productivity for East Asian societies. While this chapter has focused on the issue of gender in East Asian universities, there are obviously many other factors to consider in developing a culture of inclusive leadership. With significant numbers of students from East Asian cultures undergoing their higher education in other parts of the world, it is possible they will see the advantages of more inclusive societies and push for significant change when they return to their own country and culture. It is recommended that there be policy and institutional transformations for creating more inclusive academic environments. The transformations should be informed by women's perspectives, which see personal and professional lives, marriage and family, identity, agency and power differently from the taken-for-granted male worldviews. However, women in particular need to want to take on this challenge. East Asian universities may need to look to universities in other societies to ask how best to provide the mentoring, the development and the encouragement that is required to build more inclusive cultures. Only through a more humanistic approach to recruitment, retention and reward within the academic profession and intellectual leadership can talented academic women be attracted and retained – for a more powerful and healthier development of East Asia's academic professions.

References

Acker, S., 2014. A foot in the revolving door? Women academics in lower-middle management. *Higher Education Research & Development*, 33(1), pp. 73–85.

Aiston, S. J., 2011. Equality, justice and gender: Barriers to the ethical university for women. *Ethics and Education*, 6(3), pp. 279–291.

Aiston, S. J., 2014. Leading the academy or being led? Hong Kong women academics. *Higher Education Research & Development*, 33(1), pp. 59–72.

Aiston, S. J. and Jung, J., 2015. Women academics and research productivity: An international comparison. *Gender and Education*, 27(3), pp. 205–220.

Bagilhole, B. and Goode, J., 2001. The contradiction of the myth of individual merit, and the reality of a patriarchal support system in academic careers. *The European Journal of Women's Studies*, 8(2), pp. 161–180.

Bailyn, L., 2003. Academic careers and gender equity: Lessons learned from MIT. *Gender, Work and Organization*, 10(2), pp. 137–153.

Baker, M., 2010. Choices or constraints? Family responsibilities, gender and academic career. *Journal of Comparative Family Studies*, 41(1), pp. 1–18.

Beddoes, K. and Pawley, A. L., 2014. Different people have different priorities: Work–family balance, gender and the discourse of choice. *Studies in Higher Education*, 39(9), pp. 1573–1585.

Benschop, Y. and Brouns, M., 2003. Crumbling ivory towers: Academic organizing and its gender effects. *Gender, Work and Organization*, 10(2), pp. 194–212.

Bhalalusesa, E., 1998. Women's career and professional development: Experiences and challenges. *Gender and Education*, 10(1), pp. 21–33.

Chen, A-Y-H., 2011. Women university president work–family adaptation life journey. Master's thesis; in Chinese. Available from Airiti Library (U0021–1610201315262795).

Chen, D-I-R., 2008. Managerialism and its impact on female academics in Taiwan. *Journal of Asian Public Policy*, 1(3), pp. 328–345.

Chen, E. W. C. and Hune, S., 2011. Asian American Pacific Islander women from Ph.D. to campus president: Gains and leaks in the pipeline. In: Jean-Marie, G. and Lloyd-Jones, B. eds. *Women of color in higher education: Changing directions and new perspectives* (Vol. 10). Bingley, UK: Emerald Group, pp. 163–190.

Cheong, H. E., 1982. A study on the professional women's role at home: with emphasis on the women professor in Seoul. Master's thesis, Seoul: Hanyang University.

Chou, C. P., 2014. *The SSCI syndrome in higher education: a local or global phenomenon.* Rotterdam: Sense Publishers.

Cubillo, L. and Brown, M., 2003. Women into educational leadership and management: International differences? *Journal of Educational Administration*, 41(3), pp. 278–291.

De Welde, K. and Laursen, S. L., 2011. The glass obstacle course: Informal and formal barriers for women Ph.D. students in STEM fields. *International Journal of Gender, Science and Technology*, 3(3), pp. 571–595.

Eagly, A. H. and Carli, L., 2007. Women and the labyrinth of leadership. *Harvard Business Review*, 85(9), pp. 62–71.

Ely, R. J., 1994. The effects of organizational demographics and social identity on relationships among professional women. *Administrative Science Quarterly*, 39(2), pp. 203–238.

Fan, C., 1999. Mixed blessings: Modernizing the education of women. In: Michael, A. and Adamson, B., eds. *Higher education in post-Mao China*. Hong Kong: Hong Kong University Press, pp. 299–320.

Fu, K., 2015. Women academics and higher education leadership in Hong Kong: A case study of the Faculty of Education and Li Ka Shing Faculty of Medicine in the University of Hong Kong. Master's thesis, Hong Kong: The University of Hong Kong.

Gaskell, J., Eichler, M., Pan, J., Xu, J. and Zhang, X., 2004. The participation of women faculty in Chinese universities: Paradoxes of globalization. *Gender and Education*, 16(4), pp. 511–529.

Harley, S., 2003. Research selectivity and female academics in UK universities: From gentleman's club and barrack yard to smart macho? *Gender and Education*, 15(4), pp. 377–392.

Heilman, M. E., 2001. Description and prescription: How gender stereotypes prevent women's ascent up the organizational ladder. *Journal of Social Issues*, 57(4), pp. 657–674.

Homma, M. K., Motohashi, R. and Ohtsubo, H., 2013. Maximizing the potential of scientists in Japan: Promoting equal participation for women scientists through leadership development. *Genes to Cells*, 18(7), pp. 529–532.

Howe-Walsh, L. and Turnbull, S., 2014. Barriers to women leaders in academia: Tales from science and technology. *Studies in Higher Education*, 41(3), pp. 415–428.

Hughes, C., Clouder, L., Pritchard, J. and Purkis, J., 2007. Caring monsters? A critical exploration of contradictions and ambiguities. In: Cotterill, P., Jackson, S. and Letherby, G., eds. *Challenges and negotiations for women in higher education*. Dordrecht: Springer, pp. 131–147.

Hung, J. H., 2004. The administrative gender horizon in higher education: A study of female university deans. *Bulletin of Educational Research*, 50(4), pp. 79–113.

Husu, L. and Morley, L., 2000. Academic and gender: What has and has not changed? *Higher Education in Europe*, 25(2), pp. 137–138.

Johnsrud, L. K., 1995. Korean academic women: Multiple roles, multiple challenges. *Higher Education*, 30(1), pp. 17–35.

Kano, Y., 1988. *Academic women: Sociology of (or by?) female academics*. Tokyo: Toshindo. (In Japanese)

Kano, Y., 2007. Academic marketplace for academic women. In: Yamanoi, A., ed. *Academic marketplace in Japan*. Tokyo: Tamagawa University Press, pp. 168–189. (In Japanese)

Kim, N., Yoon, H. J. and McLean, G. N., 2010. Policy efforts to increase women faculty in Korea: Reactions and changes at universities. *Asia Pacific Education Review*, 11(3), pp. 285–299.

Kimoto, N., 2015. Gender bias: What has changed for female academics? In: Ariosto, A., Cummings, W. K., Huang, F. and Shin, J. C., eds. *The changing academic profession in Japan*. Switzerland: Springer International Publishing, pp. 89–102.

Kloot, L., 2004. Women and leadership in universities: A case study of women academic managers. *International Journal of Public Sector Management*, 17(6), pp. 470–485.

Koh, H. C., 1987. Korean women, conflict, and change: An approach to development planning. In: Kendall, L. and Peterson, M., eds. *Korean women: View from the inner room.* New Haven: East Rock Press, pp. 159–174.

Koo, J. S., 2007. The status of women professors and gender politics. *The Politics of Education*, 14(2), pp. 7–28. (In Korean)

Krefting, L.A., 2003. Intertwined discourse of merit and gender: Evidence from academic employment in the USA. *Gender, Work and Organisation*, 10(2), pp. 213–238.

Kuwahara, M., 2001. Japanese women in science and technology. *Minerva*, 39(2), pp. 203–216.

Lam, M. P. H., 2006. Senior women academics in Hong Kong: A life history approach. PhD thesis, Hong Kong: The University of Hong Kong.

Lee, Y. J. and Won, D., 2014. Trailblazing women in academia: Representation of women in senior faculty and the gender gap in junior faculty's salaries in higher educational institutions. *The Social Science Journal*, 51(3), pp. 331–340.

Luke, C., 1998. 'I got to where I am by my own strength': Women in Hong Kong higher education management. *Education Journal*, 26(1), pp. 31–58.

Luke, C., 2002. Globalization and women in South East Asian higher education management. *Teachers College Record*, 104(3) pp. 625–662.

Macfarlane, B., 2011. Professors as intellectual leaders: Formation, identity and role. *Studies in Higher Education*, 36(1), pp. 57–73.

Mackie, V., 2002. Embodiment, citizenship and social policy in contemporary Japan. In: Goodman, R., ed. *Family and social policy in Japan: Anthropological approaches.* Cambridge: Cambridge University Press, pp. 200–229.

Madera, J. M., Hebl, M. R. and Martin, R. C., 2009. Gender and letters of recommendation for academia: Agentic and communal differences. *Journal of Applied Psychology*, 94 (6), pp. 1591–1599.

Min, M. S. and Huh, H. R., 1998. *Faculty gender imbalance in Korean university: Present status and future needs.* Seoul: Korean Women's Development Institute (KWDI). (In Korean)

Morley, L., 2013. The rules of the game: Women and the leaderist turn in higher education. *Gender and Education*, 25(1), pp. 116–131.

Morley, L., 2014. Lost leaders: Women in the global academy. *Higher Education Research & Development*, 33(1), pp. 114–128.

Neale, J. and Özkanlı, O., 2010. Organisational barriers for women in senior management: A comparison of Turkish and New Zealand universities. *Gender and Education*, 22(5), pp. 547–563.

Nguyen, T. L. H., 2013. Barriers to and facilitators of female deans' career advancement in higher education: An exploratory study in Vietnam. *Higher Education*, 66(123), pp. 123–138.

Nikunen, M., 2012. Changing university work, freedom, flexibility and family. *Studies in Higher Education*, 37(6), pp. 713–729.

Normile, D., 2001a. Women academics propose steps to equity. *Science*, 292(5516), p. 416.

Normile, D., 2001b. Women faculty battle Japan's koza system. *Science*, 291(5505), pp. 817–818.

Özkanlı, Ö., Machado, M. L., White, K., O'Connor, P., Riordan, S. and Neale, J., 2009. Gender and management in HEIs: Changing organisational and management structures. *Tertiary Education and Management*, 15(3), pp. 241–257.

Pang, J. M. S. 1993. Job satisfaction of women faculty at universities in Seoul, Republic of Korea. PhD thesis, Texas: University of North Texas.

Peng, S. M., 2006. Official report: The study of teachers' evaluation mechanism in higher education. Databank of higher education in Taiwan. Available from: <http://www.cher.ed.ntnu.edu.tw/analyze/> [Accessed 12 March, 2017].

Postiglione, G. A., and Tang, H. H. H., 2008. A preliminary review of the Hong Kong changing academic profession data. In: RIHE, ed. *The changing academic profession in international, comparative and quantitative perspectives: Report of the international conference on the changing academic profession project, 2008.* Hiroshima: RIHE, Hiroshima University, pp. 227–249.

Probert, B., 2005. 'I just didn't fit in': Gender and unequal outcomes in academic careers. *Gender, Work & Organization,* 12(1), pp. 50–72.

Raddon, A., 2002. Mothers in the academy: Positioned and positioning within discourses of the 'successful academic' and the 'good mother'. *Studies in Higher Education,* 27(4), pp. 387–403.

Rhoads, R. A. and Gu, D. Y., 2012. A gendered point of view on the challenges of women academics in The People's Republic of China. *Higher Education,* 63(6), pp. 733–750.

Riger, S., Stokes, J., Raja, S. and Sullivan, M., 1997. Measuring perceptions of the work environment for female faculty. *The Review of Higher Education,* 21(1), pp. 63–78.

Savigny, H., 2014. Women, know your limits: Cultural sexism in academia. *Gender and Education,* 26(7), pp. 794–809.

Schein, V. E., 2007. Women in management: Reflections and projections. *Women in Management Review,* 22(1), pp. 6–18.

Shin, E. S., 1981. A study on the role conflict of women professors in Korea. Master's thesis, Seoul: Ewha Womans University.

Siann, G. and Callaghan, M., 2001. Choices and barriers: Factors influencing women's choice of higher education in science, engineering and technology. *Journal of Further and Higher Education,* 25(1), pp. 85–95.

Tang, H. H. H., 2014. Academic capitalism in Greater China: Theme and variations. In: Cantwell, B. and Kauppinen, I., eds. *Academic capitalism in the age of globalization.* Baltimore, Maryland: The Johns Hopkins University Press, pp. 208–227.

Usui, C., Rose, S. and Kageyama, R., 2003. Women, institutions, and leadership in Japan. *Asian Perspective,* 27(3), pp. 85–123.

White, K., 2003. Women and leadership in higher education in Australia. *Tertiary Education and Management,* 9(1), pp. 45–60.

Yu-Tull, D., 1983. An investigation of attitudes and perceptions of educators in Korean higher education toward job performance ability of women in Korean higher education. PhD dissertation, Washington, DC: George Washington University.

Zhang, J., 2000. Study of the status of women teachers in China's higher education. *Chinese Education & Society,* 33(4), pp. 16–29.

Zhang, L., 2010. A study on the measurement of job-related stress among women academics in research universities of China. *Frontiers of Education in China,* 5(2), pp. 158–176.

4

INTERSECTIONALITY AND INCLUSIVE LEADERSHIP IN THE UNIVERSITY

Case Studies from Denmark

Kirsten Locke

Introduction

This chapter has several ambitions in the context of inclusive leadership in the university. First, as a resistance to top-down transactional forms of leadership this chapter offers inclusive leadership alternatives through the voices of three women in positions of leadership in a specific university context. Second, the chapter explores the position of women in the university and the barriers women experience in attaining named and formal positions of academic leadership such as, for example, full professor and head of department respectively. While inclusive styles of leadership are not the panacea for gender equity in the university, the discussion brings in the responses of three interview participants to explore the way their experiences in leadership positions in the university have led them to value inclusivity as a fundamental leadership approach. The final ambition is a question of methodology, in which I incorporate the concept of intersectionality to explore women's leadership experiences in the university, and the space opened in their own subjective positions when viewed through this methodological lens.

The Gender (Im)Balance in Universities

The question of the impact of gender on academic career trajectories is one that has reappeared at moments of perceived acute imbalance in the last 50 years, of which the second decade of the 21st century is shaping up to be one such example. With the majority of western, developed countries pursuing an agenda of widening participation in higher education that has paralleled broader societal shifts based on human rights and discourses of equality and democracy, universities have seen a rapid rise in the number of female students and increasing numbers of female academics entering management and leadership positions in the academy. Taking New Zealand as an example to illustrate this point, women have consistently outnumbered men in attaining university undergraduate and postgraduate qualifications since at least the turn of the 21st century (Callister *et al.*, 2006; Newell and Callister, 2008). At the University of Auckland, New Zealand, women now constitute 44.7 percent of the academic staff cohort but constitute only 28.6 percent of senior academic staff (University of Auckland, 2014). This paucity of representation in senior academic positions is reflected on a national and international scale where the seemingly intractable fact remains that substantially fewer women make it to professorial level than their male counterparts (for some recent examples, see Lindberg, Riis, and Silander, 2011; Deem, 2013; Heijstra, Bjarnason, and Rafnsdóttir, 2015; Loots and Walker, 2015). Likewise, only minor gains have been made in the numbers of women appointed to the highest levels of university management and leadership. One specific observation that emerges in light of this misbalance is that there is still not a comparatively assured pathway to higher-level positions for women compared to those of men in the university, despite a clear discourse of sustained and supported participation at all levels of academic engagement. Some of the potential reasons for these discrepancies are explored in this chapter through an analysis that combines structural and socio-cultural dimensions, and their interactions and intersections with the subjective positioning of academics.

As Søndergaard outlines, taking up university positions and achieving promotion within academic hierarchies demands "at least two sets of competencies" (Søndergaard, 2005, p. 189). One set of competencies revolves around the formal expectations and requirements of academia that can be measured relatively easily through publications and other tangible outputs. These include gaining funding, winning national and international prizes, formal teaching evaluations, and citation metrics. Other evidence includes connections with larger, more prestigious, international research networks that can be evidenced by conference attendance, invitations to present in various forums, and external grant applications. This set of formal competencies can often be viewed and observed objectively, such as in the form of one's curriculum vitae and other appropriate applications and proposals that are exposed to formal assessment procedures. These competencies accumulate over the course of a career and are the observable 'facts' about the academic.

The second set of competencies however, are much harder to measure but are no less significant. These encompass the socio-cultural categories that, as Søndergaard states, "would imply knowledge about how to 'do academic'" (2005, p. 190). 'Doing academic' constitutes a set of performances that are not exposed to formal assessment procedures, but emerge in the daily lives of academics in the way they interact with colleagues, form allegiances and alliances, and broadly position themselves in advantageous ways alongside others. Søndergaard expands on these competencies as involving:

practical-social knowledge about how to behave in different situations, what to say when and in what way, how to network, how to economize information and how to handle mutual favours as well as obstructions in interactions with academic colleagues, competitors, friends, superiors and subordinates (Søndergaard, 2005, p. 190).

This academic 'know-how' works in the cracks, so to speak, of the more formalized sets of capabilities and competencies and, while not subject to formalized modes of assessment and judgement, is nonetheless a powerful source and contributor to academic subjective positioning. However, these sets of competencies do not work in isolation from another important dimension and that is the performance and articulation of gender, which serves both to mediate and dictate these informal rules of engagement. Drawing on the work of Butler (1990), the performance, or 'doing', of gender cannot be separated from the performance or 'doing' of academic if the complex ways in which each are iteratively produced as mutually constitutive articulations are taken into account. To illustrate the point as a means to move to the next layer of analyses at work in this chapter, Butler's account of gender/sex is the iterative performance of that category that lends itself to credibility, viability, and visibility, as is aptly stated in the following quote:

> 'Sex' is, thus, not simply what one has, or a static description of what one is: it will be one of the norms by which the 'one' becomes viable at all, that which qualifies a body for life within the domain of cultural intelligibility (Butler, 1993, p. 2).

In this context, practical-social knowledge in the academy is intimately embedded in the 'doing' of gender in ways that ensure cultural intelligibility, and this, as we will see, has no small part to play in the subjective negotiations of career trajectories for academics themselves.

Introducing Intersectionality

By way of understanding these informal and formal sets of competencies in academia, the concept of intersectionality will be utilized in order to make sense of the complexities at work in the processes involved in subjective academic positioning and negotiations. An understanding of intersectionality as a methodological tool for analysis is required before further explication of its relevance as a research paradigm. Emerging initially in the North American context of radical race theory to depict the marginalization and positioning of black women (Crenshaw, 1991a; 1991b), intersectionality offered a framework of analysis that considered the interrelations between different socio-cultural categories of identification and differentiation. Intersectionality provides a conceptual frame with which to explore how categories such as family, class, ethnicity, gender, religious affiliation, sexuality, and nationality, intersect and mutually construct each other in ways that position subjects in relation to discursive and societal forces of power or sub-jugation (Collins, 1998). These crossovers, repetitions, and interactions cannot be separated from each other and are to be seen as mutually constitutive elements that influence or 'tone' each socio-cultural category (Staunæs and Søndergaard, 2011). An example of this is the way the category of 'gender' when intersected with 'race' and 'socio-economic class' produces certain effects that impact both identity constitution and the interrelations between each category.

The analytical potential of intersectionality as a research paradigm has under-gone a number of recalibrations and developments to support researchers in understanding more fully the interrelations between multiple categories including gender, class, age, and ethnicity for example, in order to grasp the complexities, nuances, and dynamisms of these socio-cultural categories and their effects on identity formation and subjective positioning.

The unfolding interplay of each dimension, in the context of this chapter, of academic identity construction, offers a further analytical tool with which to understand the negotiations of the academic subject in the context of their career trajectories. It also offers an interesting lens with which to view their own lea-dership subjectivities and the ways they have incorporated inclusive leadership approaches into their leadership styles over time. It is to the notion of leadership identities and the lens of intersectionality that I now turn.

Intersectionality and Leadership

According to Richardson and Loubier (2008), intersectionality provides an inter-esting theoretical lens with which to view notions of leadership, for two reasons. First, people live multiple layered identities, therefore it is critical that we start to use multiple aspects or factors to examine leadership diversity. Second, the application of an intersectionality lens aims to reveal these multiple identities and personas of social actors in order to reveal the connections between a range of socio-cultural factors. In other words, leadership styles, identities, and subjective positioning cannot be reduced to one singular dominant characteristic or influence; they instead must be read in a more holistic and broad sense to understand distinct experiences and the effects of inextricably connected roles and situations (p. 143).

When further applied to understanding the complexities of leadership construc-tions and styles, intersectionality can be stretched beyond a singular application to identity formation, to a broader socio-cultural platform that incorporates the past histories and experiences of these identity subjectivities. This means that, when applied to understanding how women negotiate their own leadership position-ality, their past experiences of working under academic leaders such as heads of department for example, affect the way they constitute and construct their own leadership styles and agendas into the future. Manuel (2007) extends this further in the leadership literature by suggesting different policy formations, agendas, and constructions be taken into consideration within the intersectional approach. Defined by Manuel as "structural intersectionality" (p. 182), when applied to understanding the position of women as leaders (inclusive or otherwise), consideration of the structures of the university within which they are constituting themselves as leaders, whilst in turn being constituted by the university itself, must be given. According to Manuel, and important in the light of the data samples presented later in this chapter, "structural intersectionality can be dynamic (changing in different contexts) or subordinating" (p. 182). We will see for the women under consideration in this chapter, that they indeed experienced both the potentially liberating and undoubtedly subordinating and identity-negating affects throughout the trajectories of their academic careers.

When applying structural intersectionality alongside intersectionality as an identity-constituting force, barriers and challenges to women's attainment to achieve and perform leadership roles are illuminated. In the context of the wider workplace, Sanchez-Hucles and Davis (2010) offer a particularly critical application of intersectionality to explore the way in which women are often appointed to senior positions when companies have performed poorly. They observe that "women are likely to find themselves dealing with situations that have high risk and that can potentially set them up for failure" (p. 172). When referring to the 'know-how' of 'doing' academic appropriately and acceptably, this perspective of women at the top of what can be called a 'glass cliff', sheds light on the way women in academic leadership positions can be judged harshly despite their skills and credentials just for being placed in a precarious leadership role (that presumably would not be offered to an equally qualified male colleague). The point here is that structural intersectionality allows us to see the nature of this glass cliff and the intersecting categories that incorporate both the ambitions and agendas of individuals and the organizational structures of a workplace that allow such appointments to be made in the first place.

To summarize what we have covered thus far, the chapter has outlined the performative dimension to being, or following Butler, 'doing' academia as consisting of formal and informal elements that are performed on an individual subjective level but are also actioned in ways that subjectify and shape academic identities through interactions with others. The concept of intersectionality as a lens with which to view the identity-constituting forces at play allows a way in to make visible the intersecting socio-cultural categories of class, gender, and race and the way these intersecting elements produce certain subjectifying or subjugating affects that influence the negotiations women in academia make throughout their daily realities.

We have also seen the expansion of the methodological reach of intersectionality to incorporate socio-cultural categories that include academic status, age, and leadership position. Categories such as historical narratives of leadership experience extend this reach even further. Finally, intersectionality has been broadened to include the structural dimensions of workplaces and organizations that encompass the policies and forms of governance that impact the extent to which manoeuvrability, access, and sustainability of leadership positions and roles is even possible. To lend this discussion further applicability, the chapter now turns to specific interview data from three senior academic women and their experiences and current approaches with the formation of their own leadership subjectivities that lean toward inclusivity as a specific approach.

Background to the Project

The analyses presented in this chapter originate from a comparative project in which I was involved under the auspices of the EU FP7 PEOPLE IRSES project 'University Reform, Globalization and Europeanization' (URGE) that explored women in positions of academic leadership and management in New Zealand and Denmark. Alongside my co-researcher, I undertook interviews with a group of 15 women from a selection of well-established universities during October and November 2013. All of the women had reached professorial level in their university, or were working at a high level of academic leadership in research, or as head of department, head of faculty, and in one case a former pro-vice chancellor of a university. An underlying driver of the study was the very large discrepancy between the numbers of male and female professors in both the Danish and New Zealand university systems. The 2013 statistical stock take from the Danish Agency for Higher Education Statistics and Analysis put the percentage of women professors at 18.4 percent, as opposed to the male cohort of 81.6 percent (Ståhle, 2013). Likewise, the *New Zealand Census of Women's Participation* released in 2012 reported 17.22 percent of women at professorial level compared to the 82.78 percent apportioned to their male colleagues in the New Zealand tertiary system (Human Rights Commission, 2012, p. 137). This statistical imbalance set the context for the direction the data gathering would take, and all questions were shaped around exploring reasons for this statistical discrepancy.

The semi-structured interviews of all participants loosely followed the same structure that began with an introduction outlining their publicly available curriculum vitae, about which each participant was invited to comment. The participants were then asked questions about challenges and obstacles they had encountered throughout their careers. Questions were also asked about personal circumstances they considered relevant to the trajectory of their careers, whether or not they were mothers or partners, their domestic circumstances, and their general perspectives on the way they had navigated the terrain of academia up until that point. The ways in which the participants responded to these prompts garnered different reactions (Locke, 2015), but the three women in focus in this chapter all talk about career-defining moments that influenced their own inclusive leadership styles. These moments are now presented in the form of three case studies.

Case Study 1

Wearing 'Armour' to Survive: Structural Intersectionality of Governance and Personal Narrative

Denmark, like other countries such as New Zealand, has undergone a sustained period of reform over the last two decades that has radically altered the structural organization of the university. Describing governance as "the array of ways that a university orders its own affairs by managing its relations with the state; maintaining its own internal organization and, instilling certain values and expectations of individual conduct," Wright (2014, p. 295) provides an outline of the reforms and the effects these had on individuals working in the Danish university system. Moving from a democratic system whereby students, academic, administrative, and technical staff elected the leaders and decision-making bodies at every level of the university organization, Wright details the introduction of a 'new' form of university governance that replaced the democratic system with a governing board that was elected primarily from outside the university. Rather than moving accountability 'down' to the people to whom a leader was accountable, the new form of governance shifted accountability 'upwards' in a structure that mirrored the introduction of New Management policy strategies. Just one example of this is the governing board now appointed the rector (the equivalent of a position known also as vice chancellor) in the manner a company would appoint its CEO.

This first case study explores this new form of governance and its intersection with the experiences of one senior woman academic working under a more senior male to whom she reported at the time that this form of governance was first introduced into the Danish universities. As with all the case studies in focus in this chapter, this woman was herself a very senior academic occupying both a formal, named leadership position as the head of a well-established research center, and an academic leadership position by virtue of her status as a full professor. Recalling the notion of structural intersectionality, this participant describes the difficulty of working under the leadership style of a person who was not accountable to his staff, and the effect this experience had on her own development as a leader. While overcoming the challenges involved in working within a structure where academic leaders had no formal responsibility toward their staff other than managing outputs and congruent institutional values, the participant describes a very difficult period where the behavior of this leader was threatening and bullying toward her specifically. While the reasons for this were varied, the participant cites the example of introducing a new Master's level programme and not wanting to force the programme to grow too fast. The participant continues:

> I walked over to the meeting and told him that we … need to build it [the programme] … It takes time, but we are working and I tried to tell him we are loyal to what your plans are.

The response to this explanation from the male leader was:

Sometimes when I look at you I feel like beating you up.

What we can see in this shocking response, is the extent to which this senior male leader wanted his colleague to align her values and vision with those of the university and his own duties to develop and grow his department like a business. The interviewee, however, articulated clearly that she wanted to take things slowly enough to develop a program that was cohesive and well structured, and for this she needed time. When asked in the interview how she coped with this challenge, the interviewee answered in this revealing way:

For a very long time, I had a leather jacket, and I put it on very often when I was going to a meeting at the Academic Council. And I just realized why did I do that. And I felt like sort of protecting myself, yeah. Really. So it wasn't a very pleasant atmosphere. It was okay at the department mainly, but going from the department and representing it at the Academic Council, I tried to avoid having more contact than I had to with the [Head of Council] and people around him. It was a terrible psychological strain at the time.

For this participant, finding a metaphorical suit of armor in the physical form of her leather jacket signified an important piece of resistance to the style of leadership exhibited by her colleague. In the context of structural intersectionality, it is important to link the leadership style of this particular colleague to a form of university governance that endorsed a top-down approach whereby appointed (mainly male) leaders did not have to answer to those below them in the managerial hierarchy. Rather, the structures of the university endorsed a form of governance that allowed inappropriate and bullying behavior through ensuring accountability was strategically aimed 'above.' In describing this as a pivotal moment, the dawning of her own construction of an academic leader identity, the participant describes her current leadership style – that exists within the same form of governance, albeit with the benefit of a couple of years for it to develop within the structures of the university – as valuing time, attention, and transparency:

That procedures are open to the people involved, which also means that it's … not only a matter of information, it is also a matter of having enough time to have dialogues that are necessary.

Discussing the working context of the research center she now heads, the participant defines her style of leadership against the leadership she experienced, in the following way:

There's a lot of laughter, hardly any conflicts. And this may turn because suddenly we might not have enough money or whatever, but at the moment we are just building and making sure we don't grow too fast, I think.

The intersecting points of governance and personal narrative are career-defining for this participant as she navigates her own leadership capabilities and styles toward a more inclusive and even rational form of leadership. While there are markers of contemporary 'fish-hooks' in the form of tight deadlines to achieve maximum productivity, and pressures to generate income and the ever-present threat of not having enough money to run an efficient center, the form of governance that allowed the appalling behavior of her previous manager to emerge produces a completely different set of academic subjectivities when the participant herself becomes a leader.

Rather than being threatening and abusive, she is collaborative and objective; in short she incorporates the definition of inclusive leadership as a style of leadership "manifested by openness, accessibility, and availability of a leader" (Carmeli, Reiter-Palmon, and Ziv, 2010, p. 250).

Her type of resistance, in the form of metaphorical armor, engendered a pivotal moment in the formation of her academic identity as a future leader. The intersectionality of university governance and personal narrative initiated a leadership subjectivity that could withstand the institutional structural forces to produce a more collaborative and inclusive leadership approach inside the university.

Case Study 2

The 'Glass Cliff': Intersecting Gender with Institutional and Individual Power

> I think it is gender here because I simply, I couldn't play the power ... the game of power in the right way, or maybe I could, but I didn't want to do it.

Like the previous example, the interviewee in this second case study is a very senior academic woman who headed a large research department and also held a significant leadership position in the management structures of a Danish university. Also like the previous example, this participant in the study was appointed to a senior leadership position when Denmark was first instituting reforms in governance. Unlike the previous example, this participant subsequently left the university to pursue a career in her disciplinary field of expertise. Therefore this case study is more a story of inclusive leadership, as an explicit approach at the beginning, and the tensions that arose with the intersectionality of a leadership approach from a colleague who wielded institutional and gendered power over the participant in ways that were fundamental to her decision to leave the university. As the quote that leads this case study section explains, this participant was explicit in her identification of the intersecting effects the categories of gender and power had on her own leadership identity.

When describing her leadership style prior to her taking up a significant leadership position, this participant describes working as part of a team as a fundamental element. She continues:

I've been a team worker and researcher all my life ... My way of leadership is to be in a very good team and I am very good at managing a team ... I know there are a lot of things that I don't know, but I don't care because I am good at something and very good at working together with a lot of people who know these things...

A subjective marker of this participant is her robust sense of self in the context of her capabilities. Recalling Butler again, this participant can be viewed as an accomplished performer of 'doing academic' in that both the sociality involved in working well with others to succeed, and the traditional measurement of research expertise in the form of funding and output, are in abundance. When the offer of a prestigious leadership position in her university came her way, this participant expected these capabilities and her previous inclusive leadership approach to hold her in good stead. This is reinforced in the following statement:

And that is what I wanted when I became a [senior academic leadership position in the university], that we should be a team. That was why I went into it.

The reality however, was quite different:

But very quickly I found out that this was only something that was said. It was not a team. It was the [boss] who decided. And I had a male [co-leader], he was absolutely not working in a team and very quickly when we started to work ... I found out that this was more about fighting each other and getting your territory and it was about power and we had a lot of discussions about who was in charge of these things.

The intersecting categories of gender and power can be read in these responses to produce an effect on the participant that was subjugating and dominating. The performative dimension to her academic identity 'told' her to acquiesce and to force a sociality that neutralized the conflict. Yet, the participant explains she simply could not bring herself to take part in the power games of her colleagues and, as such, the well-honed capacity to engage and negotiate the sociality of academia was not utilized, arguably, to the detriment of the perceived 'success' of the leadership position. This reading of power can be extended to structural intersectionality, whereby the institutional power emerges in the metaphor of the 'glass cliff'. The participant/interviewee was placed in a role that was set up to fail in the context of the competing leadership agendas and styles that surrounded her. Describing herself as, at first, invigorated by the challenge of holding a significant academic leadership position, the participant becomes discouraged by the gendered politics and negotiations inherent in the leadership culture of the university. After a period of time in this position, the participant leaves the university to work in the private sector.

Case Study 3

The Great Seducer? Intersecting Power with Academic Subjectivities

Like the interviewees in the previous two case studies, the participant in focus for this case study is both a full professor and the head of a research center. What this participant articulates a little differently to the previous two participants is her resistance to stepping into significant management positions in the university and to, instead, approach inclusive leadership primarily through the platform of her research. The defining moment that influenced this participant's perspective on academic leadership occurred in the early stages of her career when she was first appointed as a young academic at a Danish university. Having established a scholarly reputation early in her academic career, the participant was employed in a department run by an older male head of department who was close to retirement. Describing this period of her academic life as formative and responsible for creating the desire and motivation to better understand the university, the participant describes the relationship with the head of department in the following way:

> Anyway, I think that he thought he could discipline me somehow, and I was in constant opposition to whatever and thought that I was in my good right to do research and to teach the way I wanted to ... At a particular point I went into his office and asked him 'what is it you want, what is it you want? Do you want me to make bad lectures? Do you want me to do bad teaching ...?' And I mean afterwards ... I could see that it was a stupid thing to say ... but that was what he wanted me to do. He wanted me to lie down and to accept my place in the hierarchy ... which I didn't [do].

For the participant, the leadership style of her head of department was oppressive yet stimulating in that it shaped her own subjective position as an academic as a response to the overt discipline he tried to wield over her as a young female academic. When exploring this through the lens of intersectionality, the socio-cultural categories of age and gender clearly intersect with the power on display from a more senior leader who tried, unsuccessfully, to assert his dominance over the young academic. It is also important to note the way this power relation helped solidify and define the academic identity of this participant in ways that inspired her throughout her career and that would become important as she began to build her career.

Moving to her current context as an academic leader in the sense of being a well-established scholar in her disciplinary field, the participant introduces a further dimension to structural intersectionality – that of power and age, in themselves intersecting factors – in her constitution of academic identity formation. This further dimension is the force the university brings to notions of leadership in an external sense. Academic leadership in the contemporary context involves an expectation to incorporate the dual tasks of managerial leadership positions alongside scholarly leadership in an area of expertise. The participant articulates this structural force of the organization on identify-formation as gaining much of its power through the seductive 'promises' such managerial leadership positions offer:

> And it's very energizing in many ways, and it's rewarding, I mean the feeling of being in control and being able to overview what's happening and to be able to pull strings in different places and see things grow. But also of course to do all this, in order to make other people thrive, to make other people grow … etc, it's fascinating … but it's also exhausting in a particular way.

The unstated type of leadership the university seems to favor in the above quote is not inclusive so much as 'extractive', in that the leadership styles and con- structions are based around the need to extract as much labor from workers as possible whilst also forever expanding worker capacity (Locke & Wright, 2017). The participant articulates a kind of structural intersectionality that incorporates the hidden desires of academia in the following:

> Yeah it's seductive … Whereas the kicks that you get from research are quite different. They are rewarding in quite a different way. The long periods of loneliness when you write, and there is a large struggle to be allowed to write because everyone wants you to do something else and tries to pressure you to spend your time on teaching, administration and stuff. But when you see new perspectives and actually manage to write something that's new and that's exciting, it's quite different. It's not as seductive.

To return to the pivotal event the participant describes as defining her later career, we can make visible the intersecting forces involved in the creation of an academic identity that privileged research, and her desire to research above the blatant seductiveness of brute power. The head of school's response to a young female academic was to try to subjugate and control her, and this provided a springboard to a later-career approach that resisted overt power structures in the form of university leadership positions. For this participant, withdrawal and non- engagement with named leadership positions in the managerial context of the university is itself an articulation toward a form of inclusive leadership where she sees herself as primarily 'leading' through researching and writing.

Readings of Intersectionality toward Inclusive Leadership in the University

To return to the stated ambitions of this chapter, intersectionality has been deployed as a methodological lens to analyze the position of women in the uni- versity by way of exploring the gendered discrepancy in leadership representation in the university. The theoretical coordinates of intersectionality have been discussed, particularly in the context of Staunæs and Søndergaard's (2011) analysis, on the formation of identities and subjectivities. The theoretical platform has been expanded through an inclusion of socio-cultural categories that move beyond class, age, and gender toward categories such as personal narratives and histories and status. The chapter extends this further by applying intersectionality to readings of leadership that take into consideration institutional and organizational structures of differentiation that impact on individual subjectivity formation in the context of wider forces. These forces include forms of governance and management, in this case encompassing the context of the university. The analysis then offered three case studies to anchor the theoretical discussion to the lived reality of three senior academic women who have worked, or are currently working, in the Danish system.

The case studies offered slightly different versions of inclusive leadership through the individual narratives of these three participants. All three interviewees articulated some career-defining point that was pivotal in their adoption of inclusive styles of leadership, and each of these women, in some way resisted strategies of governance within the structural platform of their working contexts. While the second case study explores the withdrawal of one participant from the university to the private sector, all three case studies provide an interesting snapshot of academic leadership subjectivities in the making. As a final engagement with intersectionality in the chapter, it is important to view the sometimes disturbing narratives of power and control that feature so prominently in the participant responses within the more dynamic potentiality of intersectionality. While it is tempting to view the number of women who attain academic leadership roles in both named and formal positions inside academia as fixed and pre-determined, when taking consideration of the often-overt patriarchies of the university context, the lens of intersectionality provides a way in which to see potential spaces of resistance and movement for women to open.

One such response is the persistent infusion of inclusive styles of leadership taken up in some form by all three participants in ways that privilege the relationality and reciprocity of the collegial working context. It is perhaps in these inclusive leadership approaches that the three participants offer the brightest spark of hope: that it is through the legacy of their leadership styles that pathways for new generations of women in academia may be traversed.

References

Butler, J., 1990. *Gender trouble: Feminism and the subversion of identity.* New York: Routledge.
Butler, J., 1993. *Bodies that matter: On the discursive limits of 'sex'.* New York: Routledge.
Callister, P., Newell, J., Perry, M., and Scott, D., 2006. The gendered tertiary education transition: When did it take place and what are some of the possible policy implications? *Policy Quarterly*, 2(3) pp. 4–13

Carmeli, A., Reiter-Palmon, R., and Ziv, E., 2010. Inclusive leadership and employee involvement in creative tasks in the workplace: The mediating role of psychological safety. *Creativity Research Journal*, 22(3), pp. 250–260. doi:10.1080/10400419.2010.504654.

Collins, P. H., 1998. It's all in the family: Intersections of gender, race, and nation. *Hypatia*, 13(3), pp. 62–82. doi:10.1111/j.1527-2001.1998.tb01370.x.

Crenshaw, K., 1991a. Demarginalizing the intersection of race and sex: A black feminist critique of antidiscrimination doctrine, feminist theory, and antiracist politics. In: Bartlett, K. T. and Kennedy, R., eds. *Feminist legal theory: Readings in law and gender*. Boulder, CO: Westview Press, pp. 57–80.

Crenshaw, K., 1991b. Mapping the margins: Intersectionality, identity politics, and violence against women of color. *Stanford Law Review*, 43(6), pp. 1241–1299.

Deem, R., 2013. Gender, organizational cultures and the practices of manager-academics in UK Universities. *Gender, Work and Organization* 10(2), pp. 239–259

Heijstra, T., Bjarnason, T., and Rafnsdóttir, G. L., 2015. Predictors of gender inequalities in the rank of full professor. *Scandinavian Journal of Educational Research*, 59(2), pp. 214–230. doi:10.1080/00313831.2014.904417.

Human Rights Commission, 2012. *New Zealand census of women's participation*. Available at: <http://www.hrc.co.nz/wp-content/uploads/2012/11/web-census.pdf> [Accessed 5 June, 2016].

Lindberg, L., Riis, U., and Silander, C., 2011. Gender equality in Swedish higher education: Patterns and shifts. *Scandinavian Journal of Educational Research*, 55(2), pp. 165–179. doi:10.1080/00313831.2011.554697.

Locke, K., 2015. Intersectionality and reflexivity in gender research: Disruptions, tracing lines and shooting arrows. *International Studies in Sociology of Education*, pp. 1–14. doi:10.1080/09620214.2015.1058722.

Locke, K. and Wright, S., (2017 forthcoming). Mainlining the motherboard: Exploring gendered academic labour in the university. In: Hudson, C. M., Rönnblom, M., and Tehghtsoonian, K., eds. *Gender, governance and feminist analysis: Missing in action?*, London, UK: Routledge, pp. 74–97.

Loots, S. and Walker, M., 2015. Shaping a gender equality policy in higher education: Which human capabilities matter? *Gender and Education*, 27(4), pp. 361–375. doi:10.1080/09540253.2015.1045458.

Manuel, T., 2007. Envisioning the possibilities for a good life: Exploring the public policy implications of intersectionality theory. *Journal of Women, Politics & Policy*, 28(3–4), pp. 173–203. doi:10.1300/J501v28n03_08.

Newell, J. and Callister, P., 2008. The gender transition in tertiary education in New Zealand and Australia. Australian Population Association Conference, Alice Springs.

Richardson, A. and Loubier, C., 2008. Intersectionality and leadership. *International Journal of Leadership Studies*, 3(2), pp. 142–161.

Sanchez-Hucles, J. and Davis, D. D., 2010. Women and women of color in leadership: Complexity, identity, and intersectionality. *American Psychologist*, 65(3), pp. 171–181. doi:10.1037/a0017459.

Søndergaard, D. M., 2005. Making sense of gender, age, power and disciplinary position: Intersecting discourses in the academy. *Feminism & Psychology*, 15(2), pp. 189–208. doi:10.1177/0959353505051728.

Ståhle, B., 2013. Videnskabeligt personale på universiteterne 2013 [Academic staff at universities 2013]. Styrelsen for VideregåendeUddannelserStatistikog Analyse [Agency for higher education statistics and analysis]. Available at: <http://ufm.dk/forskning-og-innova

tion/statistik-og-analyser/forskere-ved-universiteterne/videnskabeligt-personale-pa-univers iteterne-2013-statistiknotat-1.pdf> [Accessed 14 September, 2016].

Staunæs, D., 2003. Where have all the subjects gone? Bringing together the concepts of intersectionality and subjectification. *NORA – Nordic Journal of Feminist and Gender Research*, 11(2), pp. 101–110. doi:10.1080/08038740310002950.

University of Auckland, 2014. *University of Auckland equity profile*. Statistical Auckland, NZ: Consulting Centre for the Equity Office – Te Ara Tautika.

Wright, S., 2014. Knowledge that counts: Points systems and the governance of Danish universities. In: Griffith, A. I. and Smith, D. E., eds. *Under new public management: Institutional ethnographies of changing front-line work*. Toronto: University of Toronto Press, pp. 294–337.

5

CULTIVATING INCLUSIVE LEADERSHIP IN HIGHER EDUCATION TEACHING THROUGH ACTION LEARNING

Cathy Gunn

Introduction: Notions of Leadership and Inclusivity

Leadership in higher education in the 21st century is increasingly recognized as a collective capacity within institutions rather than a set of traits or behaviors displayed by an individual (West-Burnham, 2004; Anderson and Johnson, 2006). Common terms used to describe this concept are 'distributed' or 'distributive' leadership (Spillane, 2006). A distributed approach is considered appropriate for the complex institutions of the higher education sector, in which no one individual can be expected to have all the necessary skills and experience to lead (Gunn and Lefoe, 2013).

The approach has proved to be particularly useful for developing leadership in teaching and learning; a task that can be problematic where institutional culture and career progression pathways favor research over teaching. An innovative approach that has evolved in recent years uses a distributed leadership model with action learning as the vehicle. A common aim for initiatives is to encourage faculty to take ownership of an institutional strategic objective for excellence in teaching and learning. Programs are designed to support emergent leaders as they interpret this strategic aim within their own professional practice context. A secondary aim is to grow leadership capacity within the institution. Fostering a more inclusive institutional culture may be a third explicit aim, or at least, a very worthy by-product.

Distributed leadership is inclusive by nature, as the individuals involved in development programs are usually not in senior roles with assigned positional authority in an institutional hierarchy. However, the definition of 'inclusive' that is applied in this context is unusually broad. It adds diversity of role, experience, level of appointment, and assignment of formal authority to more widely acknowledged aspects of diversity such as gender, sexuality, religion, ethnicity, or indigeneity. Because this broad perspective on inclusiveness is unusual, it is also more easily overlooked, as I will argue.

The chapter outlines three case studies as examples of how distributed leadership development through action learning approaches works in practice. The definition of distributed leadership applied to these cases studies notes that it:

- generates broad engagement;
- acknowledges and recognizes leadership irrespective of position;
- is negotiated not delegated;
- focuses on people's strengths;
- includes shared responsibility and accountability;
- means different things in different contexts;
- requires the development of strong relationships and networks;
- is about capacity building and development; and
- assists and informs succession planning.

In the true spirit of distributed leadership, participants in one of the case study groups developed the above definition collectively.

What is Inclusive Leadership?

Popular definitions of the term 'inclusive' refer to contexts where people from different identifiable cultures and groups have access, can operate without encountering barriers related to some aspect of their identity, and feel comfortable working and/or interacting with others. This chapter extends that definition to acknowledge people in all types and levels of appointment as contributors to the organization's leadership capability. The workforce of a higher education institution typically includes a range of culturally diverse identities. However, the broad definition applied here cannot be understood in terms of identifiable groups that can be singled out, or in advantaged or disadvantaged. This lack of visibility in the form of a specific or common identity masks the problem of traditional hierarchical organizations failing to recognize the leadership contributions of people who have not been appointed to a role with formal positional authority. This is an insidious form of exclusion that runs against trends toward greater democracy in higher education, and cannot be easily addressed. In fact, champions of more traditional, hierarchical leadership would deny there is even a problem. So systems of hierarchy and assigned authority can actively suppress the potential of large numbers of faculty instead of acknowledging their contribution to an institution's overall leadership capacity. This is not only a waste of considerable talent, but also a practice that runs against the grain of strategic plans that claim to be inclusive and democratic. Such claims usually relate to students rather than to staff. However, given the high level of qualification and commitment required for employment in the academy, it would be fitting for them to apply equally to both.

Growing Leadership Capacity in Higher Education

The need to grow leadership capacity in teaching and learning in higher education has been acknowledged by initiatives from the American Council of Education (Kezar and Eckel, 2002), the Leadership Foundation for Higher Education in the UK (Bolden, Petrov, and Gosling, 2008), and the Australian Learning and Teaching Council's Leadership for Excellence (Anderson and Johnson, 2009). Distributed leadership approaches are increasingly common in this area, where the power of hierarchy is less directly influential and positional authority is less relevant to the quality of the 'product.' Distributed leadership initiatives have already proved to be a productive way to grow faculty into positions with formal authority, and thus to fill a gap that made it difficult, in the past, for institutions to recruit suitably qualified individuals for senior roles. It was noted some years back, particularly in Australasia, that a limited pool of suitable applicants was available to fill roles such as Director of Academic Development; Pro or Deputy Vice Chancellor Teaching and Learning; and Director of eLearning. The reasons for this gap in supply are complex, and include the fact that these appointments require a departure from the conventional, discipline-based academic career path which many strategically minded individuals are not prepared to take. Another contributing factor has been a lack of suitably designed professional development programs to prepare people for these types of role. A wide range of leadership workshops and short courses may have planted many seeds, but then failed to provide the breadth of experience necessary to sustain growth of leadership capabilities over time. Knight and Trowler (2001, p. 150) noted the importance of contextualized activity and networks with distributed expertise as a suitable training ground for future educational leaders. Southwell, et al. (2005, p. 61) noted the need to support capacity building based on a distributed and multi-level concept of leadership practice. These factors point to the naturalistic setting of teachers' professional practice context as an obvious choice for development initiatives to focus on.

A concurrent problem in many institutions has been a lack of opportunities to acknowledge emergent leadership capabilities in early-to-mid-career faculty, particularly for leadership in teaching and learning. Opportunities to grow this pool of emergent leadership capacity were considered desirable for a number of reasons, for example, as a practical way to promote the strategic aim to foster excellence in university teaching, as part of a long-term plan to grow future leaders, and as a way to reward innovation and emergent leadership. The strategic importance of these aims resulted in faculty or organizational development centers being charged with the task of delivering suitable programs.

The suggestion that faculty development centers with active higher education teachers and researchers produce better results in this area is based purely on anecdotal evidence at present. It would be interesting to review both the measures and the factors that contribute to the success of teaching and learning leadership development programs to see if the difference is real. However, that would be an unnecessary diversion from the aim of this chapter, which is to describe three cases in which successful outcomes have been achieved, and which happen to have been designed and implemented by faculty development centers. Two of the three initiatives were resourced at institutional level. In the third case, the aims were considered sufficiently important to attract funding at national level. The concept of distributed leadership received a major boost from the various initiatives designed to address this strategic aim. Another positive outcome was that leadership in teaching and learning in higher education became more inclusive, and institutional change took on some new directions as a result of the broader perspectives that were represented in leadership circles.

The Benefits of Inclusive Leadership

It is worth noting that the benefits of institutional change that reflect the value of diversity and inclusiveness operate far below the surface and may not be immediately apparent. An institution's values, priorities, and knowledge are all influenced by the diversity of its staff, as well as by the social and political context in which it operates. Indeed, it is the sphere of operation that determines the context-specific meanings of diversity and inclusion in any situation. Opening up the sphere of leadership to a greater variety of influences, and extending it through many layers beyond the top end of a hierarchy has far-reaching implications. It does not,

> simply attempt to add new populations towards efforts at institutional transformation. This work on diversity and institutional transformation in higher education is strengthened by emerging literature that reflects increasing attention to the embedded nature of identities in institutional cultures, practices and standards (Smith, 2014, pp. 4–5).

Regardless of whether or not the outcomes are a result of a conscious strategy, applying the principles of distributed leadership to institutional capacity building initiatives could not fail to lead to greater inclusiveness, and thus to bring greater richness and diversity to institutional values, culture, and practice. The preferred approach to implementation of these principles of inclusiveness and distributed leadership is through action learning.

Why Action Learning?

Action learning appeared in the literature in the 1970s as an innovative method of management development. Breaking with traditional approaches that relied on imparting new knowledge and training off the job, action learning involved peer-supported reflection on action by managers solving problems in authentic professional practice contexts (Revans, 1982). The method became widely known in European and Australasian management and organizational development circles over the following decades, and its use extended to other areas of professional practice.

Pedler (1991, p. xxii) described the typical six-month action learning program comprising a start-up module, monthly learning sets, occasional workshops, and a final workshop as "having almost reached the status of a new orthodoxy." Like many new ideas that produced successful results, action learning was adapted and applied in a range of different contexts with varying degrees of success. Less successful initiatives may have lost the intrinsic value of action learning by reducing the core ideas to inappropriate techniques, and overlooking key aspects of the method (Pedler, 1991). While noting how difficult it was to offer a universal definition of action learning, the defining principles were described as simple and able to be applied in any professional or organizational development context.

> Action learning is an approach to the development of people in organizations which takes the task as the vehicle for learning. It is based on the premise that there is no learning without action and no sober and deliberate action without learning (Pedler, 1991, p. xxii).

Action learning is a holistic approach. It does not aim for mastery of a body of knowledge, or to operate solely within the confines (or silos) of a formal organizational structure. It pits the sum total of an individual's skills, knowledge, insights, and experience against the complex system of an organization with a problem to solve. Pedler (1991, p. xxv) visualized it as a spiral starting with a problem, and a willingness to take ownership of both the internal and external aspects of that problem. The problem is situated within a learning system, and tackled over time by a leader with support from colleagues, exerting influence where necessary, and using available resources. Power and conflict invariably arise in learning situations, and the ability of an individual leader to wield power appropriately and manage conflict is a critical aspect of their learning. All learning involves a shift in identity, as the individual and the organization transition to a new state, before moving on to the spiral of the next problem and beginning the process again.

Solving a real-world problem in a naturalistic setting as the vehicle for learning is a core aspect of the method. Something that sounds good in discussion or looks good on paper might prove impractical in application, and so cannot be classed as action learning. The only way to test a solution, a theory, or a proposal is to apply it in a situation where all the contextual complexities of organizational culture, politics, pressures, and practice are present. The consequences of the chosen course of action will become evident, and the wisdom of the choice apparent. This kind of learning may not require the acquisition of new knowledge, but instead demand judgment and a considered response based on knowledge, experience, personal capabilities, and evaluation of a context. A solution to the problem does not already exist, and the 'best possible' course of action is open to interpretation. Personal reflection on agency and approach, and on critical feedback from colleagues engaged in solving the same type of problem is intrinsic to the experience. Reflection requires transparency and a translation of beliefs and opinions into action. Collaboration with peers or colleagues requires the building of trust, and is another critical element of the method. Collaboration also assumes that an 'expert' trying to solve a problem in one area may benefit from ideas put forward by 'experts' in other areas who will, in turn, gain insights into ways to solve similar problems in their own areas of practice. It is how learning occurs, both for the individual and the organization, and how identity is transformed.

> The micro-political skills needed to judge what is relevant to build into a decision, and to secure what is essential to implementing that decision can be significantly developed by action learning (Revans, 1991, p. 13).

Three simple questions sum up what these micro-political skills involve:

- Who knows about and has an interest in this problem?
- Who is in a position to do something about it?
- How can I recruit them into an action team?

To summarize, action learning applies the principles of organic evolution to leadership development and learning. It involves taking action rather than talking (or writing) about it. The three core aims of action learning are to apply skilful reasoning to real-world problems, to implement chosen solutions in the context where the problems exist, and to reflect on, and learn from, the outcomes. Textbook cases and the production of written reports are not action learning because they do not involve the anxieties and emotions, or the commitment, the complexities, and the risks of taking action on the real world. Further research would be required to find out when action learning was first adopted into higher education. Revans (1991, p. 12) mentioned an Inter-University Programme in Belgium, and Lefoe and colleagues (Lefoe, Smigiel and Parrish, 2007) adopted the method for an Australia-wide teaching and learning leadership capacity development program that began in 2007. Other initiatives may have taken place in the interim. However, over the past ten or so years, the method has proved both increasingly popular and effective in promoting leadership capacity development and inclusivity, as well as supporting local ownership of strategic plans and priorities (Childs, et al., 2012; Devlin, et al., 2012).

Distributed Leadership in Action

Two leadership capacity development initiatives run by institutions on different continents and based on the distributed model are the Faculty Scholars Project from the University of Wollongong in Australia, and the Scholars and Associates program at Glasgow Caledonian University in Scotland. The University of Wollongong-led project was part of a national Leading for Excellence initiative. The Glasgow Caledonian initiative was inspired by the Australian Faculty Scholars Project, and aligned with the UK Professional Standards Framework for Teaching and Supporting Learning in Higher Education (HEA, 2011). A third, more recently launched, initiative is the Teaching and Learning Fellowship Program at the University of Auckland in New Zealand, which began with a similar approach and drew on design principles from the other two. All three initiatives acknowledge the critical nature of local ownership and interpretation of national and institutional strategic objectives, and leveraged the strengths of the distributed leadership model to achieve this aim. Before outlining the structure and philosophy behind these initiatives, it may be useful to consider what leadership in teaching and learning in higher education means in practical terms.

Gibbs, Knapper and Piccinin (2008) described this kind of leadership as multi-faceted and involving various activities to suit different institutional and disciplinary contexts. Their article outlined nine specific areas of leadership activity:

- establish credibility and trust;
- identify teaching problems and turn them into opportunities;
- articulate a convincing rationale for change;
- disperse leadership;
- build a community of practice;
- recognize and reward excellent teaching and teaching development effort;
- market the department as a teaching success;
- support change and innovation; and
- involve students.

Many of these activities reflect what good teachers do, and how they might foster teaching excellence across their department, faculty, or institution. None of these activities depends on the leader having positional authority or a formal leadership role, although the ability to influence others will no doubt be enhanced if they have. The Australian Faculty Scholars Project was designed with these activities in mind. The Glasgow Caledonian Scholars and Associates and the Auckland Teaching Fellowship Program both followed this lead.

Case 1: The Faculty Scholars Project

The Faculty Scholars Project won national funding in Australia to create a framework for leadership capacity development in higher education institutions.

Based on a distributive model, and using action learning as the vehicle, the program targeted individual faculty members who were not yet in formal leadership positions. In most cases, selection was through a combination of self and head of department (HoD) nomination. The voluntary aspect of the nomination was important, because it meant the scholars felt ready to step up to the challenge of a leadership role, and had an idea for an action learning plan for the leadership development process. The importance of this factor should not be underplayed. In a small number of cases, where a head of department nominated a scholar, this produced poor outcomes and resentment of the additional workload involved. The first group of scholars selected from two universities assumed leadership roles to develop and implement plans to enhance assessment practice within their institution. They also committed collectively to disseminate their experience through national events and networking activities. Full details of the project are reported by Lefoe (2010), Lefoe and Parrish (2008), and Lefoe, Smigiel, and Parrish (2007). The year-long program aligned with institutional priorities for teaching and learning, and involved the following activities:

- submit an application and be acknowledged as someone with leadership potential;
- attend an immersive leadership development and action-learning planning retreat;
- plan and implement an action learning project to enhance teaching and learning in line with institutional strategy;
- develop and demonstrate leadership capability through the process;
- engage with senior staff to discuss progress and win support for action learning projects;
- collaborate with other scholars to plan and disseminate experience at a national event;
- engage with colleagues across the sector to foster communities of practice in discipline-based teaching and educational leadership; and
- act as mentors to new scholars and institutions.

The scholars' action learning projects were designed to demonstrate leadership by example in teaching and learning in their home disciplines. The value of action learning projects as leadership development opportunities was evident, as they surfaced real, context-specific challenges that required the scholars to use authority, deal with conflict, negotiate politics, and juggle multiple roles. These demands were addressed within a supportive context that offered leadership development workshops, personal coaching and mentoring, and reflective discussions with an inter-disciplinary group and with senior institutional leaders.

Case 2: The Caledonian Scholars and Associates

Glasgow Caledonian University's Scholars and Associates initiative was inspired by the Faculty Scholar Program outlined in the previous section. The initiative, launched in 2008, was designed to contribute to:

- a distributed leadership model for innovation in teaching and learning across the university;
- the enhancement of scholarship in teaching and learning across schools within the university;
- continuing professional development in learning and teaching aligned with an institutional framework;
- the quality of the student experience; and
- promotion criteria for academic staff applying through the learning and teaching route.

The Scholars and Associates program offered professional development opportunities for faculty at different stages of their career, as well as incentives for them to engage with the institutional Professional Development Framework for Learning and Teaching. It also provided the means for individual faculty to take ownership of ways to implement the strategic priority to promote innovation in technology-supported teaching and learning. The application process involved an element of self-nomination, with endorsement from a HoD, review by an international panel, and final approval by the Pro Vice Chancellor Learning and Teaching. The aims and selection criteria for these awards are described in the Scholars and Associates Overview published by the university, and a full description of the programme is available elsewhere (Creanor, 2014). The key aspects relevant to this chapter are the distributed leadership model the program is based on, the choice of action learning plans as the vehicle for leadership capacity development, and the requirement that scholars' action learning plans align with the university's strategic priorities.

Within this framework, scholars were expected to:

- lead an action learning project to improve learning and teaching, and embed the positive outcomes within the school/central department and/or university;
- provide leadership in the scholarship of learning and teaching, and share the experiences and outcomes of the action learning project with peers;
- cascade professional development in learning and teaching at institutional level during the action learning project and disseminate outcomes by contributing to courses, seminars, workshops, and publication in an internal learning and teaching journal;
- consider combining action research projects with an accredited programme in learning and teaching and/or scholarly activities for professional development;
- provide a project final report and disseminate outcomes and evaluation to school management and appropriate university committees; and
- explore opportunities to disseminate outcomes at national and/or international level through peer reviewed journal articles and/or conference papers.

Scholars and associates were encouraged to use the opportunity to lead upwards and sideways, to influence those in positions of power, and to make a positive difference to the student experience. They could also enhance their career portfolios through scholarly publications, networking at international conferences, and successful promotion applications (Creanor, 2014). As with the Faculty Scholars Project, any challenges encountered along the way were addressed with support from experienced project staff, colleagues, and professional networks.

Case 3: A Teaching and Learning Fellowship

The University of Auckland in New Zealand is a large, research-focused university with the strategic aim of achieving excellence in teaching. The Centre for Learning and Research in Higher Education (CLeaR) pursues this aim through 'staircase to leadership in teaching' programs designed to focus on the various stages of faculty career progression, and to complement broad spectrum leadership development initiatives offered by a Professional and Organizational Development Unit.

The 'staircase' begins with a year-long program for doctoral students planning to pursue an academic career, and includes a variety of opportunities for early, mid-career, and experienced university teachers, as well as a credit-bearing Graduate Certificate in Academic Practice (PGCert). The final step on the staircase is an 18-month Teaching and Learning Fellowship, launched in 2014, and awarded to one individual from each of the university's eight faculties who is acknowledged as an emergent leader in teaching and learning within their discipline. An ideal candidate might have engaged in other CLeaR initiatives, completed the PG Cert, and possibly have won an institutional or national teaching excellence award. CLeaR's programs, except the Doctoral Leadership Initiative (DALI), which is for graduate students, and the teaching excellence awards, are open to all eligible teachers, so a culture of inclusivity is reflected at the point of entry. The principles and practice of equity and inclusivity are implicit elements of the center's work. Two underlying principles of the Fellowship Program are to focus on developing leadership capabilities within the individual's own professional practice context, and to reflect the action learning framework within a flexible and supportive community. The Fellowship Program was resourced with one part-time staff member and offered nominal time release but no funding for participants, so expectations were set lower than for the programs outlined in Cases 1 and 2 above, where funding was more generous. The main areas of focus were on promoting the scholarship of teaching and learning, and sharing experience of innovative teaching approaches across disciplinary boundaries in a community of professional practice. Plans for individual projects were put in place and supported, though these tended to be a phase of a longer-term initiative being undertaken by the fellow rather than something designed to fit within the timeframe of the Fellowship Program. Fellows met on a regular basis to discuss and progress their plans. Sharing of ideas often helped to produce workable solutions or new ideas to try out in different professional practice contexts. Periodic attendance by the Dean who sponsored the program and the university's Director of Learning and Teaching boosted visibility and networking for the fellows. Presentations at a special event mid-year, and at an annual 'Teaching Showcase' towards the end of the academic year further supported these aims. Although the tangible outcomes of the Fellowship Program were limited to a 'Teaching Cases' publication for each of the first two years, participants appreciated the benefits of membership of an inter-disciplinary community of professional practice, as well as the boost in visibility and wider networks the program allowed them to engage with.

How Distributed Leadership Works

Evaluation of the three cases outlined above varied from formal internal and external reviews, to informal feedback provided by participants and colleagues attending scholar- or fellowship-hosted events. Overall, participants reported positive outcomes and evaluation reports noted successful achievement of program objectives. This suggests the action learning approach to distributed leadership capacity development is a useful design framework.

Participants in Case 1 reported a boost in confidence and heightened perceptions of their own identities and potential as leaders. Participation in the program had raised their visibility within their department and the institution, and allowed them to connect with different people and networks, including more senior ones. Conversations with senior leaders helped to broaden the participants' perspectives on ways that institutions work, how priorities are set, and where teaching and learning initiatives fit within the institutional, national, and global context of higher education. Being supported through the implementation of an action learning project in the context of a leadership capacity development initiative gave participants a heightened sense of agency, empowerment, and inclusion. Where specific teaching and learning enhancements were the focus of action learning projects, greater visibility within the discipline and the scholarly community was a further positive result.

A balanced perspective is important, however, and it would be disingenuous to imply that everything worked out in positive ways. Not all planned outcomes were achieved, although the failure of an individual action learning plan that was derailed by circumstances did not mean that the leadership capacity development aim also failed. The challenges faced by participants in all three cases reflected the realities of working in a high-pressure higher education environment. Securing time release was problematic in all three cases, and the usual demands of teaching, research, and service continued to require careful time management and priority setting. Departments got restructured, colleagues resigned, and jobs changed without warning. Barriers in the form of policies, politics, inadequate technology, and ingrained culture were commonplace, and participants generally benefitted from the experience of having to devise and implement solutions. A further advantage of being involved in a leadership capacity development initiative was the resilience that supportive networks help to build. Collegial support, mentors' advice, access to senior management, and feelings of empowerment all contributed to the resilience of individual members, whose experience of how institutions work in both an operational and political sense undoubtedly grew. From a management perspective, the return on a relatively small investment in emergent leaders included an increased pool of potential candidates for senior appointments in the future. Networking with participants also broadened management understanding of how things work at grass roots level. Thus, a more broadly inclusive leadership and institutional environment was a positive outcome for all stakeholders.

Discussion and Conclusions

An implicit aim in adopting the distributed leadership and action learning approaches to build capacity was to help steer institutions towards a broader and more inclusive perception of leadership. Using methods based on individual experience and action learning rather than a program-focused approach to leadership capacity development ensured direct relevance to the participants' interests and roles. It also allowed them to use the challenges arising from the richness and complexity of an authentic work environment as opportunities for personal leadership development. The action learning approach promoted the concept of a bottom–up 'social movement' to complement the top–down 'legislative movement' (Glenaffric Ltd, 2008) that created the scholars and fellowship programs in the first place. Distributed leadership is inclusive by default, and a tremendous opportunity for universities to capitalize on the broad expertise of multi-skilled faculty members. Similarly, action learning is an excellent opportunity for individuals to use their unique experiences as a basis to develop personal and institutional leadership capacities.

However, acceptance of these approaches may require an institutional culture shift because they are a departure from the common perception of leadership as something that is assigned to certain positions within a hierarchy. A shift in perception became necessary when two problems facing the higher education sector reached critical proportions (Scott, Coates, and Anderson, 2008). The first was a limited pool of qualified applicants for senior academic positions in a rapidly changing environment; the flip-side of this being that sometimes people appointed to senior positions were poorly prepared for the diverse demands of leadership in complex organizations. The second problem was a lack of effective ways to acknowledge and grow the emergent leadership capabilities of more junior staff. Addressing this problem opens up avenues for institutions to benefit from the large pool of talent that exists within the workforce. Hierarchies with elite leadership cultures tend to suppress rather than empower individuals by limiting the scope of their activities and the sphere of their influence. Senior leadership teams that adopt a more democratic approach are open to a greater diversity of opinions and points of view, and help to grow rather than suppress the leadership capacity that is unevenly distributed across an organization. It is important for clear messages about inclusivity to come from the top of an organization. However, the real value of these messages is at the point they are put into practice. Support for distributed leadership initiatives is a tangible sign of this commitment.

Blessinger and Anchan (2015, p. 216) identified higher education as a primary means through which people can achieve political self-determination, personal empowerment, and personal agency. The ultimate purpose of education at this level is to promote personal agency through the development of freedom and responsibility. Education may indeed be a powerful catalyst and vehicle to achieve these goals as the authors suggest. But, however well that empowerment agenda works when it is directed at students, it often stops short of inclusive practices designed to empower and foster the leadership capabilities of faculty. To be inclusive in this sense requires a mindset shift from elitism, power, and privilege to one that values fairness and self-determination. Only then can institutional leaders send a clear message that diversity and inclusivity are strategic goals in practice as well as on paper.

The challenge of advancing new, and more inclusive, conceptions of leadership in institutions with strong hierarchical traditions and an increasing focus on accountability is considerable. Programs of the nature described in this chapter face an additional challenge because capacity development is an organic process where fixed targets, timeframes, and performance indicators are, at least, irrelevant and, at worst, counter-productive. The aims, influences, and outcomes of action learning initiatives vary widely, and often cannot be measured within a short timeframe. Furthermore, failure to implement or achieve the anticipated results of an action learning plan does not mean that the leadership capacity development aim has also failed. Quantitative measures of capacity development are hard to produce, as Bamber's (2013) work on educational development describes. On that point, evidence (however disputed it may be) from the case studies outlined in this chapter might show that distributed leadership is effective in promoting teaching and learning enhancement as well as growing leadership capacity. However, greater inclusiveness is less easy to demonstrate, particularly when it does not relate to the more commonly discussed and salient aspects of diversity.

The opportunities to learn from diverse perspectives, including indigenous ones, to use real-world experience as a vehicle for learning, and to encourage the growth of distributed leadership models all exist within a context of global trends such as the inclusive approach to public policy development and implementation through citizen engagement that Charles Leadbeater (2008) wrote about. Institutions that lack the foresight or courage to embrace these trends will be poorer and less popular as a result.

References

Anderson, D. and Johnson, R., 2006. Ideas of leadership underpinning proposals to the Carrick Institute: A review of proposals from the 'Leadership for Excellence in Teaching and Learning Program'. Available at: <http://www.altc.edu.au/resource-ideas-of-lea dership-underpinning-proposals-altc-2006> [Accessed 10 September 2016].

Bamber, V., ed. 2013. *Evidencing the value of educational development*. London: Staff and Educational Development Association (SEDA).

Blessinger, P. and Anchan, J., 2015. *Democratizing higher education: International comparative perspectives*. New York and London: Routledge.

Bolden, R., Petrov, G., and Gosling, J., 2008. Developing collective leadership in higher education. London: The Leadership Foundation for Higher Education. Available at: <https://www.academia.edu/1004415/Developing_collective_leadership_in_higher_ education-final_report> [Accessed 28 September 2016].

Childs, M., Brown, M., Keppell, M., Nicholas, Z., Hunter, C., and Hard, N., 2012. Learning leadership in higher education: The big and small actions of many people. Available at: <http://learningleadershipstudy.files.wordpress.com/2012/12/herdsa -2012.pdf> [Accessed 12 August 2016].

Creanor, L., 2014. Raising the profile: An institutional case study of embedding scholarship and innovation through distributive leadership. *Innovations in Education and Teaching International*, 51(6), pp. 573–583.

Devlin, M., Smeal, G., Cummings, R., and Mazzolini, M., 2012. Seven insights for leading sustainable change in teaching and learning in Australian universities. Available at: <http://www.olt.gov.au/system/files/resources/LE10_1727_Devlin_Nagy_7Insights_ 2012.pdf> [Accessed 12 August 2016].

Gibbs, G., Knapper, C., and Piccinin, S., 2008. Disciplinary and contextually appropriate approaches to leadership of teaching in research-intensive academic departments in higher education. *Higher Education Quarterly*, 62(4), pp. 416–436.

Glenaffric Ltd, 2008. Formative evaluation of the eLearning transformation programme: Final report. Available at Scottish Higher Education Funding Council website: <http:// www.sfc.ac.uk/web/files/our_priorities_skills/elearning_elt_formative_evaluation_rep ort.pdf> [Accessed 23 May 2013].

Gunn, C. and Lefoe, G., 2013. Evaluating action-learning and professional networking as a framework for educational leadership capacity development. *International Journal of Academic Development*, 18(1), pp. 45–59.

Higher Education Academy (HEA), 2011. *UK professional standards framework for teaching and supporting learning in higher education*. Available at: <https://www.heacademy.ac.uk/ recognition-accreditation/uk-professional-standards-framework-ukpsf> [Accessed 12 August 2016].

Kezar, A. and Eckel, P., 2002. Examining the institutional transformation process: The importance of sensemaking, interrelated strategies, and balance. *Research in Higher Education*, 43(3), pp. 295–328.

Knight, P. and Trowler, P., 2001. *Departmental leadership in higher education*. Buckingham: SRHE and Open University.

Leadbeater, C., 2008. *We – think: Mass innovation, not mass production*. London: Profile Books.

Lefoe, G., 2010. Creating the future: Changing culture through leadership capacity development. In: Ehlers, U. D. and Schneckenberg, D., eds. *Changing cultures in higher education. A handbook for strategic change*. Heidelberg: Springer Verlag, pp. 189–204.

Lefoe, G. and Parrish, D., 2008. *The GREEN report: Growing ● Reflecting ● Enabling ● Engaging ● Networking. A report on the development of leadership capacity in higher education.* Available at: <http://www.uow.edu.au/cedir/DistributiveLeadership/docs/GREEN_Report.pdf> [Accessed 15 August, 2016].

Lefoe, G., Smigiel, H., and Parrish, D., 2007. Enhancing higher education through leadership capacity development: Progressing the Faculty Scholars model. Paper presented at the Enhancing Higher Education, Theory and Scholarship, Proceedings of the 30th HERDSA Annual Conference [CD-ROM], Adelaide, 8–11 July.

Pedler, M., 1991. *Action learning in practice.* Aldershot, UK: Gower Publishing.

Revans, R. W., 1982. *The origins and growth of action learning.* London: Chartwell-Bratt.

Revans, R. W., 1991. Action learning: Its origins and nature. In: Pedler, M., ed., *Action learning in practice.* Aldershot, UK: Gower Publishing, pp. 15–20.

Scott, G., Coates, H., and Anderson, M., 2008. *Learning leaders in times of change: Academic capabilities for Australian higher education.* Sydney: University of Western Sydney and the Australian Council for Educational Research.

Smith, D. G., 2014. *Diversity and inclusion in higher education: Emerging perspectives on institutional transformation.* London and New York: Routledge.

Southwell, D., Gannaway, D., Orrell, J., Chalmers, D., and Abraham, C., 2005. Strategies for effective dissemination of project outcomes. Available at: <http://www.altc.edu.au/resource-strategies-dissemination-uq-2005> [Accessed 12 August 2016].

Spillane, J. P., 2006. *Distributed leadership.* San Francisco: Jossey Bass.

West-Burnham, J., 2004. Building leadership capacity – helping leaders learn: An NCSL thinkpiece. Available at: <http://www.lds21.ie/lds/Files/randd-building-lead-capacity.pdf> [Accessed 12 August 2016].

6

INCLUSIVE ENVIRONMENTS IN UK UNIVERSITIES

Some Surprising Challenges for Leaders

Fiona Denney

Introduction

Over the past ten years, there has been a significant drive to make UK universities more inclusive environments in a number of ways. Major initiatives include Athena SWAN from the Equality Challenge Unit – evolved from work between the Athena Project and the Scientific Women's Academic Network (SWAN) to advance the representation of women in science, technology, engineering, medicine and mathematics (STEMM) and now expanded to other disciplines and other forms of inequality. At the same time, UK universities have had to put into place access agreements to ensure that students from widening participation backgrounds have better opportunities to get places to study at undergraduate level and, as a result, our campuses have become more diverse, and hopefully inclusive, places to work and study.

These major initiatives deal with specific perceived inequalities which, whilst very important, are not the whole story in terms of inclusivity on campus. Our universities comprise daily leadership and management challenges that directly impact on how inclusive the academic environment is for staff. For some years, I have been interested in the leadership and management experiences of academics who usually have no preparation or training for the management roles and responsibilities that they end up taking on. Often promoted on the basis of their good academic qualities, they find themselves adrift in a sea of management expectations that they had no adequate preparation for and those who do a 'good job' seem to do so more by luck than judgement. My work in preparing early-career researchers and academics for leadership across several UK universities over the past 14 years led me to lead a team bid to the Leadership Foundation for Higher Education's (LFHE) Innovation and Transformation Fund. The intended project, entitled *Developing the Next Generation,* for which the funding was sought was to uncover the reality, through individual interviews, of what academics wish they had known before they took on their first management and/or leadership position. The aim was to then use their experiences to develop training and support for those progressing into leadership and management positions (Denney, Mitchell and Wheat, 2015). The interview transcripts provided significant personal insights into the difficulties of leading and managing effectively in the modern and changing UK academic environment and threw up some surprising challenges for leading in an inclusive environment.

This chapter focuses on how these leaders cope, the strategies they employ and their views on leadership in modern universities. For the purpose of this chapter, inclusive leadership is defined by the report: *Inclusive Leadership ... driving performance through diversity,* commissioned by the Employers Network for Equality and Inclusion (ENEI) and carried out by Buckinghamshire New University (Buckinghamshire New University and ENEI, 2016).

The *Inclusive Leadership* report was commissioned to develop a robust model and definition of inclusive leadership and its perceived impacts. Following the survey and interviews across 11 public and private sector organizations, the study identified 15 core competencies to form the new model of Inclusive Leadership:

1. *Individualized consideration* – where leaders show interest in and consideration and support for people on a one-to-one basis;
2. *Idealized influence* – conveying a vision to inspire others;
3. *Inspirational motivation* – supporting those they lead to develop ideas and to be challenging;
4. *Intellectual stimulation* – encouraging creative thinking;
5. *Unqualified acceptance* – accepting each individual person without bias;
6. *Empathy* – being able to demonstrate understanding of how another person feels;
7. *Listening*;
8. *Persuasion* – being able to influence others' actions and behaviour without resorting to force or coercion;
9. *Confidence building* – boosting others' performance and effectiveness through positive feedback;
10. *Growth* – enabling all to make contributions, realize their potential and progress within the organization;
11. *Foresight* – being able to consider the views of others about possible outcomes;
12. *Conceptualization* – focusing on how others contribute to long-term objectives;
13. *Awareness* – being self-aware of how preconceived views can influence behaviour towards others;
14. *Stewardship* – a commitment to leading by serving others for the good of everyone rather than for self-promotion; and
15. *Healing* – a respect for the wellbeing of all employees.

The ENEI study found that these 15 behaviours and skills for Inclusive Leadership exist together in inclusive leaders as they take 'an holistic approach to leadership,' grounded in developing relationships with the people being led. Whilst this study did not focus on leadership in higher education per se, the 15 core competencies identified above resonate with the concept of collegiate leadership approaches in UK universities and, in this chapter, I map them against the views from the leaders interviewed in the *Developing the Next Generation* study.

Theoretical Framework

Although there is significant coverage in the education and wider management and leadership literature about the qualities of 'good' or 'effective' leaders, there is little research that considers the experience of leaders in the academic field (Peters and Ryan, 2015). Those in academic leadership positions are interesting to study, however, because they have usually reached their leadership position because of being highly successful in their discipline area – particularly regarding their research outputs – rather than because they exhibit the characteristics or skills necessary for their leadership role. Research on the role that prestige plays in academic progression indicates clearly that progression to an academic leadership position is dependent on factors such as success with grants and publications (Blackmore, 2015; Kandiko-Howson and Coate, 2015). Once acquired, however, the leadership role may then require the individual to prioritize other matters such as staff and budget management, for example. This can cause identity conflict and dissatisfaction, and is often in tension with the current efficiency and effectiveness agenda in UK universities.

The LFHE's Leadership and Management Survey (HELMs) conducted in 2014 found that the majority of respondents felt that the leadership skills and abilities required in UK higher education differed from those required for leadership and management in other sectors (Peters and Ryan, 2015). In other words, the context has a significant impact on the ability of the leader to be effective. Given this, and the drive for universities to be more efficient and inclusive, it would be reasonable to assume that the process of identifying, selecting and training successors would have a more prominent role in UK HEIs. In spite of developments in some UK universities, this is not universally the case.

Many universities in the UK are developing variations of leadership training programs for those already in key positions. Examples include the HeadStart program at King's College London for new heads of department and UCL's leadership and management programs for staff at certain grades and for those with line management responsibilities. While these interventions are positive developments to support those already appointed to leadership positions, they do not help early career researchers and academics in identifying what they need to do in order to progress (besides developing the prestige markers) and, more importantly, to be better equipped for the challenges of a future academic leadership role.

The *Developing the Next Generation* study takes the academic leadership literature beyond prestige factors to encompass the other aspects that aspiring leaders need to consider in order to be truly prepared for the future challenges of academic leadership and management.

The following sections of this chapter describe the methods and a brief overview of the key themes from the *Developing the Next Generation* study. This chapter then provides more detail on some of the challenges of leadership and management encountered by the respondents and discusses how they map onto the 15 core competencies identified in the Inclusive Leadership model.

Methods

The project received the financial resource from the LFHE's Fund for Innovation and Transformation. The project team included five UK universities and a key research partner Vitae, a national organization supporting researcher development. Following the research, the findings were tailored to be used as training materials and made freely available to the higher education sector online (Denney, Mitchell and Wheat, 2015).

Eighteen academics in various positions across five different universities participated in the study. Each individual had to demonstrate management and/or leadership (left as self-defined) in their jobs and agree to an interview. The universities were from different parts of the UK higher education sector – three from the elite, large, research-intensive Russell Group of institutions (Russell Group, n.d.); one was a 'post-1992' new university, smaller and more teaching-focused and the other was termed a 'plate glass university', which was founded in the mid-1960s, and is a small research-intensive institution. There was total agreement and buy-in from the participants and considerable interest in the project. Ethics approval for the project was obtained at the lead partner institution (Brunel University London) and then at the other universities. Total anonymity is a condition of the project and all identifying comments are redacted from the analysis of the interview transcripts.

The participants reflected the spread of leadership and management roles, disciplines, ages and genders across the universities. Table 6.1 shows these details. Most importantly, each of the respondents had to be leading or managing a minimum of a research group or be in a leadership role in an area of strategic responsibility in order to qualify for the study. Not all participants had responsibility for directly line-managing people, but a critical criterion point was that they had to have responsibility for leading something, and influencing the behaviour of other people.

Prior to the interviews, an initial set of questions was agreed and piloted (see Box 6.1). The interview approach would allow for in-depth probing. The lead researcher at each institution conducted the interviews within their

TABLE 6.1 Interviewee Data

Title / Position / Role	Number
Dean or Head of School	2
Dean or Director of Research	3
Vice, Deputy or Associate Dean	5
Senior Lecturer or Reader	2
Vice Principal, Pro Vice Chancellor, Deputy Vice Chancellor	4
Head of Department or Department Lead	2
Gender	**Number**
Male	10
Female	8
Discipline	**Number**
Arts and Humanities	5
Social Sciences	4
Engineering and Physical Sciences	4
Biological and Biomedical Sciences	5

university – partly because these were already established relationships, enabling the respondents to feel comfortable quickly and to open up. Each interview lasted approximately one hour and they were audio-recorded, transcribed and uploaded to NVivo™ for analysis.

BOX 6.1 INTERVIEW QUESTIONS

- Please give a brief description of your background and explain how you came to be at this point in your career.
- What do you consider to be the key decision-points in your career journey? What factors at the time prompted you to make the decisions you described?
- What lessons have you learned in your position(s) of leadership?
- What do you wish you had known before you moved into a position of leadership?
- What would have helped you in your journey?
- What three key pieces of advice would you give to an early career researcher (post-doc/PhD student) who wants to develop his/her career in academia and become a research leader?
- What do you do to enhance the performance of your researchers?
- If you designed leadership training for academics/ECRs, what would be the top five topics that you would include and prioritize?

The questions were designed to elicit key issues, in particular around lessons that the leaders had learned along the way and what they wished they had known before they took on their leadership role. The responses provided insights on what topics to prioritize when designing development interventions for future generations and they also served to unlock rich insights into the reality of an academic leader in a UK university today.

The responses to the questions gave us *a priori* codes for the analysis of the transcripts. Any additional information considered as insightful or potentially useful was also coded for further review. A 'peer scrutiny and internal triangulation' approach (Shenton, 2004) was applied to the data analysis and interpretation of key themes – the coding was carried out by one person initially and then reviewed by two other team members for a 'sense check.' The information was developed into eight core themes that were further reviewed in a workshop facilitated at the Vitae International Researcher Development Conference (Vitae, 2015) and amended in accordance with feedback from higher education colleagues who attended that workshop.

Findings and Conclusions

The eight themes from the above analyses divided easily into two groups as follows:

Aspects that help career progression:

- *Career Advancement and Planning* – This included using appraisals and taking the time to think and plan ahead, being resilient and being clear about the importance of personal values in career planning amongst other aspects.
- *Mentoring and Role Models* – The pivotal roles effective mentors and role models had played in helping the interviewees to develop were mentioned many times; and the interviewees were aware that they have a responsibility to act as role models in turn for the people they lead.
- *Building Networks* – The importance of building and maintaining networks, including making effective use of conferences and using networking as a career and professional development opportunity was cited as seeming to be obvious, but that its importance should not be underestimated in career development.
- *Building a Research Profile* – This essentially involved the prestige factors – the importance of doing the 'business' of research in order to progress with their career as academic leaders – publishing, winning funding and demonstrating impact.

Aspects of leadership found to be challenging:

- *Balancing Work and Life* – This included the challenge of putting appropriate boundaries in place to stop work from consuming everything. Respondents were somewhat sanguine about the hours they needed to put in and shared specific tools and techniques that they had tried in order to maintain a work–life balance of sorts. Some commented that they wished they had known just how much time the role would take up before taking the job on.

- *Impact of Culture and Environment* – Unsurprisingly, the respondents all talked about the considerable cultural changes that academia has undergone in recent decades and the impacts that they have felt personally in terms of work–life balance, management, leadership and the balance of teaching and research.
- *Working with Others* – The importance of working with other people to achieve goals was identified as being critical in an academic environment. The ability to interact with others in a way that achieves things positively is a key aspect of working in modern universities but respondents also talked about the difficulties of trying to get other people to do things without having line management authority over them.
- *Challenges of Management and Leadership* – Most interviewees cited the testing nature of managing and leading within a higher education environment, including the complexity of meeting organizational goals, working with staff with differing contributions and motivations alongside developing research.

The 'challenging' findings give an insight into the role of leadership in a modern university and the lack of preparation that the respondents felt they had experienced. Most of the interviewees found dealing with the people issues and navigating institutional politics to be significant challenges. They certainly felt underprepared for the multiple demands on their time. This information is useful across the UK higher education sector because it provides universities with the opportunity to focus on succession planning and preparation in a meaningful way, based on the real experiences of those who have gone before, which will hopefully benefit future generations.

Inclusive Leadership – An Alternative Approach for Modern Universities?

There is much evidence that the academic culture has changed significantly over the past 20–30 years and UK universities are now experiencing some of their most challenging times. A reduction in public funding, an increase in competition and a financially challenging macro-environment have all driven universities away from being collegiate environments to ones where large-scale transformational change initiatives (i.e. restructures) are common and academics are faced with needing to meet targets and Key Performance Indicators. Academic work, however, is by its very nature difficult to measure in many ways and requires knowledge creation or *critical thinking* – which are not necessarily easily performance managed. As a result, many universities appear to be increasingly managing things that they can measure easily – regardless of whether these are actually the right things to measure. The UK Government's recent white paper on the Teaching Excellence Framework (TEF) and consultation on whether 'contact hours' should be included as a measure, is both indicative of, and a driver for, this kind of quantifiable, yet quite possibly, meaningless approach (Department for Education, 2016). As a result, UK universities are tending to move away from collegiate approaches toward leadership and management. The culture has changed from 'minding the shop' to one where academic middle managers are required to implement transformational change initiatives on the ground and are held responsible for the results without necessarily being in the best position to ensure success. The fundamental structure of how academic leaders are selected has, however, in many cases not changed. Heads of department, in particular, are interesting, as they are usually chosen from 'within the available pool of potential candidates' and have a fixed term of office. Once that term is complete, they return 'to the fold' and once again work alongside their colleagues. This structure drives behaviour – it is a brave soul who takes on the challenge of addressing performance issues with the colleagues that they will have to work with on a level in the near future. Consequently, serious issues may go unaddressed and the head of department is seen to have failed.

This Catch-22 situation is beautifully articulated by one of the respondents in the *Developing the Next Generation* project:

> head of department is the most interesting role in that sense because you move from an academic in a body of people, or a colleague in a body of people into suddenly having this title that most people in the body who haven't done that role ... believes [has] some real authority and power. You have virtually none. And one of the ways that they can function is by creating a distance between themselves and the role. So you become head. And for lots of people you stop being you ... I was told that the day I stopped being head of department I would become me again. And I remember hearing that and thinking that can't be true, but for some people it was. They would come into my office and be completely different from how they were the week before when I wasn't head, because I was now head of department, and I found that absolutely bizarre.

The current model of academic middle management in the turbulent times of UK higher education may no longer be the most appropriate but we currently lack a viable alternative. In this chapter I have interrogated the experiences of those interviewed in the *Developing the Next Generation* study and I suggest that a model of Inclusive Leadership may offer us an alternative way in which we can define academic leadership in the future.

To limit the scope of the discussion here, I am referring to university academic managers as academic members of staff who hold a position of responsibility that includes managing other staff. The most obvious are heads of department and deans/heads of faculty, but others that fall into this group are principal investigators who lead research groups.

By the term university leaders, I am referring to those in the most senior leadership positions in our universities – but again limiting this to those who hold academic posts such as Vice Chancellor, Deputy Vice Chancellor, Pro Vice Chancellor, Vice Principal, etc. These people have a responsibility for setting and clearly articulating the strategy, vision and direction for the university and for establishing the 'bigger picture' of the values and standards that are expected across the campus. Both of these groups were covered by the interviews for the *Developing the Next Generation* project.

Based on this work, other collaborations with colleagues (Denney, Mead and Toombs, 2011) and my own experiences in management and leadership, I suggest here that the following elements are critical to creating an effective culture of inclusion. These sections are supported with quotes from the interviews from *Developing the Next Generation* and are compared with the 15 core competencies from *Inclusive Leadership*.

Setting Out a Clear Vision

There are two levels at which setting out a clear vision has an impact on creating an inclusive and effective work environment in academia. The first is at the senior level where the Vice Chancellor and colleagues have a responsibility for identifying how the university will develop over the next few years, and, if they are smart, working out which of the many demands and challenges in the macro-environment they will respond to. In other words, this is about the big picture of creating and developing the university that they want to see in the next five, ten or even twenty years.

The second is the 'local level' at department or research group level. This involves a process by which the smaller unit can clearly identify its contribution to the bigger picture, set out by the leaders above. That contribution is also communicated clearly to the individual staff members in the group so that they can identify their own contribution to this bigger picture.

This does a number of things: it makes setting any kind of targets or goals for each member of staff much easier, and it makes staff feel recognized and appreciated because they can see the (potential) impact of what they are doing in the bigger picture. In this way, inclusivity is defined as being integral in this process of setting out (and clearly communicating) a clear vision.

The Inclusive Leadership model identifies Idealized Influence as the provision of an appealing vision that inspires others, but I suggest here that, in addition to this, the Listening, Inspirational Motivation, Intellectual Stimulation and Confidence Building competencies are also important in creating an inclusive approach that genuinely brings people along with you.

The danger is that, if this is executed badly, then it can have the reverse effect. If senior leaders decide that they want the university to go in a direction that is counter, or only partly aligned to previous incarnations of the institution, then this has the immediate effect of disenfranchising any staff members who believe they are not included in the new model. This can also happen on a micro level within departments and research groups:

Respondents commented:

> there's nothing wrong with planning and having a strategy and knowing what it is … not sort of nailing yourself to it but knowing that there's a direction you want to go.
>
> So leadership in one sense suggests followship. And I've always thought that leadership is about having something to lead on. So you've got to have a clarity around why would anybody want to follow you? … You've got to have something compelling and whether that's about who you are as a person or what you believe in or how you set out a vision of where we're all going, you've got to have something.

It seems that the definition of an inclusive leader is: one who is prepared to set out a vision but who takes others along with them on the journey in making that into a reality. I think this can be tricky in an environment where the community is highly educated and trained to critique. The value of the Inclusive Leadership model is that it emphasizes the importance of building relationships using Empathy, Listening and a commitment to Stewardship and the fostering of a culture of inclusion relies on these skills and behaviours, modelled from the top.

Identifying Values and Reflecting Behaviours Against These

Whereas the vision is the direction for an organization, the values are the glue that holds it together. In contrast to received wisdom, an organization's values are not imposed from the top down and are not written on a piece of paper on the wall or on the website. Even if your organization has all of these, these are not necessarily its values. Values are seen in the behaviours, attitudes and actions of every member of staff of an organization on a daily basis. It is entirely possible for an organization to espouse a value of inclusivity, and yet for its members to behave in ways that are exclusive.

Values are probably the most important aspect of any organization – and are incredibly powerful in bringing people together and providing a mirror in which to reflect their behaviour. The first key is to identify the values for which the people in the organization want to be known. If they have an opportunity to input into naming the values that they want to espouse, then it becomes easier to encourage them to reflect their own behaviour in the mirror of those values and to hold up unwanted behaviours in that light.

For example, some UK universities are currently struggling with encouraging and supporting flexibility for some groups of staff whilst also creating a culture of presenteeism and long working hours because this is what is visible and measurable – but not inclusive. If this is understood in the light of values then it becomes less problematic and less of a dichotomy. If the organization, be that at a macro or a micro level, and its staff identify team working and customer service (for example) as some of those values, then this can be used to set standards for communications with colleagues, how queries from students are dealt with and accessibility to other people in the community. As well as communicating through example that this is a community (inclusive) endeavour.

Universities and their component departments are, however, not good at identifying and setting a common set of values that are integral to all staff. Instead, they produce the webpage or one printed page of 'Our Values' and somehow magically expect that this will change behaviour. Supporting inclusivity as a value requires that staff demonstrate a commitment to this through their behaviour – starting with an inclusive discussion on the nature of these values in the first place, and then ensuring that everyone realizes that their own behaviours and actions form part of this.

The ability to host effective discussions about values is not easy and requires the same skills and abilities identified in bringing people along with the vision or strategy. The commitment to leading by serving others for the good of everyone rather than for self-promotion may feel quite alien in today's university culture of targets and KPIs but is crucial if we are committed to developing a culture of inclusivity.

Establishing Clear Standards, Communicating These and Letting People Get On With It – With Support

Establishing clear standards is something that follows on from establishing the vision and values, and is another perspective on how to integrate inclusivity into everyday management and leadership practices. The problem in academia is that standards are not always clearly articulated – what do we mean by *good* research and *excellent* teaching anyway? If the university is clear on its vision and values, then the standards of behaviour should in theory follow and each member of staff should be clear about what they have do and to what standard in order to contribute to the bigger picture.

In addition, academic colleagues need support to attain the standards that are being set. The Inclusive Leadership model identifies Persuasion, Confidence Building, Growth and Conceptualization (being able to see how others contribute to long-term objectives) but in academia, they also then need to be left alone to get on with the job. Respondents from the *Developing the Next Generation* project referred to the environment in which the core work of academia takes place and how academics are best supported:

> I think every single academic and probably every single relatively intelligent functional human being has a certain amount of self-reflection. I think academics suffer from it quite badly ... academics tend to be quite self-critical

and quite introverted. Meanwhile the whole job is about being critiqued and putting your ideas out there and I know even very senior academics who still struggle with peer review and presenting and feedback and … they resent it even though they know it's important … we should be all acknowledging it and trying to do something about it and helping each other, [but] we just think well the lot of an academic is to have a bad work life balance and be quite miserable about large aspects of the job and just that's it.

This clearly demonstrates a mandate for change – that more effective academic work is promoted and supported by encouraging sharing, feedback and support – linking with Inspirational Motivation, Intellectual Stimulation and Confidence Building aspects of Inclusive Leadership in particular. There is however, a huge need to model that behaviour in order to lead the culture change. The notion that we just leave our academics to *be quite miserable about large aspects of the job* should be abhorrent to all universities. This cannot be the way to get the best out of academics and it implies leaving them on their own to figure it all out for themselves – hardly the model of an inclusive culture!

Additionally one respondent commented that:

researchers work best in a little bubble, they work best when they're in a little bubble and they don't have to engage with anything that isn't their research, and so part of your job is to keep the bubble inflated so that they can get on with it.

This highlights the ability of an effective academic leader to know their staff well and to understand the things that will help them to be more effective as well as helping them to deflect those things that will detract from effectiveness – in accord with the relationship focus of Inclusive Leadership.

Confidence Building and Growth were also evident here:

identifying opportunities for your researchers, for example, going to the key conference they should be seen at, introducing them to the right people to talk to … identifying other training events that they may need and facilitating these so that they can go and benefit.

The respondent was clear about how it was important to develop the academics in earlier stages of their careers.

Finally, one respondent summed it up as being an issue of trust. Interestingly this is not listed as a core competency in the Inclusive Leadership model, but is perhaps more of an overarching value that encompasses all of the 15 abilities:

So I think the big one is you've got to support people and trust them. You've got to give them latitude to do the work, you need to set the boundaries for that where there are boundaries and be really clear about what that is and then you've got to support them to do it, you've got to try not to interfere in it … So a big lesson I learned was to try to allow people to do their job. Don't micro manage them. Too much micro management, try not to set them targets. People will set their own targets. Set them the context in which you're going to talk about success and then they'll grow beyond any target you'll set.

Providing Ample Opportunities for Dialogue and Feedback

As mentioned earlier, the management and leadership roles for academics have become significantly more challenging in recent times, and this was something our interviewees commented on:

> Well, I think what's certainly changed in higher education in the last 30 years is the nature of leadership which is now much more like line management and much more top down than it was when I started.

Often academic middle managers are required to deliver on university strategies and implement transformational change initiatives but have had no leadership development or management training in order to fulfil these requirements. As a result, they end up with a very experiential approach to their development:

> So I know how to chair a meeting by being exposed to bad practice rather than best practice and I think a lot of things that we learn are recognizing well this thing which I'm experiencing right now isn't working that well, how can I do it better when I have to take that responsibility on?

Add into this potent mix the high probability that this academic middle manager will go back into the department and have to work effectively with their colleagues on the same level once again, and it becomes clear why transformational change initiatives often fail to get traction at a local level.

Furthermore, academic middle managers are often ill-equipped and poorly supported to engage in the kinds of effective dialogues and provision of good feedback that will help to improve the performance of their colleagues – besides possibly being unwilling to engage with this and set time aside for it.

This said, it is also true that effective dialogue and feedback are the ways of enhancing performance, gaining commitment to a set of collectively identified values and holding people to account to standards of behaviour that are required. This means having difficult conversations with people – but having them early and being very specific about the problematic behaviour and the changes that are required. Too often in academia, these conversations happen too late and too ineffectively because of the potent combination of driving forces and systems mentioned earlier in this section. If we are committed to inclusivity in our universities then effective performance management against transparent and agreed values and objective standards – which are not personalized or discriminatory – has got to be a powerful tool. Any system, however, that does not have transparency and objective standards as its cornerstones is going to inhibit inclusivity:

> I came into a department that was absolutely dysfunctional ... I sat in meetings where people would wait for head of department to say something and then write it down verbatim in their little notebooks. And ... they obviously had had a really traumatic time in the past and were struggling to trust that somebody could come in and want to do well for everybody in the department rather than just beat them up and do well for themselves. And the head created an environment that was really open and where people could say what they wanted to say and it didn't mean that they would always get their way but they would have a voice. He didn't hide things so everybody got to see the budget, everybody got to comment on the budget, everybody got to talk about how they might spend money. Again they didn't get their own way but we had discussions about it.
>
> And I learned from that, that that was a really powerful thing to do, to ... have conversations and don't think that you know the answers ... or don't think that their opinions aren't as important, just because you hold something that's positional in an organization.

This really clearly articulates some of the core competencies identified as Inclusive Leadership – the ability to encourage others to have ideas, showing acceptance of everyone, truly listening to the opinions of others and stewardship:

> And of course lots of the leadership stuff in higher education isn't leadership at all its management. It's just about effectively sitting in a chair and being responsible for some stuff. And that's not an interesting role or an interesting job I don't think. I also believe in academic leadership as being about collegiate leadership. So the idea that, and it's very unfashionable, apart from in the best institutions interestingly, it's very unfashionable to think that you would cycle this stuff between a community of colleagues who therefore see themselves as stewards of the department or an academic entity rather than leaders, the ... leader until they're killed or retire, you know that strikes me you're going to lead in a very different way if that's your mindset.

Concluding Remarks

The question for modern academia is one of how exclusive or inclusive we want our leadership model to be. The move away from the collegiate stewardship model to a culture which is business-oriented and has imported business tools for management, is not one that is right for inclusivity. As a result, there is a clash of cultures on our campuses now, which needs to be resolved in order for universities to move forward effectively to lead the knowledge-creation in the UK. The current culture of isolation, long hours and dominant poor person-management is not getting the best out of anyone, and management and leadership will be seen as exclusive domains dependent on role:

> I think there was a belief, you know, a sort of pious belief amongst Vice Chancellors that people's first loyalty was to the institution rather than to their discipline, even back in the 1980s, but I think what's happened is that that belief has gradually eaten its way down through the ranks of management so that now even people in team leadership positions believe that there's some hierarchy that gives them the source of their authority; they no longer believe that authority is something that's given to them by the people in their group.

We are failing to honour our espoused commitments to inclusivity in the very way in which we demonstrate leadership as an exclusive occupation, reserved for an exalted few.

Furthermore, the academic environment is currently not just one that is ineffective, but is also one that is putting people off from entering it at all:

> I wouldn't dream of leaving industry to come to academia now, the incentives that attracted me aren't here anymore. I certainly wouldn't dream of doing it to come in at a relatively junior level.

Yet the world has moved on – we must accept that and embrace change and I strongly advocate that we focus on developing a culture of inclusion throughout our organizations, empowering all people in academia to demonstrate leadership – and not just those in positions of authority. To start with, though, Inclusive Leadership needs to be modelled at the top and the 15 competencies identified by ENEI and Buckinghamshire New University provide a really great opportunity for academic leaders to pause and evaluate their behaviours.

Effective leadership in modern academia involves operating in a potent mix of old attitudes and a rapidly changing and evolving environment. Whilst the *Developing the Next Generation* study did not attempt to measure the effectiveness of those interviewed, their insights into the challenges they face on a daily basis demonstrate clearly an urgent need for discussions about a new leadership framework. All aspects of institutional policy frameworks need to reflect inclusivity – recruitment, recognition and reward – but the most important aspect is that the core competencies are modelled by those in management positions and that an expectation of inclusivity is set at every level.

I believe that if we are prepared to move towards a culture of inclusivity on our campuses, then the core competencies from the model developed by ENEI and Buckinghamshire New University provide a highly practical way forward. The questions for us now are: Do we want our leaders and leadership to be inclusive? Are we prepared to commit to achieving that goal?

References

Blackmore, P., 2015. Prestige in universities: In tension with the efficiency and effectiveness agenda? Paper presented at the Society for Research into Higher Education Annual Research Conference, Newport, UK.

Buckinghamshire New University, and ENEI, 2016. *Inclusive Leadership … driving performance through diversity*! Available at: <https://www.cipd.co.uk/binaries/inclusive-leadership_2016-driving-performance-through-diversity.pdf> [Accessed 21 November 2016].

Denney, F., Mead, J. and Toombs, P., 2011. *The leading researcher*. Cambridge: Careers Research and Advisory Centre (CRAC).

Denney, F., Mitchell, A. and Wheat, K., 2015. *Developing the next generation: Guidance and good practice in the leadership development of early career researchers and academics*. Available at: <https://www.vitae.ac.uk/vitae-publications/guides-briefings-and-information/developing-the-next-generation> [Accessed 21 November 2016] Cambridge: Careers Research and Advisory Centre (CRAC).

Department for Education, 2016. *Teaching excellence framework* [online] Available at: <https://www.gov.uk/government/collections/teaching-excellence-framework> [Accessed 21 November 2016].

Kandiko-Howson, C. and Coate, K., 2015. The prestige economy and mid-career academic women: strategies, choices and motivation. Paper presented at the Society for Research into Higher Education Annual Research Conference, Newport, UK.

Peters, K. and Ryan, M., 2015. *Leading higher education: Higher education leadership and management survey*. London: Leadership Foundation for Higher Education.

Russell Group, n.d. *About our universities*. [online] Available at: <http://russellgroup.ac.uk/about/our-universities/> [Accessed 21 November 2016].

Shenton, A. K., 2004. Strategies for ensuring trustworthiness in qualitative research projects. *Education for Information*, 22(2), pp. 63–75.

Vitae, 2015. Vitae Researcher Development International Conference Workshop A11 [online] Available at: <https://www.vitae.ac.uk/events/past-events/vitae-researcher-development-international-conference-2015/workshops/A11Developing%20the%20next%20generation%20of%20research%20leader> [Accessed 21 November 2016].

7

NAVIGATING THROUGH TOUGH WAVES TOWARDS INCLUSIVE LEADERSHIP

A Case Study from Saudi Arabia

Eqbal Z. Darandari

Introduction

Leadership has become a critical issue for all because of its role in enabling individuals, institutions and whole countries to achieve their missions and goals. With the impact of globalization, diverse markets and employees, increasing competitiveness and demands for democracy, the leadership of institutions has become more complex and demanding. Nowadays, to address this complexity, leaders are required not only to embrace diversity, but also to give full consideration to the concept of inclusion.

As Andrés Tapia (2016) comments, diversity is about "the mix" and inclusion is about "making the mix work" (p. 19). Diversity refers on the one hand to a wide range of both visible and invisible differences that exist among people such as values, beliefs, physical differences, ethnicity, age, gender, religion, marital status, culture, etc. On the other hand, inclusion refers to the quality of the organizational environment that includes, maximizes and leverages the diverse talents, backgrounds and perspectives of all people. An inclusive environment encourages and supports everyone to fully contribute to an organization's success.

It has become essential for leaders to embrace the diversity of their workforce, and to understand the importance of having everyone's voice heard. Leaders have to learn how to include and engage people of diverse backgrounds, experiences and thinking into conversation and decision-making processes in their own unique way. Leadership styles could be placed on a continuum of involvement ranging from autocratic (where leaders make all decisions), to information sharing, to consultative, to democratic leadership. Inclusive Leadership (IL) is a particular form of leadership behavior that has been recently proposed and has proved to be well founded. Inclusive Leaders can make a significant contribution to enhancing, not only diversity but also, the performance of individuals and institutions. Inclusive Leadership could improve innovation and competitiveness, attract and retain diverse talents and create an inclusive culture within an organization (Hollander, 2009; Carmeli, Reiter-Palmon and Ziv, 2010; Yin, 2013).

In higher education institutions (HEIs), the leadership approach is critical to the overall success of the organization. Distributed and collective leadership have become more common as a means of providing a greater sense of shared responsibility and diminishing hierarchical models of leadership (Bolden, Petrov and Gosling, 2008; Lefoe, Harvey and Ryland, 2012). Despite its importance however, it seems that many leaders in HEIs are not yet implementing an Inclusive Leadership Approach appropriately, particularly in some developing countries. This is due to a lack of consensus around the definition, concept and theory of IL. Further, the concept is still new and documented applications are few. Tapia (2016) stated that achieving true inclusion is much more difficult than achieving increased awareness, tolerance and sensitivity and indeed, diversity itself.

In the Middle East and in Saudi Arabia in particular, leadership approaches are discussed only amongst scholars and in specialized conferences. It is only recently that general training and preparation has taken place for leadership development. However, no specific attention has been paid to IL. In general, leaders depend on their own concepts and understandings of leadership, with some of them applying IL unintentionally. During the previous three decades, the author/researcher has studied and worked in King Saud University (KSU) in Riyadh and collaborated with other HEIs in Saudi Arabia through visits and workshops. The researcher observed that progress in the field of IL is like waves. It differs from one leader to another and from one institution to another. Even in one institution, one can easily notice differences in concepts and applications (Darandari & Hoke, 2013). KSU was selected as a case study for this chapter because: 1) it is the first university established in Saudi Arabia (1957); 2) it represents the best example of a university that has produced most of the leaders for the country and it values leadership, teamwork and fairness; 3) it is considered a model for other Saudi HEIs. Some major questions that are considered in this study are:

Have there always been Inclusive Leaders at KSU?
How were these leaders developed?
Did they create an inclusive organizational culture?
What aspects were considered?
What are the external and internal factors that affected the process and results?
What theories and definitions match the case for Inclusive Leadership?
What competencies were needed?
What strategies were used for change and sustainability?
What challenges and opportunities were met?

Theoretical Background

Institutional diversity and inclusiveness are becoming more important to HEIs in order to fulfill the numerous demands essential to knowledge societies. Universities are no longer limited to the traditional functions of teaching and research. Rather they have widened their remit and access in order to produce more qualified and innovative workers to work in knowledge transfer and a knowledge economy. Wuffli (2016) argues that leadership should be dynamic and change-oriented to meet the demands of markets and societies. It also should be horizontal, team-oriented and holistic to enable bridge building across different sectors of society as well as different cultures.

The concept of inclusion came to the forefront during the last decade of the 20th century through social work, social psychology and organizational literature (e.g., Brewer, 1991; Barak, 2000; Roberson, 2006). The concept has gained more attention in recent years, without consensus on the nature of the construct. Inclusion could be defined as the degree to which employees feel that they are esteemed members of the work group through experiencing treatment that satisfies their need for a sense of belonging and uniqueness. According to Pickett, Bonner and Coleman (2002), individuals socially identify with a particular group when it caters for their need for both belongingness and uniqueness. Avery, McKay and Wilson (2008) stated that inclusion is:

> the extent to which employees believe their organizations engage in efforts to involve all employees in the mission and operation of the organization with respect to their individual talents (p. 6).

Holvino, Ferdman and Merrill-Sands (2004) define the inclusive organization as:

> one in which the diversity of knowledge and perspectives that members of different groups bring to the organization has shaped its strategy, its work, its management and operating systems, and its core values and norms for success (p. 249).

It is important to indicate that the context of inclusion may vary among cultures, communities, countries and across time. What is considered an important factor for inclusion for one group could be considered peripheral for another. For example, the primary feature of North American companies is to increase diversity, while in Western European and Asian companies the focus is on improving conditions to attract and retain female employees, with less emphasis on other minority groups. In the Gulf countries it is felt that there is sufficient diversity regarding employees of different nationalities, and the focus is on improving conditions for local nationals who are often under-represented in management ranks in their own countries. Women's access to leadership is most problematic in

Western and Eastern Europe, the Middle East and South America (Hofmeyer, Sheingold, Klopper and Warland, 2015; Society for Human Resource Management, 2009).

Kraus and Riche (2016) stated that managing diversity and inclusion is about people and actual contact with them; it is intentional and does not happen as a side-effect of management. It is time consuming and labor intensive. A climate of inclusion is one in which policies, procedures and actions of organizational agents are consistent with fair treatment of *all* social groups. In HEIs, an inclusive climate involves the transformation of institutional policies, structures and activities in order to maximize the diverse talents, backgrounds and perspectives of all students, faculty, administrators and staff (Williams, Berger and McClendon, 2005).

IL is not clearly defined because much of the previous research on IL was not based on well-established leadership models and constructs. In critical theories, leadership does not reside in a position or a person, but in equitable, caring and fluid relationships among various individuals. These theories favor collaborative, reciprocal and horizontal relationships over the more traditional management hierarchies (Rusch, 1998). A number of IL theories reject the hierarchical leadership structure that accompanies bureaucratic forms of organization. Based on these theories, Inclusive Leaders need to foster equitable and horizontal relationships that also transcend wider gender, race and class divisions (Corson, 1996; Ryan, 2006). Leadership could occur in HEIs through student, faculty and staff leadership, where redistribution of power allows them to make decisions and influence processes in a variety of areas that are relevant to them (Kirby, 1992). Another perspective is introduced by the Employers Network for Equality and Inclusion (Buckinghamshire New University and ENEI, 2016), where it sees diverse talent as a source of competitive advantage that inspires diverse people to drive organizational and individual performance towards a shared vision. It issued the following statement relating to Inclusive Leaders: "leaders who are aware of their own biases and preferences, actively seek out and consider different views and perspectives to inform better decision-making."

Measuring Inclusion and Inclusive Leadership

The importance of inclusion in society today is such that there is an increasing focus on measuring inclusion. Optimal Distinctiveness Theory (ODT) is a social psychology theory that explains in-group–out-group differences through the individual's desire to attain an optimal balance of inclusion and distinctiveness *within* and *between* social groups and situations (Brewer, 1991, p. 477). Building on ODT, Shore, *et al.* (2011) presented a 2x2 framework, where uniqueness and belongingness work together to create feelings of inclusion. Individuals feel included when the team places a high value on both the unique and the belonging characteristics. Individuals need to have a sense of belonging to a group, as well as feeling valued in order to integrate differences into the functioning of a work group or organization. A diverse talent mix can enhance creativity and innovation.

In 2014, the US Office of Personnel Management (OPM) introduced the 'New IQ' or Inclusion Quotient, which is 'Inclusive Intelligence,' a set of change management tools. Inclusive Intelligence comprises the intentional, deliberate and proactive acts that increase work group intelligence by making people feel they 'belong' and are 'uniquely' valued. It is considered to be the most important intelligence of the future (Stewart, 2014; Office of Personnel Management, 2014). Prime and Salib (2014) conducted a study across Australia, China, Germany, Mexico and the United States, and identified four leadership inclusion behaviors: empowerment, humility, courage and accountability. Furthermore, Dillon and Bourke (2016) – based on their research carried out across six countries, including Canada, Hong Kong, Singapore and New Zealand, interviewing diversity and inclusion leaders in a range of organizations – offer six signature traits that characterize an inclusive mindset. These signature traits are: commitment, courage, cognizance of bias, curiosity, cultural intelligence and collaboration. Their overarching conclusion on inclusion is that if people feel that they are treated fairly, that their uniqueness is appreciated, that they have a sense of belonging, and that they have a voice in decision making, then they will feel included.

A major challenge facing organizations is how to assess for inclusion for the purpose of improving employee engagement and organizational performance. Furthermore, assessment of IL is an important issue in order to evaluate competencies and track the progress of organizations and individual leaders. Despite the fact that reliable and valid measurement tools are rare for inclusiveness and Inclusive Leadership due to prior ill-founded theories, some measures have been developed and examined.

OPM developed the Federal Employee Viewpoint Survey (FEVS) that assesses the extent to which employees feel engaged, supported and motivated. Bruce Stewart and his team in the Office of Diversity and Inclusion within OPM found that 20 items of that survey were highly correlated with participants' perceptions of what makes their organizations inclusive. They developed the New IQ inclusion index for government comparisons at all levels. Scores are calculated and metrics are separated into several factors, comprising five habits of inclusion: fairness, open-ness, cooperation, support, empowerment In addition, the Office of Diversity and Inclusion developed a D&I Dashboard government-specific tool for agency use in workforce planning and reporting. D&I provides agencies with demographic data about hiring, group attrition, employee inclusion perceptions and overall accountability efforts. Together, the tools and index help agencies with the instruments and practices necessary to support diversity and inclusion more fully (Office of Personnel Management, 2014).

Linkage's Institute for Leading Diversity & Inclusion team (Linkage, 2014) developed a model for behavioral competencies demonstrated by inclusive leaders. This model includes 11 competencies distributed into four areas (results focused; leads self; leads culture; leads relationships) and was used to build a reliable and valid *Inclusive Leadership Assessment* tool that could be used by organizations to develop and measure Inclusive Leaders and culture, to increase the degree of employee engagement and to advance institutional competitiveness.

The UK-based Employers Network for Equality and Inclusion (ENEI) examined the relationship between a range of known leadership theories and IL and found that the two widely accepted and well-established models of leadership that are compatible and fit with the concept of IL are Transformational Leadership (TL) and Servant Leadership (SL) (Echols, 2009). ENEI (Bucks New University & ENEI, 2016) then developed a new model of IL with strategic context that has 15 competencies that characterize the Inclusive Leader. ENEI suggests that all 15 competencies need to be present in order for someone to be an Inclusive Leader.

Korn Ferry, the pre-eminent global people and organizational advisory firm, has developed a Four Dimensional Executive Assessment (KF4D) for leadership performance that includes competencies, experiences, traits and drivers (Lewis, 2016). Tapia (2016) suggested a model based on Korn Ferry competencies to be used to assess and develop IL. These competencies are:

- **Open and aware:** self-aware, develops self, nimble learner, global mindset and resilient;
- **Actively promotes differences:** values differences, attracts diverse top talents, develops all talents, communicates the values of D&I effectively, drives engagement;
- **Build a trusting and open culture:** manages ambiguity, manages conflict, interpersonally savvy, courageous, instills trust;
- **Influences effectively:** organizationally savvy, situationally adaptable, persuasive, collaborates, balances stakeholders;
- **Optimizes organizational performance:** derives vision and purpose, builds effective diverse teams, builds trusting networks, cultivates innovation, drives results.

Through their research, Shapiro and Swiszczowski (2014) identified three success factors to ensure the development of IL in an organization is successful and sustainable: 1) Establishing senior leaders and managers as sponsors and role models for IL; 2) Building a group of change agents equipped to embed IL; 3) Positioning IL as part of an overall organizational program of change.

Other organizations relating to human resources and other researchers have put forward frameworks for assessing Inclusive Leaders and Leadership. Not surprisingly these models and frameworks begin to show considerable overlap. The models and frameworks being developed to explain the concept of IL provide a basis for an aspirational institution such as King Saud University to work towards.

The next section offers a case study of King Saud University's journey to become an inclusive HEI and a role model for other institutions in Saudi Arabia.

Case Study of King Saud University

The study is based on qualitative methodology using a case study with a story-telling style. Documents, studies, reports and personal experiences from over 25 years were used to follow the journey of leadership that King Saud University, as a prominent university in Saudi Arabia, has undergone. Themes were derived and patterns that explain meanings were concluded. Authenticity and verifiability were established through the congruence achieved from repeated analysis of data by another researcher (Creswell, 2007; Denzin and Lincoln, 2011).

Saudi Arabia and HE

Saudi Arabia, by nature, is set to accept and promote differences due to two factors: the first is that it has the two holy mosques of Islam, where thousands of Muslims of different ethnic backgrounds and colors, nationalities and different perspectives, come daily to perform *Omra* (the lesser pilgrimage) and come annually by the millions to perform the *Hajj* pilgrimage. The second factor is that Saudi Arabia is directed by religion to respect all human beings. The population of Saudi Arabia now is approximately 31 million, of which 21 million are Saudis (11 million males; 10 million females). Non-Saudis comprise approximately 10 million of the total population (7 million males; 3 million females) (General Authority for Statistics, Saudi Arabia, 2016).

During the past three decades, Saudi Arabia as a country and KSU as a higher education institution, have gone through tremendous waves of development including in leadership skills. At the time when this author joined KSU, it was non-Saudis who dominated all aspects of academic life. Saudi Arabian universities were full of professors from all over the world. In addition, more females joined HEIs. The major factors for inclusion were, and still are gender, nationality and area. At that time the concept of leadership was not clear. The leaders (rectors) in all universities were Saudis whereas most of the other positions were occupied by non-Saudis.

Higher education in Saudi Arabia has developed hugely during the past 25 years and in the past decade, many new HEIs have been established in different parts of the Kingdom in order to support access to a greater portion of society and to promote greater levels of equity for students. Presently, there are 34 universities in the Kingdom of Saudi Arabia (KSA), and several hundred other colleges (Research and Studies Center, 2014). Many faculty members were recruited from both inside and outside of the country to meet the high demands created by universities. In 2015, the total faculty numbers in Saudi Arabian HEIs reached 76,985 of which 45,443 (59 percent) are Saudis and 31,542 (41 percent) are non-Saudis. The gender balance is 60 percent male and 40 percent female. Across the university the percentage of Saudi faculty to non-Saudi faculty ranges from 70 percent to 20 percent. The staff complement other than faculty members, professional staff and administrators across Saudi universities' staff is 77,130 of which the majority (90 percent) are Saudis with again 60 percent male and 40 percent female staff members. The total number of students in higher education reached 157,095 in 2015 of which 73 percent are male, 27 percent female (Ministry of Higher Education KSA, 2016).

The Ministry of Education (MOE) sets the major policies for HEIs. It allocates significant funding to both government funded and private HEIs. It also funds thousands of students of different backgrounds and from different regions to study abroad to diminish social and class barriers. The MOE has provided grants for universities to develop their faculty, staff and students, and offers specialized training for leadership. It also allocates rewards for publishing in highly respected, specialized academic journals. There are no policies specified as yet regarding diversity and inclusion (D&I).

KSU as a Leading University in KSA

Most of the leaders in KSA have graduated from King Saud University, and they have an essential role in the development of the country (King Saud University, 2006). In 2015, the number of KSU faculty reached 7,548. Of this number 5,820 or 77 percent are Saudis and the other 23 percent are non-Saudis, 4,714 or 62 percent are male and 2,834, 38 percent are female. The total staff number in KSU is 15,796 with the majority (13,773) being Saudis and only 13 percent (2,023) non-Saudis. The gender balance is 51 percent male and 49 percent female. KSU students number 55,245 (48,297 are Saudis and 6,948 are non-Saudi; 58 percent are male and 42 percent are female) (Ministry of Higher Education KSA, 2016).

The Waves of Change

The waves of change that have taken place in the university during the past three decades have been viewed through the lens of the rector periods in KSU, because the rectors are essentially the driving force that moves the university and affects its policies, environment and actions, particularly regarding D&I. The institutional research carried out shows five waves of change.

The first wave started before 1990. The leadership at that time was influential, broadminded and encouraged differences among faculty, staff and students who had the talents to enrich the university. Differences included nationality, ethnicity, religion and gender. There was collaboration among groups, and students had representatives. The first woman dean was appointed and represented women in decision making (King Saud University, 2006). The KSU administration encouraged prominent graduates from different areas in the Kingdom to become teaching assistants. The researcher herself is an example of this particular development.

The second wave came between 1990 and 1995. This wave witnessed tremendous changes, due to decreases in the university budget which caused a significant reduction in international staff and students. The university became less open; differences and similarities between cultures were given no consideration. Most of the effort was focused primarily on just running the university through that tough time, and there was no room to encourage uniqueness and meet different needs. A top-down approach was dominant across the university, and important information was not disseminated. Inclusion was no longer a priority and it was a tough time for non-Saudi faculty and students. Fewer teaching assistants were sent abroad and more restrictions were put on women's education. In addition, many non-Saudi faculty members left the university because their children were not accepted at the university due to the recession. One professor was sad at that time and said to the rector in a general meeting, "I am speaking for hundreds of staff, whose children can no longer study at the university. I am very disappointed and I feel like a donkey that carries the water on its back and cannot drink from it. How can I teach students while my son can't join them?" As a female staff member, the researcher, along with five other women, had to fight for three years to get permission from the King to pursue higher education abroad.

During *the third wave*, which was between 1996 and 2007, the same policies continued, but some changes occurred. However, management was the most important aspect. The university resumed sending students abroad, and established many colleges and graduate programs. There was empowerment for Saudi nationals to take more leadership roles to replace non-Saudis who were holding these posts. Leadership opportunities continued to empower women and open more specializations for them. This offered Saudi faculty the chance to have more influence and helped build capability. New programs were established to help the students and staff with special needs with training opportunities. The communication was nevertheless hierarchical, and women had limited impact on decision making and finance decisions. During this period, the researcher/author returned from the USA having completed her PhD studies there, resumed teaching at KSU and was nominated for a significant leadership position. Towards the end of this period, KSU celebrated its 50th anniversary, and everybody felt proud of what they had achieved together. A very important book was issued on that occasion. It documented the accomplishments of leaders, and renowned professors, staff and students from different cultures. The university renewed the feeling of belonging and uniqueness at the time. The researcher/author was one of the steering committee members for the publication of the book collecting and collating the information (King Saud University, 2006). The steering committee was keen to include the names of everyone who had contributed to the university, so that everybody in the university could feel appreciated regardless of her or his position. The researcher remembers one of these summer days when she was running from building to building to verify information for the book, when suddenly one of the errand girls stopped her to say, "You are just like me ... I noticed that you run around for the whole day." It was a time of great energy and excitement!

The fourth wave came between the years 2008 and 2012. This period saw huge changes across all university levels and for all different groups. The first real strategic plan was developed during this period. It involved all different groups inside and outside the university, which impacted on the vision and objectives to represent this vision, and improved inclusiveness. Fortunately, the author was a member of the steering committee for this plan to represent women. She insisted on more female representation and managed to include two more female leaders on the committee. She managed to convince the committee and the leadership to have a female vice rector to represent women and minorities at high levels in the university. This dream came true three years after the strategic plan was approved. Some key objectives involved strategic empowerment for women to be appointed to more leadership positions and to be involved in decision making, with more powers also given to the student body. Other objectives focused on developing talent and performance among faculty and students; building bridges among communities inside and outside the university; providing an environment to attract high-level talent and appropriate rewarding. There was also a move toward reforming the organizational structure to be more efficient and horizontal, less hierarchical, to support better communication. KSU cited in its strategic plan:

> We are committed to promoting individual and institutional leadership roles, which drive social development, professionalism, responsibility, and innovation. Collaboration and cooperation are recognized as necessary means of attaining excellence; We abide by the principles of social justice, equal opportunity and cultural diversity, holding members of our community to the highest standards of honesty, respect, and professional ethics (King Saud University, 2010).

The system in the university encouraged every leader to be open and information to become more accessible. Differences were valued and talents were rewarded highly to boost performance. Engagement was high amongst all faculty members. Significant rewards were allocated to Saudis and non-Saudis with talents, which attracted diverse faculty and reduced attrition. Students had more legal rights and councils to represent them with their voices being heard through different means. Various student clubs and online forums were initiated to express student needs and interests, and faculty and leadership responded to them. Many policies were established to nominate leadership across all university levels and to represent various groups. A specialized development center was initiated, and thousands of workshops and hands-on training sessions were held for all groups. Leadership development was specified also for all groups. More leaders were developed in that positive climate, with an open and trustful, well-connected environment and encouragement and support for differences and diversity. Everyone was engaged in the goal of achieving a clear vision and objectives. More innovations and communities for learning and research appeared. As a result, the international ranking of KSU improved dramatically.

The fifth wave, between 2013 and 2016, was primarily about sustaining the positive gains that had been established. However, it was difficult to retain leaders who began to leave their positions because transparency and collaborative decision making started to fade away. Some of the highly qualified leaders were not given the positions they deserved, and centrality in decision making decreased trust. Even within a system with all information accessible, many faculty members lost their enthusiasm. This was often at the higher level. One woman leader said, "I tried ... now I lost interest ... I don't now even criticize because it is useless." However, at the lower levels, such as the departments, faculty were enjoying the openness that the system gave them and showed high respect for all groups. Students still had their rights and opportunities which had been created for them. Staff had gained more power, since large numbers were assigned new and challenging positions. Since women realized they had less power than expected, they had a strategic plan for the female section to have more leadership development in major areas. As a vice dean for development, the researcher was the leader of this strategic plan, and trained different women leaders to manage planning and execution skills.

Table 7.1 provides a summary across the five waves using a mix of IL competencies, theory KF4D and other theories that represent our case. Letters indicate the level of application based on the researcher's observations, where H stands for High level, M stands for Medium and L stands for Low level.

Lessons Learned Regarding IL

The results of the observations and data interrogation at KSU show that there had been a few Inclusive Leaders at KSU in previous years. Many of these leaders had no official training, but their natural characteristics helped them. Some of them managed to create an inclusive organizational culture to some degree, however, without strict policies, sustainability was difficult even within good structures. While the theories mentioned in the study are well stated, the case we have is better described through Dillon and Bourke's (2016) theory and Tapia's (2016) theory, because they fully connect with reality, as well as the required actions that control processes and produce results. Inclusive Leadership aspects that were considered include: decision-making processes, collaboration and information dissemination, fairness, trust and accountability. No specific strategies were in place for change or sustainability.

Trust Creates Enthusiasm, Collaboration and Results

Looking at the factors that impacted the institutional productivity, it was clear that the Inclusive Leaders were the ones who were enthusiastic and committed to the cause of diversity and inclusion with clear visions and results. Trust is

TABLE 7.1 Levels of IL Application in KSU across Five Waves

	IL competencies	Pre- 1990	1990–1995	1996–2007	2008–2012	2013–2016
		Wave 1	Wave 2	Wave 3	Wave 4	Wave 5
1	**Open and aware:** self-aware, develops self, nimble learner, global mindset, resilient, copes with change, knowledgeable of differences and similarities between cultures.	M	L	L	H	H
2	**Commitment to promote differences and reduction of biases:** values differences and different perspectives, attracts diverse top talents, develops all talents, communicates the values of D&I effectively, drives engagement, personal responsibility, treats others with fairness, employs fair, transparent, informed decision-making processes about talent, identifies and addresses organizational processes that are inconsistent with merit.	H	L	L	H	H
3	**Build a trusting and open culture:** manages ambiguity, manages conflict, interpersonally savvy, courageous, instills trust, works well with individuals from different cultural backgrounds, ensures team members have a voice and empowers to make decisions.	M	M	M	H	M
4	**Courageous and influences effectively:** organizationally savvy, situationally adaptable, persuasive, collaborates, connects others, balances stakeholders, holds others to account for non-inclusive behaviors.	H	L	M	H	M
5	**Optimizes organizational performance:** derives vision and purpose, builds effective diverse teams, builds trusting networks, cultivates innovation, drives results.	M	L	M	H	L

important for collaboration and productivity. Involving people only for their benefit will damage trust and results as well. This supports what Dillon and Bourke (2016) stated: if people feel that they are treated fairly, that their uniqueness is appreciated and they have a sense of belonging, and that they have a voice in decision making, then they will feel included. It is all about how strong and trustworthy the leader is. Without trust the practices of inclusion will be weak. As Kraus and Riche (2016) have stated, IL is intentional and does not happen as a side-effect of management.

Structure, Policies and Change Management Are Essential for Success and Sustainability

The findings indicate that, while the university believes in the importance of D&I, there is a major gap between good intentions and actions. The university went through tough times in order to improve IL practices, but without policies in place it was up to the leaders to decide and the picture of requirements was not clear. In addition, with no change management strategies, the road to IL was bumpy. As Williams, Berger and McClendon (2005) indicated, it is about transformation of institutional policies, structures and activities in order to maximize the diverse talents, backgrounds and perspectives of all students, faculty, administrators and staff.

It Is About Impact and Metrics, Not Just Inclusive Leadership Characteristics

The results also indicate that it is important to have a strategy, metrics and targets in place for inclusion, otherwise it will become just a waste of time. It is also important to assign a committee for inclusion that includes all stakeholders, to develop guidance and implementation and to evaluate evidence gathered about implementation.

Focus on Selection Practices

Even though there were criteria to select leaders in the university, the concept of inclusiveness was not one of them. It is important to have criteria for inclusion in recruitment, selection and assessment of leaders in order to achieve results, as Shapiro and Swiszczowski (2014) suggested. Awareness of IL and its implications are very important. Training is essential in order to create a culture that could support appropriate application.

Conclusion

Many changes have taken place in Saudi Arabia during the last three decades, particularly in the field of higher education. The vast expansion of higher education in the Kingdom of Saudi Arabia necessitated bringing in diverse faculty from different countries with different expertise. In addition, HEIs had to send graduates to pursue their higher education abroad and they came back with different perspectives. More women joined faculty and took up leadership positions. Students came from all parts of the country and also from other countries. KSU had always had a diverse population as the leading university in KSA. Even though no policies were set for D&I, KSU leaders had to manage without any specialized guidance or development for IL; that is why some were successful and others were not. The university went through many ups and downs, with no sustainability for gains. The findings of the study showed that, even though leaders' competencies are important, often there are humble equivalent actions. Structure, policies and change management are essential for success and sustainability. A high level of awareness is essential to building an IL culture. To date, the IL theories do not seem to cover all required actions for achieving the necessary results in practice.

References

Avery, D. R., McKay, P. F. and Wilson, D. C., 2008. What are the odds? How demographic similarity affects the prevalence of perceived employment discrimination. *Journal of Applied Psychology*, 93(2), pp. 235–249.

Barak, M., 2000. Beyond affirmative action: Toward a model of diversity and organizational inclusion. *Administration in Social Work*, 23(3–4), pp. 47–68.

Bolden, R., Petrov, G. and Gosling, J., 2008. *Developing collective leadership in higher education*. London: Research and Development Series, Leadership Foundation for Higher Education.

Brewer, M. B., 1991. The social self: On being the same and different at the same time. *Personality and Social Psychology Bulletin*, 17(5), pp. 475–482.

Buckinghamshire New University and ENEI, 2016. *Inclusive Leadership … driving performance through diversity!* Available at: <https://www.cipd.co.uk/binaries/inclusive-leadership_2016-driving-performance-through-diversity.pdf> [Accessed 3 March, 2017].

Carmeli, A., Reiter-Palmon, R. and Ziv, E., 2010. Inclusive leadership and employee involvement in creative tasks in the workplace: The mediating role of psychological safety. *Creativity Research Journal*, 22(3), pp. 250–260.

Corson, D., 1996. Emancipatory discursive practices. In: Leithwood, K., Chapman, J., Corson, D., Hallinger, P. and Hart, A., eds. *International handbook of educational leadership and administration*. Dordrecht, The Netherlands: Kluwer, pp. 1043–1067.

Creswell, J. W., 2007. *Qualitative inquiry and research design: Choosing among five approaches*. Thousand Oaks, CA: Sage.

Darandari, E. and Hoke, T., 2013. Using quality assurance mechanisms to enhance change and organizational learning. *Higher Education Evaluation and Development*, 7(3), pp. 21–33.

Denzin, N. K. and Lincoln, Y. S., 2011. *The SAGE handbook of qualitative research*. 4th ed. Thousand Oaks, CA: Sage.

Dillon, B. and Bourke, J., 2016. *The six signature traits of inclusive leadership: Thriving in a diverse new world*. Westlake: Deloitte University Press.

Echols, S., 2009. Transformational/servant leadership: A potential synergism for an inclusive leadership style. *Journal of Religious Leadership*, 8(2), pp. 32–51.

General Authority for Statistics, 2016. Saudi Arabia general statistics. KSA. Available at: <http://www.cdsi.gov.sa/en/node#> [Accessed 10 July, 2016]

Hofmeyer, A., Sheingold, B., Klopper, H. and Warland, J., 2015. Leadership in learning and teaching in higher education: Perspectives of academics in non-formal leadership roles. *Contemporary Issues in Education Research*, 8(3), pp. 181–192.

Hollander, E. P., 2009. *Inclusive leadership: The essential leader-follower relationship*. New York: Routledge.

Holvino, E., Ferdman, B. M. and Merrill-Sands, D., 2004. Creating and sustaining diversity and inclusion in organizations: Strategies and approaches. In: Stockdale, M. S. and Crosby, F. J., eds. *The psychology and management of workplace diversity*. Malden, MA: Blackwell, pp. 245–276.

King Saud University, 2006. *The golden anniversary book for KSU*. KSA: KSU.

King Saud University, 2010. *KSU strategic plan*. KSA: KSU.

Kirby, P., 1992. Shared decision making: Moving from concerns about restrooms to concerns about classrooms. *Journal of School Leadership*, 2(3), pp. 330–345.

Kraus, A. and Riche, M., 2016. Filling the gap: Principles, practices and tools for the effective management of diverse workgroups. In: Foegen Karsten, M., ed. *Gender, race and ethnicity in the workplace: Emerging issues and enduring challenges*. Santa Barbara, CA: ABC-CLIO Corporate, pp. 149–180.

Lefoe, J., Harvey, G. and Ryland, K., 2012. Distributed leadership: A collaborative framework for academics, executives and professionals in higher education. *Journal of Higher Education Policy and Management*, 34(1), pp. 67–78.

Lewis, J., 2016. *Korn Ferry four dimensional executive assessment*. Los Angeles, CA: Korn Ferry Institute. Available at: <http://static.kornferry.com/media/sidebar_downloads/KF4D-technical-brief.pdf> [Accessed 10 August, 2016].

Linkage, 2014. *How to build and measure a culture of inclusion? Develop inclusive leaders*. Burlington, MA: Linkage.

Ministry of Higher Education, Kingdom of Saudi Arabia (KSA), 2016. Available at: <https://www.moe.gov.sa> [Accessed 3 March, 2017].

Office of Personnel Management, 2014. *The new IQ: Diversity & inclusion in the workplace*. Washington, DC: Office of Personnel Management.

Pickett, C. L., Bonner, B. L. and Coleman, J. M., 2002. Motivated self-stereotyping: Heightened assimilation and differentiation needs result in increased levels of positive and negative self-stereotyping. *Journal of Personal and Social Psychology*, 82(4), pp. 543–562.

Prime, J. and Salib, E., 2014. *Inclusive leadership: The view from six countries*. New York: Catalyst.

Research and Studies Center, 2014. *Higher education in Saudi Arabia: Progression and accomplishments*. KSA: Ministry of Health.

Roberson, Q. M., 2006. Disentangling the meanings of diversity and inclusion in organizations. *Group and Organization Management*, 31(2), pp. 212–236.

Rusch, E., 1998. Leadership in evolving democratic school communities. *Journal of School Leadership*, 8, pp. 214–250.

Ryan, J., 2006. Inclusive leadership and social justice for schools. *Leadership and Policy in Schools*, 5(1), pp. 3–17.

Shapiro, D. and Swiszczowski, L., 2014. *Inclusive leadership: Culture change for business success*. Opportunity Now and Shapiro Consulting. Available at: <http://gender.bitc.org.uk/

system/files/research/inclusive_leadership_culture_change_for_business_success.pdf>
[Accessed 12 July, 2016].

Shore, L. M., Randel, A. E., Chung, B. G., Dean, M. A., Ehrhart, K. H. and Singh, G., 2011. Inclusion and diversity in work groups: A review and model for future research. *Journal of Management*, 37(4), pp. 1262–1289.

Society for Human Resource Management, 2009. *Global diversity and inclusion: Perceptions, practices and attitudes*. Alexandria, VA: SHRM.

Stewart, B., 2014. The new IQ: A new kind of intelligence for a new kind of world. *The Federal Manager*, 3.

Tapia, A., 2016. *The inclusion paradox: The post-Obama era and the transformation of global diversity*. 3rd ed. Los Angeles, CA: Korn Ferry Institute.

Williams, D., Berger, J. and McClendon, S., 2005. *Toward a model of inclusive excellence and change in post-secondary institutions*. Washington, DC: American Association of Colleges and Universities.

Wuffli, P., 2016. *Inclusive leadership: A framework for the global era*. Switzerland: Springer.

Yin, L.W., 2013. *Inclusive leadership and employee voice: Mediating roles of psychological safety and leader-member exchange*. Project submitted to School of Business in partial fulfillment of the graduation requirement for the degree of Bachelor of Business Administration. Hong Kong: Hong Kong Baptist University. Available at: <https://www.libproject. hkbu.edu.hk/trsimage/hp/10007490.pdf> [Accessed 15 November, 2016].

8

LEADERSHIP AND INCLUSIVENESS

A Perspective from Middle East and Central Asian Universities

Enakshi Sengupta

Introduction

This chapter presents case studies carried out in three different universities to examine the relationship between the leadership style and inclusive policies in these institutions of higher education. The case study approach was preferred in examining situations in the chosen institutions where contemporary events and relevant behavior could not be manipulated. The chapter reports on an attempt to study the relationship between leadership and inclusiveness by means of carrying out in-depth interviews, direct observations and interrogation of policy documents relating to what is happening from a descriptive angle rather than by conducting an experiment to draw inferences on the causes and effects of inclusiveness in such situations. The research is aimed at illuminating a particular situation in each of these universities to gain deeper understandings of that situation (Yin, 2004) with the help of data collected in a natural setting as opposed to relying solely on derived data (Bromley, 1986).

Over the years the concept of *inclusion* has developed and is now a critical issue in higher education. Inclusion urges and advocates those who are responsible for running a regular classroom to create space and include those who are categorized as exceptional or different. Organizational practice relating to inclusiveness does not lie with parents or teachers. Responsibility for an inclusive learning environment ultimately lies with principals or heads of institutions. "Leaders are called upon to support student learning in many ways ... to address critical problems of practice ... [and] to improve their knowledge about constructive educational leadership" (Firestone and Riehl, 2005, pp. x–xi). In most educational institutions, the head of the institution is accountable for the educational progress of each student with exceptionality. Nonetheless, despite being bestowed with accountability and responsibility, the only truly meaningful influence that any head of institution can exert on inclusion generally occurs indirectly (Edmunds and Macmillan, 2010). No one has ever argued against the merits of the concept of inclusion but, at all levels of higher education, the leadership has struggled to understand the philosophy and need for inclusiveness in their institution. One can rationalize such disconnect as owing to the fact that this special field may be lacking adequate research findings regarding the impact of inclusiveness on higher education and the institution.

Fraser and Shields (2010) state that: "Many current practices in education persist because of long held and unquestioned assumptions about the nature of schooling and the respective roles of educators and students" (p. 7). These assumptions originate from stereotyping and beliefs held by society. At the outset of this chapter the author would like to argue the fact that the typical concept of normality is quite often limited in its definition. This limiting view of normalcy demarcates those who fall outside its realm. While students with physical or mental disabilities are often considered to qualify for affirmative inclusive actions, not much consideration is given to students hailing from deprived socio-economic backgrounds or students who are marginalized on the grounds of gender, social class, religion or creed.

Concepts of *normality* or *normalcy* assume a core position in the definitions of inclusion. Inclusion is not an obsession with everyone somehow fitting a certain mold in order to be accepted (Fraser and Shields, 2010). It is, in essence, about the creation of opportunity and equitable distribution of such an opportunity. The case studies discussed in this chapter highlight affirmative actions, mainly for students from under-privileged sections of society owing to the geo-political scenarios of the countries being discussed.

The growth of higher education has lessened the debate and doubt regarding the right of students with exceptionalities to be given a fair chance of being included in a 'regular' or 'normal' classroom (Bunch, *et al.*, 1997), but the process still remains a struggle, deciding who these students are, how to include them and deliver programs suitable to all those who are a part of the prevalent education system. Empirical evidence in the past has revealed that the success of inclusive programs can be attributed to the leadership of the institution and his/her directional guidance in shaping an inclusive environment (Reyes and Wagstaff, 2005; Ryan, 2006; Baker, 2007). These programs often prove to be a morale booster and provide opportunities for enabling students to accomplish what was earlier considered to be not feasible. The affirmative actions in most cases have been initiated as a result of changes in the law concerning students with special needs.

In the case studies cited in this chapter, the governments of the respective countries or provinces have considered providing opportunities to students affected by incessant war, or to victims with diminished socio-economic situations in the aftermath of post-Soviet rule.

Leadership – In Pursuit of an Effective Style

Leadership has become a high priority issue in higher education (Leithwood, *et al.*, 2003). Many theorists attribute the development and operations of an institution to particular leadership styles. We see a growing body of work on instructional leadership styles: moral leadership, transformational leadership, cultural and primal leadership, and authentic leadership (Goleman, *et al.*, 2002). The list is long and still growing today! We need to question what might be considered an effective style. Is it dependent on context? Is there any single style that can fit every institution? While some leaders consider that their leadership style is independent of the context, others feel that they have to adapt their style according to the context in which they are operational.

There is a school of thought that does not attribute leadership to a particular individual but rather considers a distributive leadership model which includes teachers and staff members who impact on the student experience. A study conducted by Leithwood and Jantzi (2000) examined the effects of different sources of leadership on student engagement and found that 'total leadership' in most cases is the sum of the leadership provided from all sources and did not necessarily depend only on the head of the institution.

The Meaning of the Term 'Leadership'

The goal of leadership assumes significance primarily when it is directed at organizational improvement; it is about establishing direction and driving the institution towards excellence. Hence, a generic definition of leadership, simply stated, can be about direction and influence, leading the institution towards overall improvement. While we all believe in the potential for leadership to enhance organizational effectiveness, at times our confidence can be shaken by misplaced leadership or what has been termed the 'romance of leadership' by Meindl (1995).

> It appears that as observers of and participants in organizations, we may have developed highly romanticized, heroic views of leadership – what leaders do, what they are able to accomplish, and the general effects they have on our lives. It amounts to what might be considered a faith in the potential if not actual efficacy of those individuals who occupy elite positions of formal organizational authority (Meindl, *et al.*, 1985, p. 79).

This idea becomes even stronger when we discuss the inclusiveness of the institution as a path towards excellence created by the leader. Unplanned appointments, sudden changes of leader, leaders focused only on routine work and leaders lacking the ability to motivate and inspire others towards making meaningful changes that impact society can epitomize misplaced leadership. While interrogating the literature concerning educational leadership most research work has focused on leadership in schools. Little or no research has been carried out on universities supporting multiculturalism or universities in conflict zones trying to integrate students into mainstream society. Examining concepts of inclusion in this type of higher educational setting is the prime focus of this chapter. As the chapter progresses, certain leadership styles are highlighted which will have relevance to the cited case studies from three different universities. The main styles of leadership that will be mentioned in this chapter are transformational and charismatic leadership. Both these styles are closely related and both have a motivational dimension whereby the leaders influence their colleagues and the process is based on leader–follower relations, as was observed by the author while working in these institutions under the leadership of the institutions' heads. The commonalities of these styles are the leaders' abilities to communicate a compelling vision, convey high-performance expectations, project self-confidence, act as role models, express confidence in followers' abilities to achieve goals and emphasize collective purpose and identity. These themes of leadership and inclusiveness will be further explored in the three case studies to be described.

Distributive leadership may prove to be insufficient to effect meaningful, sustainable, organizational change. The broad objective is to find solutions to sustain inclusive learning environments which are not 'bolt-on' approaches or *ad hoc* projects taken up by the leader as a substitute for doing anything substantial

Inclusiveness needs to be embedded in the policy and practice of the institution and become fundamental to the survival of the organization, a part of the system, beliefs, values, actions and expectations of the institution. Such embeddedness is often difficult to achieve and can be merely superficial rhetoric. Developing a truly inclusive institution often requires a complete redesign of the institution which might actually shake the core of deeply held beliefs about students with exceptionalities. Inclusiveness calls for a disruption of our basic beliefs and a refocusing on what it is intended to be. The leadership team, with its directional and inspirational ideas, can call for the improvement of instruction which can be redesigned, implemented and sustained over a long period of time. A consideration for sustainability is imperative and can save inclusion from the risk of becoming the 'in thing' to implement.

Case Studies

American University of Central Asia

In 1991, as independence movements swept across many Central Asian countries, the region witnessed a fast-changing world of free markets and democracy. Imperialist power was thwarted and leadership emerged from the new generation which provided a fresh perspective on how economic resources and personal freedom can be intertwined to nurture an open society. This wave of change was also felt in the educational system resulting in the establishment of the Kyrgyz-American

School (KAS) within the Kyrgyz State National University (KSNU) in Bishkek in 1993. In 1997, by a decree of the President of Kyrgyzstan, KAS became the American University in Kyrgyzstan (AUK), and an independent international Board of Trustees was established as the governing body. In 2002, due to the university's expanded mission and future vision, the Board of Trustees changed the name to reflect the university's regional significance: the American University of Central Asia (AUCA) (https://auca.kg/en/auca_history/).

The AUCA is an international, independent, multi-disciplinary learning community. Its curriculum includes the AUCA School Bilimkana (grades 8–11), Preparatory Program, 13 undergraduate majors and 5 graduate programs. AUCA attracts students and faculty committed to critical thinking and pushing the boundaries of accepted knowledge. The university's commitment to academic innovation serves as the driving force behind bold curricular experiments, including many focused on developing future leaders who can challenge current practices and find solutions to the real social, economic and political problems of Central Asia.

With a few exceptions, all courses are taught in English, making a high-quality American liberal arts education accessible for students from across Asia. The university benefits from several major foundation grants, which allows it to deepen its liberal arts emphasis in the fine arts, history, regional studies and civic education.

AUCA maintains partnerships with a number of universities and organizations worldwide. The partnership with Bard College in the United States expands opportunities for students and faculty, as well as US-accredited degrees for most of their graduates. AUCA serves Central Asia, a geo-political area that has witnessed the growth of young democracies into nation-states that were earlier accustomed to more restrictive forms of governance. The university strives to develop the skills and the attitudes of mind that foster sensitivity to the region's rich traditions and adaptability for its democratic development (https://auca.kg/en/mission/).

Dr Andrew Baruch Wachtel has been the president of AUCA since 2010. He has been instrumental in nurturing a well-functioning and responsible administrative staff complement who are willing and able to take responsibility for student-centered learning and robust assessment of teaching and learning. He created a development operation from scratch in a country with a minimally functioning economy and little tradition of public philanthropy. He is responsible for raising $40 million of private, foundation and government funds (the largest amount ever for private higher education in Central Asia) to support scholarships, building and academic programs. He is instrumental in creating a successful foundational year program for students from disadvantaged backgrounds in Kyrgyzstan and Afghanistan (https://www.auca.kg/en/president/).

Dr Wachtel refuses to label or stereotype his leadership style and calls it: "relatively hands off with expectations. That is, my goal is to constantly expand the area of competence of the people who work under me. They become more autonomous and happier with their work and I have fewer things that require my decision." A leadership style, according to Wachtel, need not be contextual and dependent on the socio-economic or geo-political situation of a country, yet it often is. He believes that, in Kyrgyzstan, or for that matter in other countries rising from the wake of a post-Soviet world, it is often found that subordinates are less willing to take responsibility for doing things on their own and less willing to criticize their superiors than in the US: "It is significantly harder to implement my style of leadership in Kyrgyzstan than in the US." He believes that people in this part of the world have to be told what they are expected do, or else in most cases they feel that either they can do whatever they want or they feel free to do nothing: "It is hard to get them to see that they have to fit into an overall picture but within it they have a lot of freedom."

Inclusiveness and Affirmative Action

The AUCA practices various kinds of 'affirmative action', primarily socio-economic in response to the nature of the actual and potential student body. Financial aid is given to students from low socio-economic families to ensure a reasonable socio-economic mix of students. The university refuses to practice ethnic-based affirmative action for various reasons. On the level of faculty, the university emphasizes hiring the best people with an adequate mix of local and foreign faculty.

A fulsome list of scholarships and grants offered by AUCA is included in Appendix 1. Some of the main grants offered are:

Financial Aid for Students with Disabilities: Amount: up to 90 percent tuition – Available to applicants who are accepted into one of AUCA's programs as full-time students, maintain an overall GPA of at least 2.7 (as an existing student), can demonstrate financial need and have a disability category of 1 or 2.

Orphan Awards: Amount: up to 90 percent tuition – Available to applicants who are accepted into one of AUCA's programs as a full-time student, maintain an overall GPA of at least 2.7 (as an existing student) and can demonstrate financial need.

Higher Education Support Program (HESP) Scholarships: (3 cohorts, 10 female students each). These are awarded to female applicants from Afghanistan. The grant supports one academic year in the AUCA Preparatory Program. If the student is admitted and is enrolled in one of the AUCA bachelor's degree programs she will be provided with a full scholarship (free tuition, housing allowance and stipend) covering a full undergraduate study program. Applications should be made directly to AUCA.

The American University of Kurdistan

Established in 2014, the American University of Kurdistan (AUK) seeks to foster respect for learning, knowledge and genuine academic achievement. Located in the heart of Duhok, in northern Iraq, AUK strives to become a leading center of academic excellence and research. The university aims to mold the next generation of leaders through challenging courses, up-to-date methodology and qualified, experienced faculty members (http://audk.edu.krd/about). The university is relatively new and the inauguration of the main building was conducted in the fall of 2015. The total number of students at present is only 275, mostly enrolled in the first-year English Language Institute. The university will eventually comprise six colleges including Business, Arts & Sciences, Engineering, International Studies, Health Sciences and Education.

The university is committed to shaping leaders for local and regional communities by offering quality education, research and career-oriented programs. The university aims to become a prominent academic and research hub in this region and practice the highest standards of intellectual integrity and scholarship. The mission of the university as outlined by the Chairman, HE Masrour Barzani, is to create a passion for promoting education and blending intellectual substance and social action. AUK will have its own distinctive approach that offers the highest level of education in a vibrant community in Kurdistan. The student–faculty relationship works to create life-long relationships and career networks which will have a positive impact on academic achievement, career performance and students' lifetime achievements (http://audk.edu.krd/about/letter-from-chairman).

Dr Michael William Mulnix is the president of this university. He summarized his leadership style by using several key words: "democratic (good listening skills, sharing of power, inclusive/participative); charismatic (high energy, positive personality); and transformational (inspirational, intellectually stimulating)." Dr Mulnix feels that cultural variables may have a slight impact on his leadership style, but he has always remained consistent in his approach to leadership. Irrespective of geographical or cultural context, he has developed a consistent strategic vision as well as goals and objectives that allow faculty and staff to understand the vision of the institution, no matter where it is located. Working in a war zone with severe constraints does impact on one's leadership style and he feels that "certain environmental variables will necessitate that you act differently in different situations, such as confronting severe economic constraints. But, if you are more-or-less consistent in your management/leadership style, your team will gain confidence in your ability to handle even extreme situations." Dr Mulnix has been instrumental in institutionalizing inclusive policies in AUK by establishing various committees and policy-making bodies that are transparent and that welcome active and open participation by all. An Academic Council has been formed that meets on a regular basis to discuss a wide variety of policies and procedures that directly impact on all faculty. He expressed the fact that his leadership style "is best described as being democratic, charismatic, and transformational." The style adopted by him encourages and supports inclusivity in all deliberative processes at the university, "in other words, I actively encourage debate and input on all key decisions."

In keeping with the geo-political scenario of Iraq and the incessant battle fought by the Peshmerga forces of Kurdistan, several financial aid and scholarship programs are offered to martyrs' families, members from the families of prisoners of war and to children of war veterans. Merit-based scholarships are also given to deserving candidates.

The merit-based scholarships are:

- Mustafa Barzani Merit Scholarship;
- Chairman Masrour Barzani Merit Scholarship;
- Board of Trustees Merit Scholarship;
- President's Merit Scholarship;
- Dean's Merit Scholarship;
- AUDK Merit Level 1; and
- AUDK Merit Level.

Students are awarded scholarships based on their high school results. For students within Iraq the Baccalaureate percentage score will be used and for international students the equalized percentage score from the Ministry of Education will be used. Students have to meet and/or maintain the requirements below for eligibility. Scholarship students must maintain a minimum GPA for each study level. These awards and scholarships are not based on the socio-economic criteria of the students but are purely based on academic performance.

Scholarships based on socio-economic criteria are listed below:

Martyr's Aid: Children and spouses of martyrs are offered full tuition grants to study at AUK. This government grant is provided by the Ministry of Martyrs and Anfal to students within the Kurdistan Regional Government (KRG). The grant applies to the governorates operating within the KRG: Duhok, Hewler and Sulaimani. These students must be accepted to the American University of Kurdistan and approved by the Ministry of Higher Education and Scientific Research (MHESR). Students must abide by all rules and regulations set by the Ministry of Martyrs and Anfal.

Political Prisoners Aid: Children of political prisoners are offered full tuition grants to study at AUK. This government grant is provided by the Ministry of Martyrs and Anfal to students within the Kurdistan Regional Government (KRG).

Veterans' Aid: AUK understands and acknowledges the importance of the veterans that have sacrificed and continue to sacrifice. As a token of gratitude it offers veterans and children and spouses of veterans a discount of 25 percent. This discount applies to Peshmerga, children and spouses of Peshmerga, children and spouses of martyrs, and children and spouses of political prisoners. The students must apply for veterans' aid and must fulfil all requirements in order to be eligible. The students must provide valid ID (military, martyr's or political prisoner's) and any other requested ID or documents.

Apart from the grants and scholarship programs, the university building with a total floor area of approximately 30,000 square meters has been designed to offer accessibility to students with impaired mobility. The main gate has a ramp for wheelchair access with elevators allowing all students to reach their classrooms. Separate washrooms have been built in each floor with special facilities for disabled students, staff and faculty members. The university, being new, is in the process of developing policies and procedures in all departments and hopes to develop comprehensive policies in the field of inclusiveness under the guidance of its leadership team.

The American University of Iraq, Sulaimani

The American University of Iraq, Sulaimani (AUSIS) was established in 2007 to be a catalyst for innovation in higher education in the country. In 2006, the Board of Trustees of the American University of Iraq, Sulaimani set out to establish a not-for-profit institution dedicated to providing a comprehensive liberal arts education for the benefit of Kurdistan, and the wider region of Iraq.

This new university is designed to develop strengths in critical thinking, the ability to communicate well, a strong work ethic, good citizenship and personal integrity. The university opened its doors in 2007 to a cohort of ten students from across Iraq who were admitted to the first undergraduate class. The university simultaneously launched a professional MBA program for students planning to study business and leadership at graduate level. The university has grown to approximately 1,700 students and now offers undergraduate degrees in Business Administration, Information Technology, International Studies, Engineering and English and Journalism. All students at the university, regardless of their chosen field of study, pursue core courses in the humanities and sciences.

The university received recognition from the Kurdistan Regional Government's Ministry of Higher Education and Scientific Research in 2011, and in 2015, as the number one private university in Iraqi Kurdistan.

The cadre of AUIS alumni are a distinct point of pride for the university and in 2012, the university held its first annual commencement ceremony with 74 students graduating with bachelor's and master's degrees. By the beginning of 2013, the university had launched a new research center, the Institute of Regional and International Studies (IRIS) which, under the umbrella of AUIS, has become a leading hub for research, dialogue and expertise on topics such as energy studies, regional geopolitics, digital technology, security, economic development, gender and archaeology (www.auis.edu.krd/history).

Dr Esther E. Mulnix, Interim President and Vice President of Academic Affairs, describes her leadership style as adaptive in nature and she adjusts to the needs of the university. The university, according to her, is undergoing a transformational phase while facing significant external challenges: civil unrest given the proximity of ISIS (Daesh), economic turmoil, the collapse of some local banks, and low oil prices, as well as political tension and lack of unity. Her main focus has been building capacity both in the academy and in finance and administration. "During the first year I concentrated on developing existing skills, which served two goals: building trust and respect while setting the stage for increasing the use of data analysis in the decision making process." AUIS, according to Dr Mulnix, is moving (in a transformational phase) from person-based practices/decisions to policy-based implementation. The focus on inclusiveness in this university was to make existing policies applicable to all and to follow due process.

Being in the volatile region of Iraq, scholarships are offered to martyrs' families and also to families of war veterans. There is a designated staff member who fulfils the function of liaison on campus for the Ministry of Martyrs and Anfal Affairs (MMAA) students. Any student that is identified by the MMAA as belonging to this category can apply to any university. If accepted, then the student is sponsored by MMAA. In the academic year of 2015/2016, AUIS had 58 students sponsored by MMAA.

Basil Mahdi Al-Rahim Charity Foundation Scholarship Fund

This fund has been established with a generous donation from the Charity Foundation to support the education of deserving students at AUIS. The Basil Mahdi Al-Rahim Charity Foundation Scholarship Fund honours the memory of the late Basil Al-Rahim, chief executive officer of private equity group Merchant Bridge and member of the board of directors of Asia Cell, who passed away in a plane crash in Sulaimani in 2011. The Charity Foundation has pledged $87,010 to cover the education of three students at AUIS over a period of four years starting in March 2015. This is the largest donation that the foundation has ever made. The grant will be used to provide full scholarships for the students for the duration of their studies at AUIS, including residence, books and tuition. The students must maintain a minimum cumulative grade point average (GPA) of 3.0 to remain eligible to receive the scholarship (http://auis.edu.krd/tags/scholarships).

Discussion and Implications

To be inclusive, universities need to establish inclusion as an overarching goal that permeates everything they do, with the leadership team guiding efforts to specifically define and redefine the direction to be taken. This direction needs to be clear, contextualized and framed within the philosophy and policies behind inclusion. The leadership team often has difficult decisions to make when trying to ensure that their institute of higher education is genuinely inclusive, both in practice and in theory. These decisions involve allocation of scarce resources for program support and need to be stretched to create opportunities for teachers to understand the implications of becoming truly inclusive and developing ways to encourage the faculty members towards this overarching goal of inclusion.

The universities are guided and controlled by the guidelines of government policies. In both the universities in Kurdistan, the charity-giving dimension evolves from a government directive to look after its war-torn people.

What is prevalent and seems to be the umbrella motive from all three universities is the charity discourse position, especially with students hailing from weak socio-economic backgrounds. The overarching theme seems to be that these people should be cared for, protected and plucked from a world in which they lack the capacity to cope (Fraser and Shields, 2010). These students are considered victims and their conditions have evoked thoughts of suffering, incapacity and helplessness. Institutional leaders need to understand that charity giving may lead to discrimination and creation of 'out groups' and a class structure. Leaders will have to give special attention to educating their staff about these discourses and how schools can, unconsciously, perpetuate these-unethical attitudes. Institutional leaders need to promote an alternative discourse, and have clear guidelines and principles to include those with disabilities or learning needs. This seems to be lacking in each of the three universities cited. Policies on equality and minimizing segregation motives on the grounds of socio-economic disparity were also lacking in these universities.

Starratt (1991) explained the concept of 'absolute regard' while condemning the segregationist policies in educational institutions and spoke about building a community that is based on the foundations of ethics, justice and care. The school and the classroom are microcosms of society and will always represent the dominant norms of power, privilege and status, unless school leaders devise and enact specific policies to ensure social justice exists and that everyone is treated equally. One way of embedding this culture of justice is to create awareness amongst faculty and staff to promote affirmative action in the classroom leading towards social integration. Both an over-protective and discriminatory system of remuneration and financial benefits due to socio-economic conditions may result in discriminatory behavior and resentment among other students.

Ramps for wheelchair access or adaptations to bathrooms and drinking fountains to cater for disabled people are just a starting point. Some universities are doing virtually nothing beyond these basics which, in themselves, do not foster inclusion. Inclusion is truly fostered when students with disabilities can participate alongside their non-disabled peers as equals. This means that they are not isolated in the corner of the classroom with the teacher aide, separate from the rest of the class, struggling to catch up with their fellow students. Peer relationships can be enhanced through physical proximity, through cooperative group activities, through shared interests and joint projects where both sides should be encouraged to participate as equals.

Lack of friendship and being shunned due to deprived economic condition can also increase the likelihood of teasing and bullying which, in turn, creates a vicious cycle (MacArthur, *et al.*, 2005). Inclusive practices foster authentic relationships and the leaders must develop principles and guidelines and encourage faculty and staff to provide opportunities for positive relationships.

In addition to the emotional wellbeing that friends provide, there is increasing evidence to suggest that social inclusion and friendships can enhance institutional achievement (Ladd, 1990; Newcomb and Bagwell, 1996; Peters, 2000). Inclusive environments may not in themselves ensure academic progress, but "are associated with enhanced opportunities to exercise behaviours related to social, emotional, and cognitive growth" (Newcomb and Bagwell, 1996, p. 317). Selden and Selden (2001) propose the paradigm of valuing-and-integrating, which seeks to create an all-encompassing multicultural climate by incorporating individuals' pluralistic views.

Scholars are also presenting the notion of 'identity safety' as a part of the environment that institutions should seek to foster. Foldy and Buckley (2009) define identity safety as the belief that one is safe despite one's racial or socioeconomic identity. When identity safety is achieved, differences in the scope of social inclusion may highlight the different settings in which social inclusion may take place.

Two of the universities cited in this chapter are in the Middle East, in the northern region of Iraq. The absence of policies pertaining to disabled students or students suffering from learning disorders such as dyslexia for example, has been noted by Professor Eman Gaad (2011), who has written the most comprehensive monograph on inclusive education in the Gulf: "Historically the people of [the Gulf] region have not had a very open and accepting attitude towards those with special needs and/or disabilities" (p. 91). Gaad believes that the common cultural understanding in the Gulf region fosters an approach "based on supporting the 'weak and vulnerable' from a charity-based approach rather than supporting citizens with equal rights and benefits from a rights-based approach as the region is still in a transitional phase between the two notions" (2011, p. 81). Rights-based approaches to disability and special needs education are more common in western cultures which place emphasis on the individual, while in the Gulf, such students become the liability of the family or the tribe with zero expectation from educational institutions.

Sheikha Hessa Al-Thani, the UN Special Rapporteur on Disabilities, noted in 2007: "the general condition of children with disabilities in Arab societies is invisibility" (cited in Al-Kaabi, 2010, p. 20). With inadequate support and with negative social attitudes towards the disabled in most Arabic-speaking countries (in this case a Kurdish-speaking region), disabled children are often isolated from society within families and the presence of disabled facilities in institutions of higher education is rare. According to Qatari Assistant Professor of Social Work, Ibrahim Al-Kaabi, historically in the region: "these children are considered sources of shame and a burden on their families. Families with children with disabilities experience multiple stress factors, including psychological and economic pressure" (Al-Kaabi, 2010, p. 20).

A paradigm shift in attitude is expected to occur as all Gulf countries have embraced the theoretical framework of education for all and providing educational opportunity for all citizens, broadening the definition of inclusion to embrace gifted individuals, returning adult learners, socially and economically disadvantaged individuals as well as physically disabled or mentally impaired students.

The condition in Central Asia is no better:

> [M]any children with disabilities in former Soviet states are placed in special institutions. Families who choose to raise children with disabilities in the home face a lack of adequate resources that exacerbate already poor economic circumstances. Due to low expectations, children in segregated institutions are often given a second class education, which poses a barrier to the attainment of higher education. Architectural barriers also pose a barrier for children with physical disabilities in primary, secondary, and post-secondary general education settings (Johnson, 2007, p. 10).

The case study cited from Central Asia witnesses no exception to this condition.

Conclusion

Inclusion is increasingly seen as a key challenge for educational leaders. Leithwood, *et al.* (2003) suggest that, with continuing diversity, institutions are increasingly coping with uncertainty. Fullan (2001) describes five mutually reinforcing components necessary for effective leadership in times of change: moral purpose, understanding the change process, relationship building with members of the institution and the community outside, knowledge creation and sharing, and coherence-making of the problems in hand. Lambert, *et al.* (1995) argue for a 'constructivist' view of leadership. This is defined as the reciprocal processes that will help enable participants in institutions of higher education to construct common meanings that lead toward a common purpose for education.

Leadership and inclusion is not the journey of a lone individual at the helm but includes an interactive process entered into by both students and teachers. At the same time, there is a need for shared leadership, with the principal seen as a leader of leaders. Borders defining hierarchical structures have to become blurred and need to be replaced by shared responsibility in a community that becomes characterized by agreed values and hopes. These are by no means easy tasks and put tremendous strain on existing resources alongside routine work. Success in these areas relies on the willingness and ability of staff with different specializations to work together for 'blending' the support services to be made available for students with special needs. Leaders committed to inclusive values are crucial to promoting and supporting collaboration by developing formal and informal opportunities for staff who can realize the importance of distributed leadership and participative decision making for creating a better institution.

References

Al-Kaabi, I., 2010. The socio-family and care staff opinion of services and role of children with special needs in Qatar. *International Journal of Business and Social Science*, 1(3), pp. 8–25.

American University of Central Asia, n.d. Available at: <https://www.auca.kg/> [Accessed 2 July 2016].

Baker, D., 2007. The principal's contribution to developing and maintaining inclusive schooling for students with special needs. Master's thesis. Ontario, Canada: University of Western Ontario, London.

Bromley, D. B., 1986. *The case-study method in psychology and related-disciplines*. Chichester: John Wiley & Sons.

Bunch, F., Lupart, J. and Brown, M., 1997. *Resistance and acceptance: Educator attitudes to inclusion of students with disabilities*. North York, Canada: York University.

Edmunds A. L. and Macmillan R. B., eds, 2010. *Leadership for inclusion: A practical guide*. Rotterdam, The Netherlands: Sense Publishers, pp. 7–18

Firestone, W. A. and Riehl, C., eds, 2005. *A new agenda for research in educational leadership*. New York: Teachers College Press.

Foldy, E. G. and Buckley, T. R., 2009. Colour minimization: The theory and practice of addressing race and ethnicity at work. NYU Wagner Research Paper no. 2010–2001, SSRN. Available at: <http://ssrn.com/abstract=1532302> [Accessed 10 August, 2016].

Fraser, D. and Shields, C. M., 2010. Leaders' roles in disrupting dominant discourses and promoting inclusion. In: Edmunds, A. L. and Macmillan, R. E., eds, *Leadership for inclusion: A practical guide*. Rotterdam, The Netherlands: Sense Publishers, pp. 7–18.

Fullan, M., 2001. *The new meaning of educational change*. 3rd ed. New York: Teachers College Press.

Gaad, E., 2011. *Inclusive education in the Middle East*. New York: Routledge.

Goleman, D., Boyatzis, R. and McKee, A., 2002. *Primal leadership*. Boston, MA: Harvard Business School Press.

Johnson, A., 2007. Disability rights. In: Nowakowski, A., ed. *Topical research digest. Human rights in Russia and the former Soviet republics*. Denver, US: Graduate School of International Studies, University of Denver.

Ladd, G. W., 1990. Having friends, keeping friends, making friends and being liked by peers in the classroom: Predictors of children's early school adjustment? *Child Development*, 61(4), pp. 1168–1189.

Lambert, L., Walker, D., Zimmerman, D. P., Cooper, J. E., Lampert, M. D., Gardner, M. E. and Szabo, M., 1995. *The constructivist leader*. New York: Teachers College Press.

Leithwood, K. and Jantzi, D., 2000. The effects of different sources of leadership on student engagement in school. In: Riley, K. and Louis, K., eds, *Leadership for change and school reform*. London: Routledge, pp. 50–66.

Leithwood, K., Riedlinger, B., Bauer, S. and Jantzi, D., 2003. Leadership program effects on student learning: The case of the Greater New Orleans School Leadership Centre. *Journal of School Leadership and Management*, 13(6), pp. 707–738.

MacArthur, J., Kelly, B. and Higgins, N., 2005. Supporting the learning and social experiences of students with disabilities: What does the research say? In: Fraser, D., Moltzen, R. and Ryba, K., eds, *Learners with special needs in Aotearoa New Zealand*. 3rd ed. Southbank, Victoria: Thomson, pp. 49–73.

Meindl, J. R., 1995. The romance of leadership as a follower-centric theory: A social constructionist approach. *The Leadership Quarterly*, 6(3), pp. 329–342.

Meindl, J. R., Ehrlich, S. B. and Dukerich, J. M., 1985. The romance of leadership. *Administrative Science Quarterly*, 30(1), pp. 78–102.

Newcomb, A. F. and Bagwell, C., 1996. The developmental significance of children's friendship relations. In: Bukowski, W. M., Newcomb, A. F. and Hartup, W.W., eds, *The company they keep: Friendship in childhood and adolescence*. Cambridge: Cambridge University Press, pp. 289–321.

Peters, S., 2000. 'I didn't expect that I would get tons of friends ... more each day.' Children's experiences of friendship during transition to school. Paper presented at the New Zealand Association of Research in Education conference, Hamilton, New Zealand.

Reyes, P. and Wagstaff, L., 2005. How does leadership promote successful teaching and learning for diverse students? In: Firestone, W. and Riehl, C., eds, *A new agenda for research in educational leadership*. New York: Teachers College Press, pp. 101–118.

Ryan, J., 2006. *Inclusive leadership*. San Francisco: Jossey-Bass.

Selden, S. C. and Selden, F., 2001. Rethinking diversity in public organizations for the 21st century: Moving toward a multicultural model. *Administration & Society*, 33(3), pp. 303–330.

Starratt, R. J., 1991. Building an ethical school: A theory for practice in educational leadership. *Educational Administration Quarterly*, 27(2), pp. 185–202.

The American University of Iraq Sulaimani, n.d. Available at: <http://auis.edu.krd/> [Accessed 7 July 2016].

The American University of Kurdistan, n.d. Available at: <http://audk.edu.krd/> [Accessed 4 July 2016].

Yin, R. K., 2004. *Case study methods: Complementary methods for research in education*. 3rd ed. Washington, DC: American Educational Research Association.

9

INCLUSIVE LEADERSHIP

Lessons from South Africa

Brenda Leibowitz

Introduction

When I was asked if I was interested in writing a chapter for this book on inclusion in higher education, I was bemused, and replied to the editors, "this is an intriguing proposition. The irony is that in my country, I don't believe there has been much successful inclusive leadership, especially with regard to teaching and learning. This would make a case study difficult!" It was September 2015, student protests against proposed fee hikes and a colonial institutional culture were sweeping the country. I reasoned that, if students were protesting so emphatically, united across political, racial and class divides, there must be something that the leadership of our country, and of higher education institutions, are doing wrong. What, then, can I offer on this topic to an international audience? This chapter is an account of my further reflections on this question of what South Africa can teach the world, and of a set of interviews I conducted on the issue with a small number of significant leadership figures in the country. The discussion that follows suggests that there is, indeed, much that South Africa can teach the rest of the world about inclusive leadership, especially under challenging contexts.

The key point that I hope to illustrate is that whilst inclusion – and inclusive leadership, therefore – is highly contextual in relation to space and time, it remains embedded within social forces in the regional setting (South Africa) and internationally. The chapter looks specifically at the role of institutional leaders who constitute an extremely significant lever for ensuring inclusion in higher education. However, given the role of context, especially in challenging times, responsibility for educational development lies with all those who are in a position to exercise influence in this domain, as we are all interdependent.

The 2015–2016 Context

Higher education in South Africa post-apartheid has been slowly making changes in terms of governance, unification of the sector, diversification of the student cohort and, to a lesser extent, diversification of the staff cohort at an aggregated level. According to the CEO of the Council on Higher Education (CHE) Professor Narend Baijnath, it is "perhaps the part of the entire education sector that has advanced most in terms of achieving national goals of quality, equity and transformation" (CHE, 2016, 'A word from the CEO'). Despite this, the sector remains influenced by the inequalities inherent in the society. With regard to the student cohort, for example, the size of the cohort has increased from half a million in 1995 to 'almost a million' in public higher education in 2015 (CHE, 2015, p. 6). There are more black students in the system, but the participation rate differs: 55 percent for white students and 16 percent for black students in 2013 (CHE, 2016). There remains a racial differentiation according to discipline and student success continues to be differentiated along the lines of race (Scott, Yeld and Hendry, 2007; Cooper, 2015) and social class (Soudien, 2008; Cooper, 2015). Individual institutions continue to be influenced by disparities in funding, geographic location and institutional history (Bozalek and Boughey, 2012). South Africa has featured consistently amongst countries showing the greatest disparities between rich and poor in the world (Bhorat, 2015) and thus poverty influences which students are able to attend university, as well as the material resources they draw upon when learning. University curricula remain in thrall to international or Western norms and standards (Badat, 2009). There has been a drop in subsidy in real terms for students in higher education (CHE, 2016). Despite the increase in student numbers, higher education remains underfunded at 0.75 percent of the GDP in 2011 as compared with the world average of 0.84 percent (CHE, 2016). Finally, the society in which the institutions are located is presently volatile: dissatisfaction with service delivery and the persistent level of inequality has led to an increase in social unrest and protest, such that it has been argued that protest has possibly doubled between 2010 and 2015 (Demian, 2015).

A nation-wide wave of student protest began in 2015, centring on the need to 'decolonise' the university. The claim was most strongly expressed in two of the previously white or advantaged universities, but took hold more visibly in the Historically Advantaged Universities (HAUs). The call became 'Rhodes must fall', with reference to the British coloniser, Cecil John Rhodes, after whom one of the HAUs, Rhodes University, was named, and who bequeathed the land for the University of Cape Town. A second spark igniting protest was the announcement that all universities were to increase fees, an annual occurrence. This led to a broad coalition of student groupings across the country who protested at universities and in front of the government buildings in Pretoria. The protest was sufficiently broad-based and clamorous that the President, Jacob Zuma, agreed that all universities would not increase fees for 2016, and that various means would be found to support universities to make up their shortfall in funding. A third demand emerged at many universities: to end the outsourcing of workers. At the time of writing this chapter there is an unclear outcome, as students have been calling for no fees at all, and a commission set up by the President has not yet produced its findings. There are also universities where destructive protest has led to disciplinary hearings (Chabalala, 2016), the outcomes of which are not yet known. A significant feature of the protest is the students' contesting of the legitimacy of many of the leadership figures, both at the level of Vice-Chancellor, and of intellectuals advising these figures. Most of these leadership figures and intellectuals are black and saw themselves as victims of the apartheid dispensation. Many participated in the struggle against apartheid and continue to advocate for social justice in South Africa, but the vocal students have cast these leadership figures as representatives of the oppressive system (see, for example, Mangcu, 2016).

Interview Process

In order to shed light on the challenges facing leaders in challenging times, I decided to interview several of these leaders. My choice of interviewees was motivated by a desire to learn from individuals who had acquired a vast amount of experience in relation to inclusion in higher education, and whom I believed would provide valuable insight about leadership in the current context. I managed to secure interviews with five South African individuals who have been involved in the sector for the last one to three decades in one form of senior leadership or another. Sizwe has served as Vice-Chancellor at a rural research-oriented university in the Eastern Cape for the past two years. Ihron has served as Vice-Chancellor at an urban comprehensive university for the past ten years. Narend served as Deputy Vice-Chancellor at two distance universities for 14 years, before joining the Council on Higher Education as CEO in 2016. Adam has been the Vice-Chancellor at an urban research-intensive university for the past three years, and Ahmed served as Vice-Chancellor at an urban University of Technology for five years, before being appointed as the CEO of the Council on Higher Education in 2016.[1]

The group is by no means representative according to race or gender, as all are 'black' in South African terminology (one coloured, two Indian and one African) and all are male. All became academics during the anti-apartheid period, prior to 1994, and as is evident from their biographies as well as interviews, all were influenced intellectually and morally by their involvement in education and the struggle against apartheid during this period. They were selected as I hoped they would help me think through the question of what South Africa can teach the world with regard to inclusive leadership. The audiotaped and transcribed interviews were short, lasting between 30 and 90 minutes. Each of the interviewees has written and spoken publicly as leadership figures over the past decades, and my understanding of their views is thus not limited to these brief interview sessions.

I devised a set of questions, which form the subheadings of the following section. In the next section I discuss the answers to these questions, as I made sense of them subsequent to the interviews.

Views on Inclusive Leadership

1 What do you understand inclusion in higher education to mean (in South Africa and internationally)?

Dimensions of Inclusion

Inclusion is seen as contextual, relational, in relation to the past, present and the future: "Inclusion means a lot in terms of our history of being kept apart" (Sizwe). It means working for a new society, "it is our constitution which is compelling us, encouraging us to nurture the new society, inclusive, caring, democratic society, non-sexist" (Ihron).

Inclusion is understood both in terms of the process of teaching and learning, as well as the outcome – not unlike a distinction between teaching *for* social justice, and teaching *in* a socially just manner (Leibowitz and Bozalek, 2016). With regard to the process or condition of inclusive higher education, this pertains to various dimensions: physical access to the institution, all-encompassing support for learning, a sense of belonging and identification with the cultural and knowledge practices. All of these dimensions are to cater for the various identity categories outlined by Ihron above, although there has been a recent addition of 'rural' or 'regional' to these categories. According to Ihron, inclusion must be seen in terms of three dimensions: access in terms of being admitted to a university, material and social support so that one can be physically and emotionally comfortable and help so that one can manage the transition from school and home knowledges to university knowledge systems. As Narend pointed out, access is to the physical institution, to the knowledge and to various forms of material support such as food, transport money, residence fees and so on. Inclusion is not something that one should 'pay lip service' to, as some universities and lecturers do; it should be systemic, articulated in policies and plans and "saturated in the consciousness of all of your staff" and it is a 'web' of issues that need attention including content, curriculum, funding, language, culture (Narend).

Inclusion and Culture

One should also respect the diversity of views and cultures: "make sure you embrace the diversity of the student population, recognise they bring certain knowledges, lived experiences, dip into the tapestry to create a rich experience, make sure they are recognised and they are affirmed" (Sizwe). Inclusion is not a matter of targets, where only numbers of black students or staff are worked towards – it is about the processes and meanings, not just the concretely measurable or outward signs. Both Adam and Ahmed used the word 'thoughtful'. According to Ahmed there should also be thoughtfulness in the transformative acts the institution engages in. For example, there is a current trend to rename locations to celebrate individuals or struggle heroes but this is out of line with indigenous practices of using fauna or flora for place names, thus one should proceed 'thoughtfully'. One should proceed in a manner that unites people, "we are influenced by indigenous as well as Western. How do you create the mix, done in the way that unites people? That kind of conversation is not happening" (Adam).

An important dimension of inclusion is a sense of belonging and affirmation, where the rituals and symbols should make students and staff feel they belong: "the ceremonies, how we conduct them, are they inclusive, are they providing everyone to celebrate in the best ways they know how?" (Sizwe)

Inclusion and Knowledge

With regard to the curriculum, inclusion means considering how to respond to the alienating nature of the curriculum, not purely by introducing indigenous, local or relevant knowledges, but by considering how teaching occurs such that knowledge becomes "less opaque – whether it is Fanon or Chaucer" (Sizwe). Echoing calls for cognitive justice (Visvanathan, 2007), Sizwe says that we should draw on a "diversity of knowledges." We should resist the notion that the local, therefore familiar, is necessarily the way to go:

> To recognise students bring with them certain knowledges, certain experiences, but we should not end there, we should push them to a stage where they should feel comfortable about being uncomfortable, they should feel uncomfortable about being comfortable.
>
> *(Sizwe)*

With regard to inclusion in relation to outcome, 'inclusion' implies that the university plays a meaningful role in society, by the kinds of graduates it produces:

> [Y]ou are able to produce young people who are able to solve problems that are not yet formulated ... young people who will understand that their education is for the greater good and not just for themselves.
>
> *(Sizwe)*

In other words, inclusive education is a public good, in that it engenders in students the capabilities for human flourishing, and for contributing to a flourishing society (Nixon, 2015).

Finally, inclusion implies that the 'South African university' pays attention to the kinds of knowledge it shares with students and the knowledge it generates:

I am 100% committed to the idea that we should be players in the global space as far as knowledge is concerned. … however the one responsibility that our universities have to bear is to produce knowledge about our context and to then enter the global knowledge system on the basis of that knowledge.

(Ahmed)

Ahmed illustrated how the production of useful local knowledge is related to the demographic composition of this cohort, and the relationship of local or 'indigenous' academics to the unearthing and mining of the value of local knowledge. A bio-technology lecturer who had recently completed his PhD at the university, was Zulu speaking and grew up in a nearby semi-rural community, conducted a study on the indigenous fermentation techniques for making beer, with the help of some of his fourth-year students. They returned with the information to further their investigations in the laboratory. The function of this anecdote was to emphasise the benefit of the lecturer's deep understanding of the cultural practices of the area, and his ability to interview people in the local language. This would not have been possible, according to Ahmed, had the student population all been elite and English speaking.

Inclusion and the Broader Community

An inclusive university is not an autonomous entity, but is an institution that can be owned, and be perceived as relevant to a broader community:

[Y]ou have to see higher education not as something that's kind of isolated from society and in the ivory tower, but ultimately it is about the university and higher education being seen by people around the university here as a common good.

(Ahmed)

According to Ahmed, proof of the way that the university is seen by people in the surrounding areas as a common good is the fact that the university he led until recently is in the heart of one of the most dangerous spots in a major urban area, and a major thoroughfare for domestic workers walking from the station to the suburbs where they worked – yet the workers felt safe walking through the university. This was, further, an argument used at the university pertaining to not closing the roads off from pedestrians.

2 What does this require from leadership (at the VC level and more broadly)?

Leadership and Decision Making

There is no doubt that at this level, leaders have responsibility – they are 'in the middle', reporting to those below as well as boards and/or government (Smith,

2012). A Vice-Chancellor, as a CEO, has to report to the Council and therefore one must exercise authority where necessary,

> A Vice-Chancellor is called the Chief Academic Officer, the Chief Admin Officer, the Chief Accounting Officer ... it means there is authority resident in the position and therefore that authority must be used wisely.
>
> *(Ihron)*

Yet not all the Vice-Chancellors interpreted this responsibility in the same way, Sizwe emphasised consultation and vulnerability:

> I do not believe in authority. I try to engage many people and we all collectively arrive at a decision, that places me in a vulnerable position, because Council will come to me, I am the accounting officer.
>
> *(Sizwe)*

An inclusive leader must also not be afraid of taking what appear to be unpopular decisions. An example Ahmed gave is that, on learning that members of the Students Representative Council were serving their own interests whilst on the Procurement Committee, he terminated their membership:

> [T]here was a group that was really incensed. But almost immediately I did that I discovered that the number of demonstrations around catering and residences, slipped to zero.
>
> *(Ahmed)*

One must stand firm when necessary:

> [T]here are moments when you have to hold this line and say, 'beyond this line I will not go' and 'challenge thoughtless extremism ... from the left and the right.'
>
> *(Adam)*

One must be prepared to "make trade-offs" between uncomfortable choices (Adam) as one is responsible to the council, parents, all students, not only those who are protesting. In a similar sentiment, Narend felt one must "avoid populism" and not be naïve, as students will push their advantage where they see weakness. Realpolitik is necessary, "Gramsci requires you to grapple with the strictures that exist" (Adam), and to find bridges that tide one over challenges. For example, the Vice-Chancellors went to negotiate with the banks about delaying student payment of debt. Realism is also required, but the converse too, "that requires imagination, thoughtfulness and trade-offs" (Adam).

Leadership and Mobilising Support

At the same time, one leads by being inspiring, by 'making the case', mobilising support from above but also from below, leading from the front, "being a rower of the boat" (Ihron). Having visionary documents is not enough (Ihron). One is the 'servant' and should be 'vulnerable' (Sizwe).

One does not always have good ideas as a leader, but when others produce good ideas or strategies, one should champion these. An example from one HAU was a lobby group in the Health Sciences faculty which cited research that students from rural areas are more likely to go back to work in those areas after graduating. Adam supported this position that there should be a quota for entry for these students. He had to challenge academics who felt this would pose a risk to the academic program, and middle-class black parents who feared this might deprive their children of access to the program. One has to be firm, but also respond to the needs of those who become anxious about changes:

> [Y]ou can't say to the guys, 'it can't be done' you have to confront their concerns and find a solution to their concerns.
>
> *(Adam)*

Leadership and Trust

In times of instability or when risk taking is necessary, trust becomes a crucial component in enabling or constraining innovation (Tierney, 2008). In the context of this study, instability or risk would apply to the need to implement reform and innovation pertaining to inclusion, as well as to respond creatively to student protest. Tierney distinguishes between *interpersonal* trust and *organisational* trust. It would appear, from these accounts, that interpersonal trust in the leader is necessary, not only trust in the organisation. One needs to be a role model and to be trusted by one's team and by others in the institution. For Ahmed this meant that people should accept him for what he is:

> I would be very uncomfortable if I had to play a leadership role which was somehow really kind of divorced from who I am.
>
> *(Ahmed)*

This, for him, included resisting his Chair of Council insisting he drive a smart car, because that is the symbol of wealth that should be associated with a Vice-Chancellor.

One should also be available to staff and students, but proximity can lead to its own dangers:

> It almost sounds so paternalistic, I really did feel that there was a need for students to see me as a father figure, so I gave everybody my e-mail address. Sometimes [the e-mails] were dire, somebody who's sleeping in the lecture theatre, the other times they were 'Dear Mr Bawa, I got this award', of course

it would cut the other way too, during demonstrations, students would say 'you are our father, why are you treating us like this?'

(Ahmed)

Leadership and Participation

A 'participative approach' (Gumport, 2012) is required. One should model inclusivity, for example by consulting colleagues. Sizwe ensured his staff understood the decisions and important issues at the university, which he believed they appreciated. This he learnt from his history during the anti-apartheid struggle:

> That was instilled in me in my student days. I went to university and if you look at the history of the liberation movement the kind of leadership that was practised was one that ensured that everyone knew what had to happen, what was to be done because if information resided with just a few people, if those people would be arrested or would disappear, that would be the end.
>
> *(Sizwe)*

Neumann (2012) writes that leaders come to view themselves as facilitators of a 'thinking team' which can be real or nominal. Sizwe's passion for having all his deans and senior leaders involved in decision making, does not appear to be nominal.

Leadership and Creativity

Rationalist approaches towards strategic planning (reviewed in Gumport, 2012) and modern managerialist practices such as mid-term reviews need not be avoided, but they are insufficient, and should be complemented by one's creativity (Ahmed) and by turning these managerialist measures around so that they become meaningful:

> [O]ur council is very adamant that we should develop a risk analysis approach at the university. At first I really had to adapt to it, but thankfully we had a really good guy there who was able to think about risk ... we turned it on its head, we said to ourselves, 'what is the overall strategy of the university?' Can we think about how we deal with the risks, entertaining that overall strategy? And it turned out to be quite a lot of fun actually. The council bought into it.
>
> *(Ahmed)*

3 Regarding current student protest in South Africa, what does this reveal about the nature of higher education in South Africa, how inclusive it is, and about what 'inclusion' in higher education means?

Change as Transformative rather than Ameliorative

Answers to the above question point to the need for change towards social justice and inclusion that is deep and transformative, rather than ameliorative, as Fraser

(2009) and Badat (2009) have argued. The Vice-Chancellors gave examples of the attempts their institutions have made to diversify their student populations and to increase support for students from various disadvantaged backgrounds, including the categories mentioned above, such as race, gender and more recently, rurality:

> The university has deliberately sought to increase its first-year enrolment from schools that serve the poorest in our nation. And in a decade's time we had increased that percentage from quintile one and two schools from 8% enrolment to 28% enrolment and that has changed the demography and the dynamics and extraordinary challenges that come with that.
>
> *(Ihron)*

But this is not enough:

> [W]ealth, distribution, affordability of higher education, sustainability of higher education … for [students] to be successful they need enabling conditions … they can't just have their fees paid and then starve. You can't study that way.
>
> *(Narend)*

Thus, despite a change in the profile of higher education in South Africa, there is still much inequality both in the system and in the broader society and changes ("the durability of the old order is extraordinary" (Ihron)). The changes might even give cause for celebration but they lead to the need for deeper change. Sizwe noted that it is paradoxical that, although Rhodes university, previously mostly white, is now majority black, there is still a strong sense of alienation amongst students and staff, who protest against what they perceive to be a dominant colonial culture at previously white institutions.

Ahmed pointed out that, although the student protests were relatively new in the previously advantaged institutions, that there had been consistent protests at the previously disadvantaged institutions, each year, in fact. The problems of poverty and lack of access to fees or food were more prominent in protests at some of the historically disadvantaged rural universities and universities of technology:

> Durban University of Technology, Twane University of Technology, the Universities of Limpopo, Zululand and so on, this has just been going on for years. They just had a different take. The focus was very much on financial aid. There's just no money to get students into the classes and into lectures.
>
> *(Ahmed)*

Recognising the Need for Flexibility

There is also the sense that educators and leaders had been displaying a level of complacency, as well as a measure of just continuing as before. This inured leaders in higher education (in a broad sense) from seeing the looming crisis for what is was. Vice-Chancellors and other leaders had shown concern with inequality and injustice, but was this in a form that was ossifying? Perhaps the formal, institutional rules and procedures have their limitations. According to Narend:

> [T]he whole idea of organisation is to formalise things and if it's not working or if it's being disruptive it's a futile conversation to have. Because then you need to be sitting out in the quadrangle with students and say, 'what is the sentiment?' from moment to moment ... It requires immense political acumen.
>
> *(Narend)*

The limitations of the formal practices are alluded to by Ihron. He described the outcome of the student protest – that the state capitulated to student demand for a zero fee increase in 2015 – as extraordinary:

> So an extraordinary accomplishment ten years of action by Vice-Chancellors did not achieve.
>
> *(Ihron)*

One of the lessons of the student protest is its demonstration that higher education is embedded (Gumport, 2012) and co-dependent with society. Neumann (2012, p. 318) uses the phrase "expanded view" to argue that higher education institutions are partial expressions of a larger constellation of forces and organisations.

The Connection between Universities and Society

However, this interrelationship is not optimal currently. Narend pointed out that education has become a battleground over inequality in society. This is linked to the belief in the power of the university as an institution, that it can operate above societal forces and lead to the resolution of problems:

> Some people think the University of the Witwatersrand, the University of Johannesburg, are going to resolve society's problems, there is a myth in the system that you can create an island.
>
> *(Adam)*

Furthermore, the disconnect between higher education and society is demonstrated, according to Ahmed, by the fact that parents are not coming to the defence of the university. He did not clarify whether this defence was against the onslaught of student protest or the state's neglect of funding for the institutions. He contrasted this with the period of the anti-apartheid struggle, where parents came to the defence of higher education institutions, even though they were regarded as apartheid creations. His explanation for this is the divorce between popular needs and knowledge systems, and those of academia.

The need for a greater connect between higher education and society was acknowledged by all the leaders. The current crisis of funding and legitimacy is not something Vice-Chancellors can resolve on their own:

> We are in an exciting moment in the history of our education system, but we are also in a very precarious position because if we do not navigate our way very carefully we may just witness a collapse of our education system. We all have a responsibility: it is the students, it is academics, it is workers, the state, the private sector, the general South African society. We all need to come together to decide what we want to make of the higher education system.
>
> *(Sizwe)*

4 What in your view are solutions to the current challenges to higher education in South Africa, and whose responsibility are these solutions?

> There are simple lessons, for example that one has to prioritise amongst the many competing needs for change, and hold people to be accountable to get things done ... be intentional.
>
> *(Narend)*

Role-players such as the state, industry and education each must play their part, even if it is to be combative. Whilst the state must lead, leaders in education in South Africa should perhaps have made a much stronger play for more funding for higher education. Universities in the country should also be more collaborative, working together as peers (Ihron). This underscores Neumann's injunction for leaders to work with others: "to survive and thrive is about college leaders and others, in and outside traditional college and university organizations working together" (Neumann, 2012, p. 319).

One solution is for leaders to take control or agency:

> How do we mobilise all of these parties and players? Which raises interesting questions about the role of the Vice-Chancellor and of the management, executive management of the university. Are we simply fellow rowers on the ocean? ... or are we the ones who must take the lead and create conditions far more deliberately, far more effectively, and more deeply and inclusively. I certainly don't believe we are just fellow travellers.
>
> *(Ihron)*

Whilst higher education its constrained by its context, it has a leadership role to play, in ensuring its own vitality and ability to play a leadership role in society. There are two valuable views about agency that are useful in relation to the role of inclusive leadership. The first, posed by Margaret Archer, makes a strong argument for reflexivity and self-conscious conversation as a mediating force between the individual or actor, and the context, which can be either constraining or enabling (Archer, 2000). This is not unlike many of the views expressed by these leaders: that leadership must be intentional, and involved in deep reflection about the purpose of higher education. Archer maintains, however, that the circumstances one inherits are not of one's choosing, and most constraints (except the most dire) can be circumnavigated, but with varying degrees of effort (Archer, 2000). The second view, expressed by feminist materialist Karen Barad (2007) and others, is that the world is not pre-ordained and there is always the chance for 'free acts' (Grosz, 2010), creativity and the capacity for imagining the world to be otherwise, but that this is accompanied by taking responsibility for ethical action. This view of agency as entangled within webs of relations has also been suggested by many of the comments above.

5 What are the relevant lessons emanating from this protest for an international audience (pertaining to inclusion in higher education)?

The Limits of a Rationalist Approach

Other than the danger of complacency, what are the lessons that can be learnt about the current situation in South Africa? One lesson is of the limits of a rationalist approach to leadership. Especially when a crisis is upon the sector, it is necessary to step beyond customary rules and procedures. Extreme challenges require careful deliberation by leaders, who "face stark choices ... one day the appropriate response might be to call in the police, another day it might be to negotiate" (Narend). According to Narend, the government was faced with stark choices too:

> [D]o you want a totally destabilised higher education system or do we spend two-and-a-half billion rand to make the problem go away, at least momentarily? Take the pressure off. That's what they did. And that's a choice faced by leaders on a daily basis on institutional level.
>
> *(Narend)*

The Interconnectedness of Regions

What is happening in the South Africa context is, in the first instance, not unique to this region, and therefore the current trends are of relevance to others elsewhere:

> [I]t is really interesting to see just how widespread the student actions are around the world. If you look at the World University News, in the first week of May, there are about eight or ten articles there, about Japan, Germany, the UK, USA.
>
> *(Ahmed)*

And yet, in one sense local events *are* unique to the region, in that inclusion is related to context – in terms of time, as discussed earlier, as well as geographical location. For Adam, what South Africa has to teach the rest of the world based on the current situation, is about the importance of context:

> [I]nclusion is about context. That is not sufficiently appreciated by international audiences and ideologues.
>
> *(Adam)*

According to Narend, problems in the developing world are *not* the same as problems in the developed world. In the developed world, doctors cannot get jobs, whereas in South Africa we cannot graduate enough doctors.

On the other hand there is an interconnection between world regions, "National systems of higher education ... are affected by the global relational environment at many points" (Marginson, 2016, p. 13). The mutual co-dependency of regions is with respect to world peace:

> If there's inequality here, it threatens the developed world because disruption here [means] ... their investments are not safe and secure.
>
> *(Narend)*

Social problems in one area have an impact on others:

> You cannot be complacent and say, 'Oh we've got a long history and traditions and that it's not our problem, it's their problem.' The problem of inequality threatens sustainability, it threatens stability, it threatens peace all over the world. If there's inequality here, it threatens the developed world ... When people are desperate and have nothing to lose, they are prepared to risk everything ... So we're creating, so we're feeding desperation by not being inclusive.
>
> *(Narend)*

Institutional Change and Time

Another lesson is about the importance as well as complexity and interrelatedness of time. One requires an awareness of the past but, at the same time, an awareness that there is no stillness and certainty. The ground is constantly moving beneath our feet. A teleological mode of change, reflecting intentionality (Kezar, 2012), is inadequate to shape how we think about institutional change. According to Sizwe:

> History is not something that has happened in the past, it continues to be part of us, and it continues to be interrogated, it must be interrogated, as we move forward, we must always move back and ask some pertinent questions.
>
> *(Sizwe)*

And yet one has to move beyond the present time, too:

> It is tempting to be parochial and to be preoccupied with the here and now. I am simply saying we should be responsive to the challenges we face, but at the same time fulfil the prophetic role of higher education, to respond to problems that have not yet been formulated.
>
> *(Sizwe)*

The nature of social challenges and a struggle for justice is part of history and time in this sense, but is somehow outside of time as well. Hindsight, especially hindsight that sits in judgement, is not helpful, in that precisely the context that existed at a particular point, means judgements cannot pronounce on what one believes ought to have happened. For example, in 2016 critics are dismissive of the change that was brought about in South Africa in 1994, at the advent of democracy:

> They too easily look at it from the perspective of 2016. They look at 1994 and say it was a sellout, they too easily look at it from the comfort of the present. 1994 was a fundamental advance on 1992 when people were dying, in prison without trial, it is too easy to look at it with hindsight.
>
> *(Adam)*

Change is Never Complete

Tierney (2012, p. 177) reminds us that "colleges and universities are not static entities, they are in constant redefinition." Change is not linear (Nieuwenhuis and Sehoole, 2013), and unpredictable. The context is ever changing with new challenges (Ahmed). According to Adam, in 2000 a course on Fanon was introduced at Wits and students were not interested. Now students call for the decolonisation of the curriculum, citing Fanon. A non-teleological approach to time allows us to accept that:

> Inclusion is never an end in itself, it is always a project in the making, one kind of inclusion you require in 2000 is not going to be the same, it is never a moment when it is going to be enough, there are moments of upsurge that will deepen it, that will undermine it, a never-ending project.
>
> *(Adam)*

Conclusion

To return to the questions I asked myself about what South Africa might have to offer when I considered my assignment of writing this chapter, there are indeed many lessons in the accounts of the five leadership figures who so generously shared their time and reflections. One of the lessons learned concerns the attributes of leaders themselves. Amongst the attributes of inclusive leaders are the need for thoughtfulness, to be firm and resolute, but also to be humble, vulnerable, to encourage trust and participation. Another lesson concerns rational approaches to leadership which are useful, but at times it is also useful to subvert rationalist and managerial processes, especially when these create stasis and complacency.

Furthermore, leadership to encourage inclusion is complex and demanding. Recipes for how to lead in an inclusive way are not going to be sufficient to guide leaders through extremely challenging times. One of the reasons accounting for the complexity of the challenges facing leaders, is that inclusive leadership is relational and contextual, involving relations with people within and without the organisation. A key lesson is for responsibility across contexts. This is usefully summed up by the concept of 'entanglements', which are "relations of obligation ... being bound to the other ... irreducible relations of responsibility" (Barad, 2010, p. 265).

Finally, the influence of societal forces and broader contextual conditions on the university should not be underestimated. In South Africa these forces have been couched in the discourses of race and class and capitalism, with the assumption by protesting students that our society has not changed much since the demise of apartheid. However, this is not unlinked to international processes of neoliberalism and neoliberal globalisation, which Santos (2006) maintains have been imposed since the 1980s. Whilst it is laudable for institutions and their leaders to strive for "participation, community, empowerment and respect for different identities" (chapter 1, this volume), this cannot occur outside of the maelstrom of broader conditions, and simultaneously, the university has to take the broader conditions into account, as well as to attempt to influence these conditions, in the interest of inclusion in society. Leaders who strive for inclusivity need to build alliances and seek input from role-players inside as well as outside the institution.

Note

1 In the US context these would be Presidents or Chancellors.

References

Archer, M., 2000. *Being human: The problem of agency*. Cambridge: Cambridge University Press.

Badat, S., 2009. Theorising institutional change: Post-1994 South African higher education. *Studies in Higher Education*, 34(4), pp. 455–467.

Barad, K., 2007. *Meeting the universe halfway: Quantum physics and the entanglement of matter and meaning*. Durham: Duke University Press.

Barad, K., 2010. Quantum entanglements and hauntological relations of inheritance: Dis/continuities, spacetime enfoldings, and justice-to-come. *Derrida Today*, 3(2), pp. 240–268.

Bhorat, H., 2015. Factcheck: Is South Africa the most unequal country in the world? *The Conversation*. Available at: <https://theconversation.com/factcheck-is-south-africa-the-most-unequal-society-in-the-world-48334> [Accessed 14 November, 2016].

Bozalek, V. and Boughey, C., 2012. (Mis)framing higher education in South Africa. *Social Policy & Administration*, 46(6), pp. 688–703.

Chabalala, J., 2016. University of Johannesburg identifies students in arson attacks. *News 24*. Available at: <http://www.news24.com/SouthAfrica/News/university-of-johannesburg-identifies-students-in-arson-attacks-20160805> [Accessed 14 November, 2016].

Cooper, D., 2015. Social justice and South African university student enrolment data by 'race', 1998–2012: From 'skewed revolution' to 'stalled revolution'. *Higher Education Quarterly*, 69(3), pp. 237–262.

Council on Higher Education (CHE), 2015. *Annual Report of the Council on Higher Education (South Africa)*. Available at: <http://www.che.ac.za/sites/default/files/publications> [Accessed 7 March, 2017].

Council on Higher Education (CHE), 2016. *South African higher education reviewed: Two decades of democracy*. Pretoria: Council on Higher Education.

Demian, M., 2015. Have protests in South Africa nearly doubled since 2010? *Africa Check*. Available at: <https://africacheck.org/reports/have-protests-in-south-africa-nearly-doubled-since-2010/> [Accessed 14 November, 2016].

Fraser, N., 2009. *Scales of justice: Reimagining political space in a globalizing world*. New York: Columbia University Press.

Grosz, E., 2010. Feminism, materialism, and freedom. In: Coole, D. and Frost, S., eds. *New materialism: Ontology, agency and politics*. Durham: Duke University Press, pp. 139–157.

Gumport, P., 2012. Strategic thinking in higher education research. In: Bastedo, M., ed. *The organisation of higher education: Managing colleges for a new era*. Baltimore: Johns Hopkins, pp. 18–44.

Kezar, A., 2012. Organizational change in a global, postmodern world. In: Bastedo, M., ed. *The organisation of higher education: Managing colleges for a new era*. Baltimore: Johns Hopkins, pp. 181–221.

Leibowitz, B. and Bozalek, V., 2016. The scholarship of teaching and learning from a social justice perspective. *Teaching in Higher Education*, 21(2), pp. 109–122.

Mangcu, X., 2016. Students shouted me down. *IOL*. Available at: <http://www.iol.co.za/sundayindependent/students-shouted-me-down-2027581> [Accessed 14 November, 2016].

Marginson, N., 2016. Global stratification in higher education. In: Slaughter, S. and Taylor, B., eds. *Higher education, stratification, and workforce development: Competitive advantage in Europe, the US, and Canada*. Dordrecht: Springer, pp. 13–34.

Neumann, A., 2012. Organizational cognition in higher education. In: Bastedo, M., ed. *The organisation of higher education: Managing colleges for a new era*. Baltimore: Johns Hopkins, pp. 304–331.

Nieuwenhuis, J. and Sehoole, T., 2013. Access in higher education in South Africa. In: Meyer, H., St John, E., Chankseliani, M. and Uribe, L., eds. *Fairness in access to higher education in a global perspective: Reconciling excellence, efficiency, and justice*. Rotterdam: Sense, pp. 189–202.

Nixon, J., 2015. Inequality and the erosion of the public good. In: Filippakou, O. and Williams, G., eds. *Higher education as a public good: Critical perspectives on theory, policy and practice*. New York: Peter Lang, pp. 163–177.

Santos, B., 2006. The university in the 21st century: Toward a democratic and emancipatory university reform. In: Rhoads, R. and Torres, R., eds. *The university, state, and market: The political economy of globalization in the Americas*. Stanford: Stanford University Press, pp. 60–100.

Scott, I., Yeld, N. and Hendry, J., 2007. *Higher education monitor 6: A case for improving teaching and learning in South African higher education*. Pretoria: Council for Higher Education.

Smith, D., 2012. Diversity: A bridge to the future? In: Bastedo, M., ed. *The organisation of higher education: Managing colleges for a new era*. Baltimore: Johns Hopkins, pp. 225–255.

Soudien, C., 2008. The intersection of race and class in the South African university: Student experiences. *South African Journal of Higher Education*, 22(3), pp. 662–678.

Tierney, W., 2008. Trust and organizational culture in higher education. In: Välimaa, J. and Ylijoki, O., eds. *Cultural perspectives on higher education*. Dordrecht: Springer, pp. 27–42.

Tierney, W., 2012. Creativity and organizational culture. In: Bastedo, M., ed. *The organisation of higher education: Managing colleges for a new era*. Baltimore: Johns Hopkins, pp. 160–180.

Visvanathan, S., 2007. Between cosmology and system: The heuristics of a dissenting imagination. In: de Sousa Santos, B., ed. *Another knowledge is possible: Beyond northern epistemologies*. London: Verso, pp. 182–218.

10

TO BE THE AFRICAN UNIVERSITY IN THE SERVICE OF HUMANITY

Mandla Makhanya

Leaders who develop coherence around shared values are likely to deepen the sense of community within an organisation – a sense of being in relationship with others who are striving for the same goals.

(Grogan and Shakeshaft, 2011, p. 6)

Introduction

The University of South Africa (Unisa) has a vision statement which is captured in the title of this chapter. It is pithy and precise, known by every staff member of the university, and it has two distinct elements: an aspirational one which gestures towards the future of its academic position and status on the continent of Africa while also capturing its African corporate identity, and an ethical element which describes Unisa's avowed intention to serve people. As is well known, however, organizational mantras are often glibly recited at public events, graduation ceremonies and in conference papers with little relation to, or impact on, their lived reality. This chapter casts an uncompromising gaze upon Unisa's intentions and ideals in relation to its current organizational culture in order to uncover its manifold complexity and test its declared ethics, framed as inclusive practice, as a university that serves its staff and students as well as the wider community on the African continent.

Unisa's History and Context

The University of South Africa has a long history extending over a period of 143 years. It began its life in 1873 as the University of the Cape of Good Hope segueing into South Africa's first examining and certification body in 1918. During the period 1947–1952, it operated a division of external studies from a motley collection of ten buildings in Pretoria, the administrative capital of South Africa at the time, and in 1959, through an act of government, became South Africa's only correspondence university, closing down all other colleges that could compete with its primary business, and making use of textbooks, study guides and later, cassette tapes, to transmit its learning material. Unisa's history designates the institution as authoritative and juridical, enmeshed, from the outset, in considerable controversy. It is important to keep this in mind as it makes Unisa's transformation (which will be described in a later section) all the more remarkable. In 1973, Unisa moved its offices to a grand central campus on top of one of the higher hills in Pretoria, now the City of Tshwane, where it still stands, the first building one sees when travelling by road into the city from the south.

In 1997, again by an act of government, Unisa merged with two other distance-education institutions, Technikon SA and Vista University Distance Education Campus (Vudec) to become what Sir John Daniel (1996) calls a 'mega' open and distance institution. Shortly after that, Justice President Bernard Ngoepe became Unisa's first black Chancellor and Barney Pityana its first black Principal and Vice-Chancellor. Pityana held the position for ten years (2001–2010) and oversaw Unisa's merger and transformation, including the shrinking of ten faculties into five colleges, and a bold bid to make Unisa a truly African university. This involved strategic partnerships with the African Union, the Southern African Development Community, the Association of African Universities and the African Council on Distance Education, among others.

In 2007, after an agreement between the two governments, Unisa opened a campus in Addis Ababa, Ethiopia, with the intention of supporting and increasing the number of master's and doctoral students in that country. While causing considerable tension, this expansion was in line with the Africanization policy of the university. Africanization is not only about strategic partnerships and expansion. The university was serious about curriculum transformation and set about looking critically at what was being taught. In 2008, Unisa announced that it was underpinning an Africanized syllabus with African scholarship which embedded indigenous knowledge systems in its academic repertoire.

This brief contextual history shows what I inherited in 2011, when I became Principal and Vice-Chancellor. Together with my management team, I have initiated further transformational changes, including two new colleges, a global compact with the United Nations, a Living Green project and the institution of six entirely online 'Signature Courses'. The entire organizational architecture of the university has been reconsidered and reframed, and a number of significant research chairs have been instituted. Unisa is the largest university in Africa with 80 percent of its students drawn from the black population. At present, Unisa educates approximately 40 percent of the teachers in Africa, testifying to its importance as a leader of social change. One could say that Unisa is, in its very nature, an inclusive organization.

However, I also inherited a troubled university, one that is driven by a silo mentality and competing constituencies. The challenges have been considerable and they are not abating. Indeed, in line with more general change and upheaval, they are increasing and changing in character. Strong unions, forceful angry students, demands for swifter change (often outside the control of the institution), increasing numbers of students (at the time of writing, Unisa has grown to over 300,000 students), an ageing professoriate, unexpected changes owing to top management retirements and resignations: all these have occupied my time. But, while this forms a necessary contextual explication, this is not the main concern of this chapter.

In order to exemplify a particular form of leadership within an inclusive organization, my focus from here on will be on people. And I have a view from the Muckleneuk Hill.

> Great places to work show a strong commitment from CEO and senior management (who walk the talk), a genuine belief that people are indispensable for the business, active communication among the entire organization, the perception of a unique culture and identity, a well-articulated vision, and values that are lived and experienced at all levels of the organisation.
>
> *(de Vries, Ramo and Korotov, 2009, p. 3)*

From where I sit, at the top of one of the highly visible buildings I mentioned earlier, I can see a narrow bridge which has been constructed over the road to allow pedestrians to cross from the railway station to the campus. On any given day, one sees multitudes of students crossing the bridge to reach the campus, despite the fact that Unisa is a distance education university which does not offer face-to-face tuition. As I will show, its history, architecture, position and strange and unexpected identity influence the way it operates at the present time. The complexity correlates with its current reality, making the leadership of this vast and convoluted institution a monumental task, fraught with challenges. I hope to show that despite its rather grim, authoritarian architecture, the university is a busy and bustling campus. It is a place where the workers and students who occupy its offices, boardrooms and library (often in more than one sense) are reachable through a simple and direct channel: a short walk. My vision of inclusive leadership involves taking that walk, as I will show in the next section.

Servant Leadership

Servant leadership begins with a person and a set of beliefs. I have been fortunate in my upbringing which has been saturated by cultural and family norms and values, all of which embrace the idea of inclusivity even though it never had that appendage when I was in my formative years. Even my 'choice' of university, Fort Hare in the Eastern Cape, was both fortuitous and formative. The scare-quotes require an explanation for non-South African readers. When I was about to enter tertiary education, there was no choice for people of color. Universities, like everything else in apartheid South Africa, were strictly segregated and demarcated. My natural preference would have been for the (then) University of Natal, as it was situated conveniently in my home town and had a sound reputation. But that was reserved for white people. The University of Fort Hare was a considerable distance from my home and family, yet it proved to be a fertile source of intellectual ideas and political ideologies which added to my already established pool of values.

My major in Sociology further endorsed what was already a way of being: a sense of belonging, a belief in equality, the values of family and community, respect for others, recognizing the dignity of others – these values translated into what I later adopted as my leadership *raison d'être*, servant leadership. Much later in my career, I was fortunate to attend Harvard's advanced leadership training which added to, and confirmed, my beliefs in servant leadership and gave me the conviction I needed to diffuse this philosophy in my work practice. I believe that I am blessed in being able to follow a leadership style that is so intimately connected, and intrinsic to, a personal arsenal of beliefs.

Immersion conjures images of sinking under water, including the practice of baptism. It leads to a further meaning: deep mental involvement in something. As I have shown, I was already 'baptized' into a pool of values by the time I came to my present office. Inclusivity is a natural extension of those values, a vision that leads to a value chain that is immersed in what we do, how we behave and how we relate to each other at the university and beyond. But is this enough? My job is to move inclusivity from immersion to infusion in an institution which is composed of individuals who may not necessarily hold the same values. How does inclusivity endure when it meets major challenges and stumbling blocks?

For the purposes of this chapter, I will assume a modicum of familiarity in my reader with the term 'servant leadership'. Robert K. Greenleaf (see Parris and Peachey, 2013), who is acknowledged as the progenitor of the name, not necessarily the practice, described the servant leader as someone who lives their values, has an authenticity, is observant, connected and open to others, with a high degree of personal responsibility. Daniel Wheeler (2012, p. xii) commented as follows:

> I was searching for a philosophy that would preserve the best of higher education. When I speak of the best of higher education, I am referring to the sense of community based on learning and developing together, empowerment, embracing curiosity and innovation, and making society better.

With humility high on the list of attributes of the servant leader, it is obviously difficult and a little ironic, to write of oneself in this manner. True servant leaders are reluctant to claim a label that proclaims them as different or special. I would be more comfortable, therefore, in talking about servant leadership as a way of leading a university in difficult times. I will, from here on, adjust the nomenclature accordingly to show how Unisa embodies an ethic of service in its people, its policies and its actions.

The first principle of servant leadership is, obviously, service to others. In the realm of higher education, this means recognizing potential in others, fostering their growth, ensuring that they reach their potential. Sen Sendjaya's working definition of servant leadership, adapted for my purposes, reads as follows:

> Servant leadership is a holistic approach to leadership characterised by service orientation, a focus on authenticity, an emphasis on relationships, moral courage and a desire to transform both self and other towards their highest capabilities. (Sendjaya, 2015, p. 1)

Primarily, servant leadership is characterized by relationships between leaders and followers and is linked closely in my mind with the idea of stewardship. A steward, in its original sense, was the guardian of a house. More recently it has accumulated further meanings: one who administers anything as the agent of another, or a trustee, someone whom one can trust. Senge (1990) makes an important contribution in understanding stewardship when he distinguishes between stewardship of the people one leads and stewardship for the larger purpose of mission. The two concepts are conjoined usefully by Reinke (2004): A servant leader acts as a steward who holds the organization in trust.

There is a subtle linkage in these explanations of the terms, servant leadership and stewardship, between the private and the public, between the individual and the community. The word 'steward' has its origins in the domain of the private house, albeit that of a wealthy landowner. It does not require too much of a stretch of the imagination to extend this idea to a university in which the Principal is the steward of both the people who work and the people who study. These dual but intertwined communities are the responsibility of the steward and his/her management teams. How this happens is the topic of the next section.

Infusion is the introduction of a new element or quality, such as mint leaves soaked in hot water to make a tea. The two elements, mint and water, retain their individuality yet are fused to form a third substance. Infusion of the ethics of servant leadership was a first step after I took office and it was done by fairly simple means: collaborative drawing up of a charter, whose words were carefully chosen by a large group of university staff members at a *legkotla*[1] some distance from the campus. Once the principles of servant leadership in relation to the university had been framed, they were transcribed into direct and simple statements that could fit on one page. This page was printed onto a large placard and placed on the stage of Unisa's main auditorium where various management groups were gathered. These included both the administrative and academic staff who were in leadership positions either as Deans or Heads of Department. Once the principles of servant leadership had been read out, each member of the group who had been part of its compilation was asked to come to the stage to sign the charter.

An Inclusive Transformation Charter

Since the principles of servant leadership are recognizably fused with Unisa's vision statement (in the service of humanity), signing a charter was an important and fairly uncontroversial first step in saturating the ideals within the organization. Yet, these signees were the managers who had already been immersed in the creation of the charter. There still remained the process, far more difficult, of trickling down through lower staff echelons the principles that would hopefully bind the staff of Unisa together into a 'servant organization' (see Laub, 2010, p. 105). To this end, we jointly developed a further set of principles called, initially, 'The Six Cs' consisting, amongst others, of caring, connection, collegiality and creativity. Once again, these principles were publicly debated in each College (Faculty), and during the discussion several more 'C' principles were suggested. As an inclusive gesture, these further Cs were added to the charter, increasing the number to around a dozen. The Cs speak to a culture of common purpose in which the kingpin is connection – to the people and to the institution and its goals.

Ideally, by infiltrating the Cs throughout the university, the principles of connection seep into the attitudes and actions of the people who work there. The 'Cs' initiative resonates with the idea of generative metaphors suggested by Bushe (2013) as a practice where a group of people "discover, create and/or are present with an image that allows them to experience their work and their organization differently" (2013, p. 3). With its simple formula, the Cs facilitate a strategy that aims to include Unisa's staff in institutional thinking and behaving. They are a reminder that connection is important in an environment that, on the whole, militates against conversation and cohesion. Within its concrete walls, long passages stretching from west to east form the backbone of the older buildings housing the academic staff (the newer buildings have been designed differently to encompass open spaces and seamless offices).

I have observed in my personal career, from faculty member to Dean to Pro-Vice-Chancellor to Principal, a persistent decline in movement and congress and a steady incline towards isolation and privacy. Corridors of closed doors confront the visitor, concealing the academics working within. Collegiality does not emerge naturally from closed doors. Then too, the increasing propensity of people to stay glued to their computer screens, sending e-mails when they could walk ten paces to communicate with their colleagues does not engender true connection. How is such a culture to be changed and enhanced?

The values, norms and beliefs that inform Unisa are a necessary, but not sufficient, framework for a successful organization. They are, if you will, the ship that floats quietly in the dock waiting to begin the journey. In order to get from A to B, the ship must be peopled with a competent crew who are skilled in sailing and servicing and equipped to look after the passengers. Someone is in charge but also relies on others to sail the ship towards its destination. Leadership is both an individual and a communal process. One person cannot lead an organization without the involvement of other leaders in different ranks, despite the number of books and articles that claim otherwise. The idea of the heroic leader, the strong leader, the captain (the 'great man' theory) acting in magnificent isolation is, and has always been, a myth. It has depended on recognizable traits held up as individual and aspirational attributes, including intelligence, courage, drive, confidence, persistence and so on (Stogdill, 1974; Gardner, 1993). When we speak of inclusive leadership we should lean rather towards the ideas of relationship and interdependency as part of a process playing out in a flattened ethnography.

A more apposite leadership model for the 21st century than previous models of hierarchy and authority embodied in a 'great man' therefore is servant leadership, closely linked to transformational leadership where the leader is a role model for others, provides meaning, vision and tangible goals, enhances team spirit, stimulates creativity and innovation and acts as a mentor of individual improvement (Derungs, 2011). The ship floating in the dock, to continue the analogy, is a finished product yet she has still to sail. Similarly, the university under new leadership may be imbued with core values and vision, yet it must be steered through processes within a stable yet flexible structure: a rigid ship cannot withstand too strong a gale. In other words, the values and vision have mapped the journey; the people and processes will ensure that we reach the destination provided that they are enabled through effective communication.

Inclusivity

Inclusivity in higher education is primarily about access. Who is allowed to study? Who will help with funding? What processes can be put in place to facilitate student success?

Achille Mbembe (2015), one of South Africa's leading public intellectuals, had this to say in a public lecture presented at the Wits Institute for Social and Economic Research (WISER):

> When we say access, we are naturally thinking about a wide opening of the doors of higher learning to all South Africans. For this to happen, SA must invest in its universities. For the time being, it spends 0.6% of its GDP on higher education. The percentage of the national wealth invested in higher education must be increased. But when we say access, we are also talking about the creation of those conditions that will allow black staff and students

to say of the university: 'This is my home. I am not an outsider here. I do not have to beg or to apologize to be here. I belong here'. Such a right to belong, such a rightful sense of ownership has nothing to do with charity or hospitality. It has nothing to do with the liberal notion of 'tolerance'. It has nothing to do with me having to assimilate into a culture that is not mine as a precondition of my participating in the public life of the institution. It has all to do with ownership of a space that is a public, common good. It has to do with an expansive sense of citizenship itself indispensable for the project of democracy, which itself means nothing without a deep commitment to some idea of public-ness.

This comment was made at a time when students across South Africa (and the movement spread to the University of Oxford in the United Kingdom) were taking part in the '#RhodesMustFall' campaign (later to become the '#FeesMustFall' campaign) to remove offensive statues of historical figures who were plainly racist imperialists, but also to wholly transform the curriculum and teaching practices at universities across the country as well as their staff profile. The swift momentum of this movement, prodded in the main by social media, took South Africa by surprise with its segue into a demand for free education and, from there, a much more serious expectation of total transformation of higher education in South Africa.[2] While it is possibly too soon to expect a thorough and objective analysis of the groundswell that flows beneath these demands and outbursts of anger which more and more frequently spill over into violence against people and property, both Mbembe and Ndlovu-Gatsheni gesture towards a deep and compelling need for change in South Africa. Achille Mbembe, an influential historian and political theorist at WISER, has consistently argued that the archive has to be broadened to reflect African and Southern scholarship. For him this is essential for curricular transformation. Northern epistemological hegemony has, in his view, marginalized African voices. Ndlovu-Gatsheni takes a more radical Afrocentric and nationalist position. This is clear from the quotation which follows. Their respective calls to re-think the idea of the university in African and Global South contexts have, however, lessened these differences in favor of advocating thorough-going transformation of the academy through a sincere search for epistemic justice.

Ndlovu-Gatsheni situates the current social movements within a broader canvas of 'decoloniality':

Decoloniality is brewing like a heavy storm and is at the moment manifesting itself as a psychic state of both 'agonism' and 'antagonism.' Universities, as part of those global institutions that continue to reproduce coloniality, alien cultures and 'whiteness,' are legitimate targets of decolonisation. Deep frustrations over the slow pace of transforming and decolonising universities have produced the current student- and youth-led decolonial movements in South Africa. For black students, universities have remained alienating spaces and sites in which they have to undergo a form of epistemicide and linguicide (emptying of heads and change of language) in order to fit in. Curriculum has remained Eurocentric. Africa-centred knowledges remain marginalised. Africanisation initiatives have not resulted in decolonisation.

(Ndlovu-Gatsheni, 2015, p. 26)

Higgins and Vale (2016) speak of a 'state of urgency' in their eponymous editorial to *Arts and Humanities in Higher Education* (p. 3), as they try to make sense of the deep unrest that prevails in South Africa:

Central to this moment are the related questions of tradition, transition and transformation. Twenty years ago, the question of South Africa's transition would readily have been understood as one from apartheid state to constitutional and non-racial democracy.

What impact does this have for ideas on inclusivity at Unisa, which is not a face-to-face institution, yet which has a vibrant and vociferous student population that is organized politically and has links with labor unions equally vocal on the campus?

In order to answer this, we must return to Unisa's institutional history, which is complex and layered and tautly imbricated in the political history of South Africa. Indeed, its identity that shapes its staffing composition, its formal policies and processes, its organizational architecture and its institutional ecology has shifted, formed and reformed according to the political will of the time. Each turn in the history of Unisa's identity, from examining body, to correspondence institution, to a mega merged comprehensive university, to an open distance university, and, in recent years, towards a fully digitized, online university, has echoed not only global advances in distance education but, closer to home, changes in government policy. Yet, despite this historical tension, Unisa has consistently been an open (inclusive) university, enrolling students of all races, cultures and creeds. It is famous for having as one of its prized alumni, Nelson Mandela, and many of the political prisoners on Robben Island studied through Unisa whilst incarcerated. Moreover, Unisa is the cheapest university in South Africa with the lowest fees, and allows entrance to students who are over 21 who may not necessarily have university entrance qualifications.

Significantly in the current debate about offensive statues in South Africa, Unisa set about changing the names of its public spaces at least a decade ago and consistently seeks public consensus on naming new buildings with a concomitant sensitivity to local cultures and language groups.

Inclusive Change: Young Academics Program, Signature Courses and Decoloniality School

Given the limitations of space, I must confine myself to three concrete examples here, but they conveniently represent two important pillars of inclusive practice pertaining to staff and students at Unisa. The first is the Young Academics' Program (YAP), which is an annual event aimed at introducing new members of the teaching and research staff to the culture and ethos of their university. Serving as far more than an induction program, YAP asks for nominations from each College at the beginning of the academic year. Once these are received from the Deans, a comprehensive program is devised that aims to cover every aspect of university life, including research, teaching, community life, governance, management, ICTs, the library and so on. Young academics are taken out of their academic departments for a specific period (usually spanning four months) and out of the university to a nearby venue where they are coached by experienced members of staff and nurtured into university life. They are also encouraged to work in interdisciplinary teams on a project of their choosing which they present to the Principal at the end of the program. These projects are invariably innovative and geared towards the improvement of university functioning. Not only does this program introduce the university and its functions to young members of staff, it widens their frame of reference beyond the border of their department and College, thereby encouraging inclusivity and collegiality. Our young academics frequently continue the relationships they have made during the program, since they find commonality and connections across their disciplinary fields. The program has assisted in changing the institutional culture to reflect constitutional transformation in respect of race, gender, sexual orientation and disability. It has also helped new academics to move diversity towards inclusivity. Diversity is sometimes simply tolerance of others; inclusivity, on the other hand, questions power relations and entrenched patterns of authority which reflect the deep inequality of South African society, even post-apartheid.

The second example involves a new pedagogy and practice for Unisa: the Signature Courses. These were devised and designed collaboratively in teams from two continents, Africa and North America. Both teams visited each other's spaces over a period of three years, resulting in a mutual exchange of knowledge about university practices in the North and the South. Of benefit to Unisa were those team members who were especially knowledgeable about e-learning and in pedagogies that were adaptable to an e-learning context in South Africa. The pedagogy finally adopted a heutagogical approach that is suitable for teaching and learning practices for adult students (the majority of students registered at Unisa are over the age of 25) and aims at helping students take control of their own learning through an inclusive methodology that caters for proactive leadership. Not only are the Signature Courses designed with local habitats and customs in mind, but they are highly adaptable for teaching groups of students in small, intensive, online classes in which students are encouraged to apply their learning to their 'life-worlds' and so learn to be ambassadors in their own communities.

Unusually for Unisa, learning is both structured and ongoing, with writing or other creative tasks taking place once each week or fortnight, instead of once a semester. In addition, peer-learning and peer-assessment motivate students to take responsibility for themselves and others, and opens a space for new leaders to emerge. The Signature Courses have had a considerable impact on Unisa as a teaching and learning organization. In order to devise Unisa's first truly online courses, several key processes in the administration had to be invented or adapted. This resulted in real transformation which occurred through a careful and sensitive change management process in which not only academics involved in curriculum change were included on team visits to the USA, but also administrative managers and staff who sat in formative discussions in which they could voice their misgivings and open themselves to difficult change. The academics involved in the Signature Courses from their inception took on the role of change agents, encouraging others to shift their ideas on pedagogy from lecturing to partnering – a challenging change in mindset for a lot of people.

Students too, were involved from the early stages of the project. Student leaders were initially mistrustful of the dramatic transformation involved both in pedagogy and in practice and were particularly anxious about the move towards wholly online learning. Yet, when they became involved in the process and learnt of the broader aims of the Signature Courses and were party to the excitement of devising an online module, they climbed on board and began sharing their knowledge with their peers. Once the Signature Courses passed the planning phase, several public demonstrations were held at Unisa to which the entire staff was invited.

The six Signature Courses have been running since 2013 and show a pleasing improvement in success rates and participation. They serve as an example of how inclusivity functions in curricular processes and practices, but also point the way to a new future for the university, one that is intimately tied to the new Sustainable Development Goal 'Education 2030' which encourages universities to use new technologies to expand open and inclusive practice. As the incoming President of the International Council for Open and Distance Education (ICDE), I shared the following belief with the Executive Committee in January 2016:

> The opportunities delivered by digital, open and flexible learning will increase access, equity, quality and relevance, and narrow the gap between what is taught at tertiary education institutions and what economies and societies demand.

Further global initiatives pledged by the ICDE at this meeting included a global Doctoral Consortium to support doctoral students and innovation.

The third and last example is an epistemological one, already briefly alluded to earlier in this chapter: the closely aligned agendas of decoloniality and transformation. The #RhodesMustFall campaign began in 2015 when students at the University of Cape Town called for the removal of the statue of Cecil John Rhodes at the bottom of the steps leading to the Jameson Hall on the university's main campus. The statue was a symbol of dominant white power and the colonial nature of the university. The movement sparked widespread student protest at the lack of social, material and intellectual transformation in higher education. This grew into the #FeesMustFall violence of 2016 as students advocated free education for all and the decolonization of universities to reflect African contexts and experiences. This has amounted to an 'empire strikes back' enterprise that challenges the conventions, conceits and commodification of universities in the post-apartheid era. It claims to represent democratic values which have been discounted by political corruption and patronage, as well as corporate greed. Unisa's response to the unrest provoked by the #RhodesMustFall movement has manifested on several levels: control of the disruption caused to the main campus in Pretoria; consultation with students and workers; strategic thinking and public utterances, amongst others, but essentially, like other South African universities, Unisa's leadership has been acting independently and without inter-institutional or government support until very recently, when university leaders collaborated in forming an inter-university task team, under the auspices of the umbrella body, Universities South Africa (USAf), to assist each other and to lobby government for resources:

> As universities navigate through this uncharted terrain which is politically charged and volatile they will have to contend with a complex issue of institutional autonomy in face of understandable government intervention in an effort to resolve the current crisis.
>
> *(Makhanya, 2016, unpublished report)*

It is obvious that this is a charged period in the history of South African universities and much depends on the approach taken to student and worker unrest, whether independent or collaborative. And while decisive action and intelligent decision-making are now needed, the outcome will depend on the extent to which strategic management pays heed to epistemic justice and challenging the Northern dominance of scholarship. Epistemic justice refers to the results of the challenge of Southern scholarship against Northern canons which dominate curricula and marginalize Southern, especially African, knowledges. The purpose of curricular transformation is to widen the epistemological repertoire of university courses and programs to include the research of African and diasporan theorists as a counterpoint to European and American authorities. In this way, epistemic virtue would result. Prinsloo (2016, p. 165) argues:

> [there are] deeply intellectual questions that require complex understanding to subvert the current techno-bureaucratic approaches to transformation.

One such meeting place where thinking shapes action may be found in the African Decolonial Research Network (ADERN) project at Unisa, which each year hosts the International Summer School on Decolonising Power, Knowledge and Identity. Inaugurated in 2013, this initiative has already produced notable results in that students who attended are at the forefront of the current student movement for change and transformation of South African universities (Ndlovu-Gatsheni, 2015, p. 45), and are thus shaping future thinking about decoloniality and epistemic justice. The other is perhaps more telling, since it is closely aligned to Unisa's institutional and strategic journey towards deep transformation, not only of its structures and personnel but of its epistemological foundations (what it thinks, what it communicates, what it teaches and researches).

I have instituted a new unit in the office of the Principal and Vice-Chancellor to focus on change management and to assist the university "to shape futures in the service of humanity" by bringing together its disparate elements, its strategic goals and its scholarly pursuits in exploring knowledge production, epistemic re-alignment and multilingualism. The unit has three pillars which support curricular change in the interests of asserting Africa-centered knowledges; technological change to realize the potential of open, distance and e-learning pedagogies; and cultural change for diversity and social transformation at Unisa.

One of the early initiatives of the Change Management Unit is the Charter on Transformation which is not only a leadership initiative, but also an institutional response to the swelling political and social movements in South Africa. Enshrined in South Africa's Constitution for a just democracy, it encourages institutional introspection and self-critique in ensuring that Unisa's assumptions, thoughts and practices are closely aligned to the university's transformational goals. This may invoke what Pillay (2015) calls 'epistemic violence', in that ideas around transformation and decoloniality are embedded in disruptive thinking about necessary change both institutionally and epistemologically. The Charter on Transformation identifies several key focus areas for transformation at Unisa:

- staff equity, development and work experience;
- student equity, development and outcomes;
- students' lived experiences, including their socialization;
- knowledges, epistemologies, methodologies and languages;
- governance, leadership and management experiences;
- funding and resource allocation; and
- infrastructure, including buildings, facilities and ICTs.

Beyond these, the Charter will focus on a rigorous program to decolonize scholarship, thus aligning strategically with the ADERN project which has brought African and Latin-American scholarship together in a combined research partnership that attempts to mobilize the intellectual armory of Ramón Grosfo-guel, Walter Mignolo and Nelson Maldonado Torres in support of an Africa-centered challenge to Eurocentrism. The aim is to engage the 'grammars' of transformation, Africanization, indigenization and decolonization which are all critical of inherited 'ways of knowing' that privilege European and American authors. ADERN draws on Fanonian, Mazruian and Mamdanian philosophy to profile continental African ideas in dialogue with authorial views.

Concluding Thoughts

Were I to have written this chapter six months ago, my concluding remarks would, I suspect, be somewhat different to what you have read here. South Africa is going through a time of troubling, some might say tumultuous, change and, for the first time since the late 1960s and especially 1976, at the time of the Soweto Uprising, that change is being expressed by our university students. Their demands for complete transformation in the higher education sector have forced those in the top management of universities to focus their minds on what this might really mean. We have been speaking about transformation since the mid-1990s, but we have not, up to now, been tasked with the urgent need to put our words into action. We should be grateful to our students for raising the bar, yet these times lure us into deep introspection about our role and function in the university.

For me, inclusive leadership is profoundly personal. It is about humility and self-examination. It has to mean a change of attitude on the part of leadership, especially in the current environment of student protest, widespread violence and political flux. It also has to be vicarious, stepping into the shoes of others – students, academics, members of civil society. No less, it is about students understanding the contradictions in higher education which structurally pit Vice-Chancellors against students. Politicians have to accept the righteousness of the cause of free education. They should not leave the solution to university management and student representative councils. Inclusivity is not possible if we deny the huge inequality that keeps raising race and class as the inhibitors. Government and the private sector owe our democracy greater commitment to higher education. Inclusive leadership is not only the responsibility of university managers.

Jonathan Jansen (2014), the outgoing Rector of the University of the Free State, describes the difficult task ahead in this way:

> This is a difficult dimension of change – how to open the university to full political expression yet at the same time allowing for other kinds of social activism (cultural, sports, the arts, environmental, etc.) that is not reduced to party politics and that does not trap students in racial categories of organisation? How, moreover, does a university insist on its autonomy in the face of dictates from the dominant political party in the country?
>
> *(p. 42)*

I use Jansen's following words to conclude this chapter. His sentiments closely echo my own thoughts, which I hinted at earlier, on the interplay of the personal and the political and of the necessity for humble introspection:

Throughout I am conscious of my own troubled history, my own wound-edness, my own sense of the need for personal transformation. It is, para-doxically, that sense of weakness that gives me strength. It is that awareness of incompleteness that seems to draw people to engage their personal jour-neys within a broader institutional journey. It is not self-confidence but self-criticism that enable rites to suspend judgment and to allow introspection. That acute sense of personal weakness conveys a deep understanding that you cannot presume to change others unless you have confronted your own demons, and that you cannot lead alone.

(Jansen, 2014, p. 43)

Notes

1 Legkotla is a South African term describing a meeting place for village assemblies. It is now frequently used to describe strategic planning sessions for organizations.
2 It may be prudent to provide an explanation of this term as it is perceived by propo-nents of its use in higher education in South Africa: In South African debates on higher education, the term 'transformation' is generally held to refer to a comprehensive, deep-rooted and ongoing social process seeking to achieve a fundamental reconstitution and development of our universities to reflect and promote the vision of a democratic society. This entails a simultaneous process of eradicating all forms of unfair dis-crimination and creating a higher education sector that gives full expression to the talents of all South Africans, particularly the marginalized and poor. The transformation of higher education therefore refers to the active removal of any institutional, social, material and intellectual barriers in the way of creating a more equal, inclusive and socially just higher education system. As such, our understanding of the concept is one of designating a range of social, economic, cultural and political conditions and their institutionalized settings that should be reconstituted if higher education is to fulfil its democratic mandates (Higher Education Transformation Summit, 2015, p. 2).

References

Bushe, G. R., 2013. Generative process, generative outcome: The transformational potential of appreciative inquiry. In: Cooperrider, D. L., Zandee, D. P., Godwin, L. N., Avital, M. and Boland, B, eds. *Organizational generativity: The appreciative inquiry summit and a scholarship of transformation (Advances in appreciative inquiry,* Volume 4). Bingley, UK: Emerald Group Publishing Limited, pp. 89–113.

Daniel, J., 1996. *Mega-universities and knowledge media: Technology strategies for higher education.* London: Kogan Page.

Derungs, I., 2011. *Trans-cultural leadership for transformation.* London: Palgrave Macmillan.

de Vries, M. K., Ramo, L. G. and Korotov, K., 2009. In: Cooper, C., Quick, J. and Schabracq, M., eds. *International handbook of work and health psychology.* 3rd ed. London: Wiley-Blackwell.

Gardner, H., 1993. *Frames of mind: The theory of multiple intelligences.* New York: Basic Books.

Grogan, M. and Shakeshaft, C., 2011. *Women and educational leadership.* San Francisco: Jossey Bass.

Higgins, J. and Vale, P., 2016. State of urgency. *Arts & Humanities in Higher Education,* 15(1), pp. 3–6. Available at: <sagepub.co.uk/journals> [Accessed 14 November, 2016].

Higher Education Transformation Summit, 2015 (15–17 October). Annexure 5: Reflections on higher education transformation. Durban, Kwa-Zulu-Natal, South Africa. Available at: <http://www.dhet.gov.za> [Accessed 16 November, 2016].

Jansen, J., 2014. Skin apart: On the complexities of institutional transformation in South Africa. In: Smith, D. G., ed. *Diversity and inclusion in higher education: Emerging perspectives on institutional transformation.* London: Routledge, pp. 29–44.

Laub, J., 2010. The servant organization. In: Van Dierendonck, D. and Patterson, K., eds. *Servant leadership: Developments in theory and research.* New York: Palgrave Macmillan.

Makhanya, M., 2016. Reflection on current developments within the higher education sector in South Africa. [Unpublished report] 23 January, 2016.

Mbembe, A., 2015. Decolonizing knowledge and the question of the archive. A Public Lecture given at WISER (Wits Institute for Social and Economic Research). Available at: <http://wiser.wits.ac.za/system/files/Achille%20Mbembe%20-%20Decolonizing%20Know ledge%20and%20the%20Question%20of%20the%20Archive.pdf> [Accessed 2 March, 2016].

Ndlovu-Gatsheni, S., 2015. Decoloniality in Africa: A continuing search for a new world order. *The Australasian Review of African Studies,* 36(2), pp. 22–50.

Parris, D. L. and Peachey, J. W., 2013. A systematic literature review of servant leadership theory in organizational contexts. *Journal of Business Ethics,* 113(3), pp. 377–393.

Pillay, S., 2015. Decolonising the university. Available at: <http://africasacountry.com/2015/06/decolonizing-the-university/> [Accessed 8 March, 2016].

Prinsloo, E. H. (2016) The role of the humanities in decolonising the academy. *Arts & Humanities in Higher Education,* 15(1), pp. 164–168.

Reinke, S. J., 2004. Service before self: Towards a theory of servant-leadership. *Global Virtue Ethics Review,* 5(3), pp. 30–57.

Sendjaya, S., 2015. Conceptualizing and measuring spiritual leadership in organizations. *International Journal of Business and Information,* 2(1), pp. 104–126.

Senge, P., 1990. *The fifth discipline: The art and practice of the learning organization.* New York: Doubleday.

Stogdill, R. M., 1974. *Handbook of leadership: A survey of the literature.* New York: Free Press.

Wheeler, D. W., 2012. *Servant leadership for higher education: Principles and practices.* San Francisco: Jossey Bass.

11

UNDERSTANDING THE GRIT AND GRAVITAS UNDERLYING CULTURALLY SUSTAINING INCLUSIVE LEADERSHIP IN ACADEME

Lorri J. Santamaría and Andrés P. Santamaría

Introduction

Although educational leadership has been studied in theory and practice for over a century, educational leadership specific to higher education has been and remains on the margins of scholarly exploration (Santamaría, in press). Research on educational leadership for an increasingly diverse society is even more rarified and further removed from studies in the field of educational leadership and higher education in general (Santamaría and Santamaría, 2016). In this chapter we consider a closer and more responsible look at what we, in the past, have called culturally responsive leadership and instead continue the conversation about what it means for leadership to be culturally sustaining and inclusive (Paris, 2012; Paris and Alim, 2014). We do this as an integral part of scholarly discourse to further define and implement more humane approaches to diversity and inclusion in higher education.

Here, the authors address ways in which inclusive leadership can be cultivated at all levels in higher education. We begin by defining what is meant by inclusion as it relates to diversity and the ways in which these concepts play out in the academy. The notions of 'grit' and 'gravitas' in educational leaders are juxtaposed against the backdrop of diversity and inclusion as necessary characteristics of educational leaders in a variety of higher educational settings. To provide context for this inquiry, literature and research featuring the inclusive and culturally sustaining educational leadership practices of 25 leaders working with systemically, institutionally, and socially excluded populations in diverse tertiary settings in the United States, New Zealand, Canada, Australia, and South Africa are presented and examined. These inclusive educational leadership case studies in higher education have been thematically analyzed to determine ways in which cultures of inclusion are created and sustained. Findings from theses analyse serve as exemplars contributing to a model for educational leadership in academe. A conclusion offers implications for application that promotes access, equity, and improvement for leaders in higher education who wish to integrate inclusion principles into their policies, structures, and activities for better experiences for all involved.

Unpacking Inclusion, Diversity, Grit, and Gravitas

Tienda (2013) argues that enrollment of a diverse student body is nothing more than a baby step toward broader social goals of inclusion, and, therefore, diversity does not equal inclusion. Her assertion is the premise for this brief, definitive section laying the groundwork for this chapter. Further, we define inclusion and diversity in academe and consider ways in which they relate to what is needed from educational leaders in diverse educational contexts. We also highlight the characteristics for grit and gravitas references.

Inclusion and Diversity

There tends to be the assumption that diverse environments are automatically inclusive, however, authors such as Tienda (2013) have conducted research revealing the contrary. Where inclusion may mean one or many things at once, notions of diversity may insinuate something else altogether. Culturally sustaining leadership practices are more than culturally responsive when they are grounded in and arise from diverse individuals and are, thus, inherently inclusive. We begin this inquiry by taking a closer look at these two constructs to further clarify this distinction.

Inclusion

Often comprised of organizational strategies and practices promoting "meaningful social and academic interactions among students who differ in their experiences, views, and traits" (Tienda, 2013, p. 467), inclusion also alludes to educational access beyond secondary schooling (Archer, Hutchings, and Ross, 2005) and integration into society for individuals with disabilities (Silver, Bourke, and Strehorn, 1998). Access, participation and success for the disenfranchised, marginalized, and otherwise socially excluded lie at the crux of inclusionary practices in higher education (Gidley, et al., 2010). Policies in most institutions of higher learning now make references to inclusion as wide-ranging, goal-spanning structures and actions, while maintaining inclusion as a goal or ideal.

Many inclusion policies find their legs in pastoral programs for student success, beginning with recruitment and continued-retention activities targeting students representing specific backgrounds who may require additional support in post-secondary institutions. These supports include writing or academic assistance centers, in addition to student centers designed to foster a sense of belonging for culturally and linguistically diverse students attending predominantly white institutions (PWIs). Where there are culturally specific centers on campus, there are also often women's studies centers and sometimes centers to support lesbian, gay, bisexual, transgender, questioning, or intersex (LGBTQI) students present. These kinds of gathering spaces are often constructed, nominally funded, and legally *responsive* to diverse populations on the margins in PWIs. This response comes from a deficit mindset and a way of thinking about providing what is needed to students who are lacking. Instead, these centers of belonging could be authentically more inclusive to sustain the richness of what diverse students bring to the university. They could strive to ensure that the added value that diverse communities bring is both acknowledged and valued. This is a strengths-based position. The distinction requires a mindset shift from deficit thinking to a perspective where diversity is considered desirable, a priority, and worthy of investment. The inclusion and diversity intersection appears in literature, policy, and practice but there are important idiosyncrasies that warrant closer examination.

Diversity

Attention to, and provisions for, diversity are requirements of the law in institutions of higher learning in the United States and similar countries. As the editors of this volume maintain, in many universities it is illegal to discriminate against students based on aspects of their identity (e.g., race, ethnicity, nationality, sex, gender, sexual orientation, marital status, religion, beliefs, disability, and age). Therefore, attention to diversity in academe has come about as a response to legal challenges to affirmative action in race-based considerations and college admissions (Gurin, *et al.*, 2002). This is exacerbated by social unrest among many African American groups in response to disproportionate arrests and police officer-involved shootings of Black African American men in the United States in particular. From their research using single and multi-institutional data garnered from African American, Asian American, Latino/a and white students in their study of democracy outcomes, Gurin, *et al.* (2002) provide evidence for the importance of sustained affirmative action and diversity efforts in higher education. The authors suggest these efforts would increase access to higher education for as many students as possible and contribute to students' academic improvement.

It is clear that diversity is the law and inclusion can be considered the manifestation of this law if educational leaders in higher education are able to morally and ethically shift policy and law into practice resulting in the breaking down and removal of the structural and, sometimes practical, barriers present in higher education today. We argue that, in order to cultivate, create, and sustain organizational cultures that are increasingly inclusive of all types of diversity in the academy, individual leaders need to critically and unapologetically examine their assumptions and practices on personal and professional teaching, research, service, and administration one situation at a time. Leaders looking inward towards a change of heart and mind is the only way to foster change of practice from being difference *responsive* to being difference *sustaining* and thus *inclusive* (Santamaría, et al., 2016). This kind of approach takes individual leadership commitment and engagement toward sustainable educational change.

Grit and Gravitas

We propose grit and gravitas as characteristics of staunch commitment and steadfast engagement inherent to educational leaders who are able to embody leadership practice that cultivates strengths-based inclusivity in higher education. Each are defined as a point of reference and related to previous research featuring applied critical leadership undertaken in a variety of diverse and international contexts wherein individuals draw on positive aspects of their identities to strengthen their leadership practice in educational contexts (Santamaría and Santamaría, 2012; 2016). Tables 11.1 and 11.2 provide examples of grit and gravitas gleaned from current research findings.

Grit

Courage, resolve, strength of character, commitment, and passion are ways to describe the kind of non-cognitive personality traits needed by leaders who challenge status-quo higher educational practices and work toward sustainable change and improvement. A philosophical positioning of sorts is to suggest that reflecting grit as an educational leader means that one is confident in his or her ability to lead and in what he or she brings to the table. In the extensive and growing research base on applied critical leadership, findings indicate that leaders who are themselves diverse (e.g. race, ethnicity, nationality, gender, sexual orientation) and work closely with, and on behalf of, diverse peoples or those who have overcome an adversity, disadvantage, or social justice inequity tend to exhibit elements of grit in their leadership practice (Santamaría and Santamaría, 2012; Santamaría and Jean-Marie, 2014; Santamaría, et al., 2014).

Previous research findings reflect that educational leaders who exhibit grit are more prone to initiating and engaging in critical conversations on behalf of disenfranchised and marginalized groups. These leaders tend to assume a critical race (or otherwise critical) lens to inform decision-making, particularly when decisions have to do with inequities. Another example of grit is these leaders' documented consciousness of 'stereotype threat' and their own or others' unintentional fulfillment of tokenistic behaviors associated with systemically underserved individuals as expected by those who shape the dominant culture within their context. Finally, culturally sustaining leaders with grit exhibit steadfast motivation in

TABLE 11.1 Case Studies for Inclusion, Diversity, Grit, and/or Gravitas

Location and diversity addressed	Leader role and identity	Example of inclusionary practice (grit and/or gravitas)
Midsized teaching university: Southern CA. More than 25 percent Latino/a students matriculated. Growing numbers of students who are Asian Pacific Islander (API). Small populations of American Indian and African American students.	Director Student Affairs, API Post-op transgender woman (N=1)	Served as faculty advisor for the API and a LGBTQI student group as well as expanding definitions of diversity to include students who are LGBTQI (Grit: critical stance).
	Dean, Mexican descent Chicana woman (N=1)	Created conditions to increase cultural competency for faculty working with diverse student populations (Gravitas and Grit: servant leadership for greater good).
	Provost, White woman (N=1)	Immersed self in life experiences of underserved, under-represented, and marginalized individuals with the intent to understand others while advocating with them and on their behalf (Grit and Gravitas: critical stance to serve greater good).
	Director Multicultural Student Center, Arab descent (Iraqi Chaldean) American woman (N=1)	Brought together teachers, faculty, and administrators to form multidisciplinary groups of individuals working together toward a social justice and educational equity (Grit and Gravitas: consensus as norm to serve greater good).
	Student Leader and Project Director, two Latina women (N=2)	Utilized identities and experiences to serve strategically in their roles as both 'outsiders' and 'insiders' of institutional margins to benefit other marginalized learners (Grit: conscious of tokenism).
Large research intensive (RI) University: Southern CA. More than 25% students who are API. Smaller population of Latino/a and lesser numbers of American Indian and African American students.	Directors Student Centers, API man and Latina lesbian woman (N=2)	Deliberate creation of safe spaces, community, and resources to enhance identity development, sense of belonging, mattering, and retention for underserved students (Grit and Gravitas: critical stance and servant leadership).
	Doctoral Student of educational leadership, Black African American woman (N=1)	Brought opportunities to the attention of underserved students that might benefit them in reaching educational and professional goals (Grit: conscious of tokenism and critical conversations).

Large RI University: Southern CA and large Ivy League University Mid-West USA. Large and increasing numbers of API students. Smaller population of Latino/a and smaller numbers of American Indian and African American students.	Directors Student Centers, White gay man, Black African American woman, Filipino American woman (N=3)	Engaged in sustained dialogue and shared stories and shared struggles with people with different perspectives and experiences in public spaces as an example of what it means to be a community (Gravitas: building trust and inclusion of multiple voices and perspectives).
Large RI university, New Zealand. Indigenous Māori and Pasifika students who have low post secondary completion rates as compared to their peers including students who are immigrants and recent arrivals to New Zealand.	Student Leader and Academic Leader, Tongan New Zealander woman and European New Zealander woman (N=2)	Opened up and provided academic spaces for mutual reflection using poetry as a conduit and part of the process (Grit: critical stance and critical conversations).
	Academic Leader, Tongan woman (N=1)	Relied on employing student voice in order to inform content and delivery in higher education course work for diverse students (Gravitas: inclusion of multiple voices and perspectives).
	School University Community Partnerships Leader, European New Zealander woman (N=1)	Worked deliberately to build long-standing sustainable relationships with people within the community setting, even those for whom there was not an affinity (Gravitas: building trust and inclusion of multiple voices and perspectives).
	Academic and Professional Staff Leaders, Indigenous Māori women (N=2)	Valued contributions of academic and professional staff in parity while grounding all leadership decisions and actions in Kaupapa Māori: Māori ways of being (Gravitas: servant leadership and inclusion of multiple voices and perspectives).
Five research intensive universities in New Zealand, Canada, Australia, and South Africa. Systematically underserved, socially excluded and marginalised students who are typically first in their families to attend university.	Academic Research Leaders, Tongan, Black/Indigenous African American, Indigenous knowledge, Pasifika, White European Australian, Egyptian descent Australian, and White European South African women (N=7)	Deferred and adapted to integrating and infusing Indigenous methodologies to match student groups being served (e.g., Kaupapa Māori and Pasifika Talanoa in New Zealand; Participatory Learning Activity in South Africa, etc.) (Gravitas: inclusion of multiple voices and perspectives).

Note: All participants are heterosexual unless otherwise indicated in the table.

TABLE 11.2 Sample Evidence of Inclusive Culturally Sustainable Leadership, Grit, and Gravitas

Grit, gravitas, and applied critical leadership	Leader	Leader quotes
Grit: Initiating and engaging in critical conversations on behalf of disenfranchised and marginalized groups.	Academic and Professional Staff Leaders, Indigenous Māori women	"Kaupapa Māori is the framework that enables us to research, participate, and work together as Māori and as Indigenous people in ways that are culturally appropriate, ethical, safe, and sustainable for us as a people" (Santamaría, Lee, and Harker, 2014).
Grit: Taking on a critical race or otherwise critical lens to inform decision-making.	Student Leader and Project Director, two Latina women	"I think I still continue the MEChA[1] Philosophy in all the work that I do, and that is keeping the door opened to our community and fighting injustice" (Zavala and Tran, 2016, p. 100).
Grit: Consciousness of 'stereotype threat' and unintentional fulfilment of token behaviors associated with marginalized individuals.	Provost, White woman	"To keep my social justice and educational equity work pure and authentic, most efforts are undertaken with individuals in one-on-one conversations, in meetings, or in casual coaching sessions in personal or professional settings" (Santamaría and Santamaría, 2012, p. 138).
Grit: Motivation is achieving goals and objectives to serve the greater good.	Directors Student Centers, Filipino American women	"Working closely with two people in similar positions brings it together for me. It brings in a level of comfort and I have two other people to bounce ideas off of making me feel safe" (Travers, Welch, and del Peña, 2016).
Gravitas: Use of consensus as a preferred strategy for decision-making.	Director Multicultural Student Center, Arab descent (Iraqi Chaldean) American woman	"We strategically use our alliances to strengthen our power when we know they can move issues of diversity, equity, and social justice to the forefront of the operations at the university" (Dauod, 2016, p. 190).
Gravitas: Active acknowledgement and inclusion of as many members of constituency as possible when making decisions.	Academic Research Leaders, Tongan, Black/Indigenous African American, Indigenous knowledge, Pasifika, White European Australian, Egyptian descent Australian, and White European South African women	"We are committed to the legacy of research that includes a growing pool of Indigenous and underserved researchers to undertake quality research for improving higher education's performance for systemically underserved students" (Bell, et al., 2016, p. 116).

Grit, gravitas, and applied critical leadership	Leader	Leader quotes
Gravitas: Express need to build an established trust when working with constituents who do not share viewpoints, values, or experiences.	Doctoral Student of Educational Leadership, Black African American woman	"Engage with whomever necessary to follow up, participate in, or engage with opportunities that might result in a positive change to current circumstances" (Stiemke and Santamaría, 2016, p. 87).
Gravitas: description of self as servant leader giving back to underserved community.	Academic Leader, Tongan woman	"There is a need for institutions to provide a learning environment where the implicit is made more explicit, especially for students who are first in their family to attend university" (Wolfgramm-Foliaki, 2016, p. 134).

Note: Applied critical leadership characteristics adapted from Santamaría and Santamaría, 2012; 2016.

achieving goals and objectives in order to serve the greater good (Santamaría and Jean-Marie, 2014).

Gravitas

A Roman virtue, gravitas is an extension of grit associated with a leader being present, in the moment, available, or engaged and more action-oriented than its philosophically-based cousin. A leader of gravitas is one who is willing to seriously and piously consider what is at stake in education from a big picture as well as a local and/or short-term perspective. Research findings indicate these leaders exhibit decorum and are trusted in all matters. When leaders exhibiting this characteristic are engaged in discussion, debate, or action involving the parsing and teasing out of issues related to inclusion and diversity, they are taken seriously and trusted by constituents and stakeholders as well as other members of the educational community (see Santamaría, *et al.*, 2016). These leaders are said to embody leadership in word and deed (Santamaría, *et al.*, 2015).

Additional examples of gravitas in action found in the research reviewed include educational leaders' use of consensus as a preferred strategy for decision-making. This finding indicates leaders of gravitas are also more "compelled to or make empirical research based contributions to their educational context by adding equity issues" (Santamaría, 2015, p. 130). These leaders are known to be inclusive by actively acknowledging and including as many members of their constituencies as possible when it comes to making leadership decisions for the community. For these culturally sustaining leaders, multiple perspectives are highly valued. Leaders of gravitas additionally expressed the need to build and establish trust when working with constituents' PWIs where diversity is marginalized or increasing, as well as when working with other partners with whom they do not share an affinity.

Finally, these leaders often describe themselves as servant leaders who 'give back' to the communities from which they have arisen. It is clear from the research considered that leaders with grit and gravitas are needed in order to cultivate inclusive and culturally sustaining leadership at all levels within higher education. These leaders do so by following the letter of the law as well as following through with courageous actions through their identity and agency in order to positively influence a more effective redistribution of power in higher education.

Scholarly Approach Taken

This chapter builds on tested and innovative research methodology employed by Santamaría and Jean-Marie (2014) and Santamaría and Santamaría (2016) promoting the use of conceptual inquiry as a viable research design. Utilizing this qualitative methodological approach, the authors entered into critical discussions bridging educational leadership with inclusion and diversity issues specific to higher education. More specifically, research analyzed for this contribution applies the characteristics identified in applied critical leadership research (stereotype threat, group consensus, trust with mainstream, critical conversations, critical lenses, honoring constituents, academic discourse, leading by example, and servant leadership) in order to yield results to further inform higher education where diversity and inclusion are major areas of concern.

Data Sources

Over the course of a semester, the authors, through the process of conceptual inquiry, engaged in critical discourse and analysis regarding their own research undertaken in higher education contexts, inquiry processes, and a growing body of extant research findings to identify interdisciplinary themes and relationships connecting applied critical leadership to inclusion and diversity in higher education. Data sources included 13 case studies featuring 25 educational leaders in positions ranging from Director, to Dean, to Program Leader, to Professor each situated in a variety of higher education settings (e.g., research intensive, teaching university, student center). Eight of these case studies were based in the US, four in New Zealand, complemented by one comparative international study featuring post-secondary students in Canada, Australia, Spain, and South Africa.

Mode of Inquiry and Analysis

We utilized aspects of applied critical leadership as a dynamic working framework to examine data previously collected through 13 qualitative case studies of educational leadership in diverse higher education settings in the United States and similar countries (Santamaría and Santamaría, 2012). The case studies included were primarily analyzed for evidence of the leaders' cultivation of inclusionary practices as well as the intersection of these practices with different kinds of diversity using the constant comparative method (Glaser, 1965). Elements of grit and gravitas were also sought through the tested lens of applied critical leadership as a conceptual frame. Finally, themes were discussed in order to shed light on culturally sustaining leadership practices.

Salient Culturally Sustaining and Inclusive Educational Leadership Practices

Following an analysis of the unique, and oftentimes very different, case studies under consideration, it was determined that each case exhibited a particular diversity representative of the context featured worthy of exploration, as well as the grit and gravitas discussed in this chapter. Table 11.1 reflects each case for location and type of diversity addressed, the leader role and identity, and evidence of commitment with examples of inclusionary leadership practice. The table includes aspects of grit and gravitas as aligned with aspects of applied critical leadership in parentheses. All case study institutions are predominantly white, meaning the majority of students in attendance are White (of European descent) representing the middle-class or mainstream, with the exception of the university in South Africa where the majority of the student body is Black South African. Each university offers some semblance of services for students with special needs, culture-based student centers/supports, women's centers, and LGBTQI Centers. Still for each, there is evidence that students who are not White and are not representative of the mainstream population are systemically and institutionally underserved (e.g. successful application, admission, matriculation, and graduation) and in need of inclusionary and culturally sustaining leadership as a result.

Examples provided ranged from service as advisor for marginalized student and faculty groups, to the facilitation of social justice and equity discussion among constituents from different cultural, linguistic or social groups, to integrating indigenous methodologies when working with students first in their families to attend university, as well as others recorded in the table. Each exemplar further illustrated what is suggested as the presence of grit and gravitas through the framework of applied critical leadership exhibited by the educational leaders involved. These are indicated in parentheses in the table.

The sections following provide evidence of shared, culturally sustaining practices across cases of inclusionary leadership. These also include patterns of leader grit and gravitas found in teaching, research, service, and administration in the institutions considered.

Teaching

Many of the academic leaders presented in the data, even professional staff members, were involved directly in teaching coursework to students in bachelor's, master's level, and doctoral programs. Curriculum taught was often centered on leadership and issues related to diversity in educational contexts. Because of this, the leaders were compelled to remain knowledgeable on topics such as Universal Design, inclusionary practices in higher education, and legal policies, procedures, and implications associated with diversity.

Exemplars of Grit or Gravitas in the Inclusive Tertiary Classroom

Research findings indicate that, when teaching, the leaders included often made a case for diversity to students, stressing that it is compelling and in need of attention in the 21st century. They often used current events, demographics, and test scores citing accountability measures to make their point. Others, particularly those in California and New Zealand, grounded their classroom instruction and critical conversations within socio-historical contexts in attempts to make curriculum more relevant to learners. Data revealed these academics made it a common practice to 'see the world through others' and their students' eyes in order to interact and adjust their teaching appropriately. These leaders were careful to adjust and differentiate their thinking and expectations of students' ability to engage with the content in a manner to refute commonly held stereotypes about particular groups. Leaders were also careful not to fulfill or exhibit common stereotypes associated with aspects of their own identities whilst teaching. Rather, they drew on positive aspects of their identities while, at the same time, presenting material that often went counter to commonly held stereotypes expected for particular groups. For example, a few participants of Mexican descent communicated that they were always careful to be present and to begin class on time to counter beliefs that Latino/as run late or are laid back. Others discussed dressing professionally or speaking articulately using 'good' English to counter stereotypes about people of color and immigrants. Finally, those who exhibited inclusionary leadership practice in teaching were looking to achieve academic success for underserved students as well as all of the students in their classrooms. One Māori academic said it best by emphasizing that, if her Māori students are able to achieve success, she was confident other students in her course would also be as successful (if not more so) as a result of her differentiated and culturally inclusive teaching practices. She was not satisfied with academic achievement unless all students achieved success.

Research

Scholarly activity was the norm for all of the participants in each case study considered, however, there was considerably more funding for those leaders in research intensive (RI) institutions. Incidentally, these institutions had less cultural and linguistic diversity in their student body by virtue of more stringent admissions policies. Much of the research undertaken by leaders engaged in inclusionary and culturally sustaining leadership practice was comprised of studies toward improved practices regarding educational needs resulting in reciprocal research giving back to underserved communities supporting their students' success. It is important to note that, regardless of whether leaders were from RI institutions, every leader featured in this chapter "made empirical contributions adding research-based information to academic discourse regarding underserved groups" (Santamaría and Santamaría, 2012, p. 82). Some of the leaders were students involved in conducting research as part of their doctoral studies while others were academics conducting research as part of their publication expectations.

Exemplars of Grit or Gravitas in Inclusive Research

Data indicated that much of the research carried out by the leaders in this study was conducted through highly collaborative research teams. As such, consensus was ingrained as common practice in many of the important decisions made regarding aspects of research such as methodology, ethics procedures, participants included, analyses, and publication/dissemination activities. Making sure that all of the voices of all of the researchers, including students and colleagues without tenure, were included in research actions was of importance to the researchers involved. Working together with individuals from diverse backgrounds with different perspectives and life experiences required a considerable amount of trust-building among the research teams. Being present and willing to commit to the research for extended periods of time was imperative for those involved. Because much of the research was centered on issues of social justice, educational equity, inclusion, or culturally appropriate practices, the topics were not always popular nor were they well funded. The data revealed that many of the researchers became involved because of their commitment to improving education and providing a voice for those who had been historically voiceless.

Service

Other activities academics and professional staff engage in, but are not specific to research, for teaching are often categorized as 'service'. Some institutions of higher learning consider democratic participation such as meeting attendance, leadership, and supporting student groups as service. This may be true for academic staff, however, it is important to recognize that most professional staff participate in service-rich activities as part of their regular day and administrative duties or expectations.

Exemplars of Grit or Gravitas in Inclusive Service

Deans and directors in student affairs, as one example, who serve as faculty advisors and student advisors in cultural centers, often find themselves engaged in critical conversations on the inclusion of marginalized learners within higher education contexts as part of their work. These individuals are hard pressed to not take a critical stance when making important decisions. This is not to say that academics do not often engage in service of this nature, as the data suggests that several of the leaders in the studies considered also worked with students as faculty advisors for cultural, women's, and LGBTQI centers. Additionally, some presented keynote speeches and conference presentations promoting the benefits of inclusion as the desired norm for students attending universities. Again, serving the greater good by working to benefit specific groups as well as mainstream constituencies, these leaders worked hard on themselves, as well as on behalf of others, to improve educational and social experiences and outcomes for as many students and colleagues as possible.

Further Evidence of Inclusive Culturally Sustainable Leadership

Applied critical leadership (ACL) is one way in which to think about grit and gravitas as desirable characteristics of educational leaders who promote inclusivity and cultural sustainability through their practice. Table 11.1 reflected some examples of these intersections in the last column. Using ACL as a conceptual frame, Table 11.2 provides additional evidence integrating the leaders' reflections on their practice and ways in which they cultivated inclusive leadership. The table is not exhaustive but contributes to a model for thinking about more appropriate and culturally sustaining leadership practices for an increasingly diverse society.

The voices of each leader presented provide strategies that leaders in diverse contexts can adopt and adapt to meet their needs. These participants referenced working together, fighting against injustice, and working in inclusionary ways that are authentic to not only themselves, but also the students they serve. They each spoke about using alliances strategically in order to strengthen and redistribute power, as well as commitment to the educational improvement of all learners. These leaders worked tirelessly toward change and unveiling 'hidden curriculum' which often remains a mystery to educationally and socially excluded learners (Santamaría and Santamaría, 2012; 2016; Santamaría, et al., 2016).

Final Thoughts Moving into the Future of Educational Leadership in Higher Education

In this chapter we have made the case for thinking about inclusion and diversity separately and together in order to better understand each construct to advance leadership practices in higher education for socially and educationally underserved learners, indeed for all students in tertiary institutions. We have identified theory and literature undergirding inclusive leadership for diverse societies across the globe and provided examples of what it takes to cultivate and provide inclusionary leadership in a variety of settings. A case has been made for developing a new model for inclusive educational leadership, but we are not sure a new model is needed. Educational leaders can look to existing data as presented here, as well as research-based tenets of applied critical leadership (Santamaría and Santamaría, 2012; 2016) and a moral leadership imperative (Fullan, 2003), complemented by Argyris and Schön's (1974) theories of action for direction. We encourage 21st century leaders and future-minded leaders promoting inclusion in increasingly and in increasingly complex, diverse societies to reflectively look inward to identify, understand, and/or realign their own values, beliefs, and assumptions prior to looking outward toward inclusionary leadership practice.

More specifically, in the data presented in this chapter, leaders who promote inclusion in universities from the United States, to Canada, to South Africa, to Australia, and to New Zealand, do so from a critical stance and a perspective based on their own personal experiences with diversity as a moral imperative toward social justice in the face of inequity. We argue that the reason policies rarely impact practice is because leaders' individual 'espoused theories' (what they think they do and their 'theories-in-use', or what really occurs) are grossly misaligned (Argyris and Schön, 1974). This is the same case for legal diversity policies that do not result in inclusionary practices. Individuals in leadership roles need to examine their hearts, their motivations and intentions, and engage in interrupting the ways in which they have been raised and taught to think in order to change their practice to become increasingly able to lead in diverse contexts (see Santamaría, Santamaría, and Jeffries, 2016). To change institutional culture and render it more inclusive and culturally sustaining, as the leaders in each case study featured here have, leaders need to recognize inequities, interrupt them, and engage in leadership practices such as applied critical leadership that are reparative and transformative in nature. Taking a cue from the data considered, and drawing on the most positive aspects of their identities, we suggest educational leaders in higher education do this work within themselves prior to (or at the same time as) engaging in inclusionary leadership practices within small affinity group contexts; to establish allies and a core community before taking the work into broader arenas. The journey, we propose, is a long and arduous one, but well worth the work and the wait. Like anything else, changing the hearts and minds of those serving and leading in higher education will take time. We assert that grit and gravitas, characteristics embodied by the diverse array of inclusive and culturally sustaining leaders in this chapter, are needed to ensure that the journey we embark on leads us in the right direction. After all, as the Hopi American Indian elders have shared, we are the ones we have been waiting for.

Note

1 Movimiento Estudiantil Chicana/Chicano de Aztlan – a national student organization that invites all Chicana/o students in their quest to enhance the development of their society.

References

Archer, L., Hutchings, M., and Ross, A., 2005. *Higher education and social class: Issues of exclusion and inclusion*. London: Routledge.

Argyris, C. and Schön, D.A., 1974. *Theory into practice: Increasing professional effectiveness*. San Francisco, CA: Jossey-Bass.

Bell, A., Wolfgramm-Foliaki, E., Airini, Kelly-Laubscher, R., Paxton, M., Pukepuke, T., and Santamaría, L. J. 2016. Together to the table: Applying critical leadership in cross-cultural, international research. In: Santamaría, L. J. and Santamaría, A. P., eds. *Culturally responsive leadership in higher education: Promoting access, equity, and improvement*. New York: Routledge, pp. 106–119.

Dauod, A., 2016. From ideas to actions: Institutionalizing diversity, social justice and equity efforts. In: Santamaría, L. J. and Santamaría, A. P., eds. *Culturally responsive leadership in higher education: Promoting access, equity, and improvement*. New York: Routledge, pp. 180–193.

Fullan, M., ed., 2003. *The moral imperative of school leadership*. Thousand Oaks, CA: Corwin Press.

Gidley, J. M., Hampson, G. P., Wheeler, L., and Bereded-Samuel, E., 2010. From access to success: An integrated approach to quality higher education informed by social inclusion theory and practice. *Higher Education Policy*, 23(1), pp. 123–147.

Glaser, B. G., 1965. The constant comparative method of qualitative analysis. *Social Problems*, 12(4), pp. 436–445.

Gurin, P., Dey, E., Hurtado, S., and Gurin, G., 2002. Diversity and higher education: Theory and impact on educational outcomes. *Harvard Educational Review*, 72(3), pp. 330–367.

Paris, D., 2012. Culturally sustaining pedagogy: A needed change in stance, terminology, and practice. *Educational Researcher*, 41(3), pp. 93–97.

Paris, D. and Alim, H. S., 2014. What are we seeking to sustain through culturally sustaining pedagogy? A loving critique forward. *Harvard Educational Review*, 84(1), pp. 85–100.

Santamaría, A. P., Webber, M., Santamaría, L. J., Dam, I. L., and Jayavant, S., 2016. Te Ara Hou–A new pathway for leading Māori success as Māori. *Evaluation Matters–He Take Tō Te Aromatawai*, 2, pp. 99–129.

Santamaría, L. J., 2015. Culturally responsive educational leadership in cross-cultural international contexts. In: Erbe, N. D. and Normore, A. H., eds. *Cross-cultural collaboration and leadership in modern organizations*. Hershey, PA: IGI Global, pp. 120–139.

Santamaría, L. J., (in press) Theories of educational leadership. *Oxford bibliographies*. Oxford: Oxford University Press.

Santamaría, L. J. and Jean-Marie, G., 2014. Cross-cultural dimensions of applied, critical, and transformational leadership: Women principals advancing social justice and educational equity. *Cambridge Educational Journal*, 44(3), pp. 333–360.

Santamaría, L. J. and Santamaría, A. P., 2012. *Applied critical leadership: Choosing change*. New York: Routledge.

Santamaría, L. J. and Santamaría, A. P., eds. 2016. *Culturally responsive leadership in higher education: Promoting access, equity, and improvement*. New York: Routledge.

Santamaría, L. J., Lee, J., and Harker, N., 2014. Optimising Maori academic achievement (OMAA): An Indigenous led, international, inter-institutional higher education initiative. In: Cram, F., Phillips, H., Sauni, P., and Tuagalu, C., eds. *Maori and Pasifika Higher Education Horizons*. Bingley, UK: Emerald Books, pp. 201–220.

Santamaría, L. J., Santamaría, A. P., and Jeffries, J., 2016. Unpacking hidden institutional culture: Strategy for gaining access to the leadership pipeline. In: Santamaría, L. J. and

Santamaría, A. P., eds. *Culturally responsive leadership in higher education: Promoting access, equity, and improvement.* New York: Routledge, pp. 17–30.

Santamaría, L. J., Santamaría, A. P., Webber, M., and Pearson, H., 2014. Indigenous urban school leadership (IUSL): A critical cross-cultural comparative analysis of educational leaders in New Zealand and the United States. *Comparative and International Education (CIE)*, 43(1), pp. 1–21.

Santamaría, L. J., Santamaría, A. P., Webber, M., and Pearson, H., 2015. Ethnicity, embodiment, and educational leadership: Indigenous and multicultural perspectives in Aotearoa-New Zealand and the United States. In: Fitzpatrick, K. and O'Connor, P., eds. *Embodiment and education.* University of Auckland Faculty of Education Research Monograph. Melbourne, VIC: Pearson Books, pp. 91–114.

Silver, P., Bourke, A., and Strehorn, K. C., 1998. Universal instructional design in higher education: An approach for inclusion. *Equity & Excellence in Education*, 31(2), pp. 47–51.

Stiemke, K. and Santamaría, L. J., 2016. Hope remains: Barrier transcendence, access, and opportunity in higher education. In: Santamaría, L. J. and Santamaría, A. P., eds. *Culturally responsive leadership in higher education: Promoting access, equity, and improvement.* New York: Routledge, pp. 76–92.

Tienda, M., 2013. Diversity ≠ inclusion: Promoting integration in higher education. *Educational Researcher*, 42(9), pp. 467–475.

Travers, S., Welch, E. F., and del Peña, E. A., 2016. Social justice leadership: Silos to synergies. In: Santamaría, L. J. and Santamaría, A. P., eds. *Culturally responsive leadership in higher education: Promoting access, equity, and improvement.* New York: Routledge, pp. 194–207.

Wolfgramm-Foliaki, E., 2016. "Do not assume we know": Perspectives of Pacific Island first in family students. In: Santamaría, L. J. and Santamaría, A. P., eds. *Culturally responsive leadership in higher education: Promoting access, equity, and improvement.* New York: Routledge, pp. 123–135.

Zavala, M. and Tran, N. A., 2016. Negotiating identities, locations and creating spaces of hope for advancing students of color in university settings. In: Santamaría, L. J. and Santamaría, A.P., eds. *Culturally responsive leadership in higher education: Promoting access, equity, and improvement.* New York: Routledge, pp. 93–105.

12

INCLUSIVE INSTITUTIONAL LEADERSHIP THROUGH COMMUNITY ENGAGEMENT

John P. Anchan

Introduction

The relationship between a university community and surrounding, external communities varies from one institution to another. This chapter will present an argument that the degree and success of an institution's inclusivity and commitment to the community depends on an involving process that entails a multi-dimensional spectrum of participants – from the President to the front-line staff. With the support of the community-at-large and the university community (students, staff, faculty, and administrators), purposeful strategic planning that is built upon genuine participation and meaningful measures can allow any institution to create an inclusive culture promoting successful community engagement. The leadership required to achieve the goal of an inclusive learning organization is not vested in a heroic individual, rather it requires leadership and leaderful behaviors to be promoted, valued, and modelled across the entire enterprise.

Increasingly, post-secondary institutions have special relationships with their surrounding communities. Although the nature of these may vary between institutions and even among countries, there has been a positive move towards acknowledging the need to further strengthen such relationships (Anchan, 2010). Besides the moral and ethical commitment, public universities are non-profit organizations that have responsibilities beyond the academic communities. Yet, the success of an institution's inclusivity strategy and commitment to the community is subject to the overall commitment of the institution – from the senior administration to the front-line staff. The success of such community relationships is dependent on inclusivity during planning, implementation, and evaluation phases. Universities have been considered as relatively elitist institutions, where only those who can afford the luxury of higher education can be found

(Blessinger and Anchan, 2015). Especially in the case of inner-city universities, the disparity between a campus community and the surrounding low-socio-economic communities can be quite evident. Many universities and schools around the world have initiated special projects to address this issue (Olowu, 2012; Martinez *et al.*, 2013; Hopson, Miller, and Lovelace, 2016). One question for us to address is: How can institutions genuinely address inequality and create an inclusivity that provides some of its unique benefits to the surrounding communities? Traditionally, the notion of 'inclusion' is understood as including community activities to showcase the 'other side of privilege'. Even K–12 schools have begun to recognize this aspect of community engagement. According to Curcic *et al.* (2011): "studies have been conducted on the role of public schools in relation to their responsibilities to surrounding communities" (p. 133). More research has been carried out in this area of interest in a range of universities that have subsequently offered different models for implementation and different ways to evaluate the success of university–community projects (Duke and Moss, 2009; Shannon and Wang, 2010; Coetzee, 2012).

Structural inequities and injustice are seldom addressed through seasonal cultural showcasing or inclusion of activities that may translate into mere tokenism. Addressing the issues involves going beyond the superfluity of ubiquitous diversity celebrations. Despite sincere attempts, many such festivities can seem to function as the introduction of the exotic 'Other', a term popularized by Edward Said (1979) in his classic book, *Orientalism*. It is akin to a museum of esoteric presentations that subjectivizes the 'alien' as a 'dysfunctional difference' from the dominant accepted norms. Addressing incongruities in the system can only happen when the underlying traditional assumptions are challenged. In fact, the notion of what I call the 'representation game' of including token individuals without addressing the underlying assumptions could only further perpetuate tensions. Similarly, inclusion of some at the exclusion of others can only cause further dysfunctionality. One might be reminded of Freire's famous argument that, if rectification of injustices entails the oppressor being oppressed – or in this case, a perceived dominant/existing culture being replaced by another without concern for those who are being displaced – it merely perpetuates inequality in a different form (Freire, 1986). A good example is where many mainstream or common traditional festivals are curtailed due to political correctness and yet, this is followed by the introduction of new and different festivals. This is a sure recipe for antagonizing the now newly excluded culture!

More recently, a welcome change occurred when a university added a number of religious festivals in its calendar to recognize celebrations of various religions. This would serve as an appropriate university guide to allow students' requests for alternate assignments and accommodation of routine classroom activities. Unfortunately, the university excluded the more commonly celebrated Christmas to avoid offending those who did not celebrate this tradition. Understandably, this created a furore among those who were now being excluded; Christmas was replaced by other, new religious celebrations. The space for such contestation under the premise of equality and fairness tends to ignore token changes made without planning. This is an example of how not to address inequality: thoughtless policies implemented without careful analyses. Unless an existing practice is unfair or inappropriate, inclusion should never imply replacing one for another. The introduction of commonly understood issues surrounding human rights, diversity, and equity and so on are less problematic compared to the introduction of one religious practice that replaces another. Inclusion by exclusion can lead only to dissension and friction.

While we may be tempted to think of dualities, top-down vs. grassroots for example, complex humans make societies. A leadership that recognizes this can engage beyond these two-directional schemes. In fact, a committed leadership is critical to successful university and community engagement (Gunasekara, 2004; Bernardo, Butcher, and Howard, 2014). One needs to consider the barriers that affect university and community relationships before embarking upon such civic engagements (Cherry and Shefner, 2004). The success of a cultural shift is dependent upon the players or, to use the much bandied-about term the 'stakeholders', who are affected by those changes. If true change is to occur, it needs to be purposeful, meaningful, and relevant to those who will be affected by the change (Polyzoi, Fullan, and Anchan, 2003; Schwartz et al., 2016). The task of understanding change is by no means a simple one. Change is a complex process involving the interaction of multiple variables (including unit of analyses, the nation's history, politics, economics, and many others). But, another (more profound and subtle) reason exists for the difficulty: our understanding is conditioned inescapably by our own subjectivity. Nevertheless, in the case of extraneous structural changes beyond immediate personal impact, the university community tends to be more adaptable and understanding than the community-at-large. It is the place where new ideas are formed based on informed discourse and polemics. It is the locale that nurtures the dialectic to challenge existing structural and systemic inequities. The institutions of higher education are better venues, offering freedom to engage in critical thinking and resistance to stagnation. Many creative changes can occur with insightful leadership and a receptive academic community. Change can be extremely difficult without the active participation of this academic community.

The Idea of Community

A brief interrogation of the term 'community' will help this discourse before we consider community or communities as discussed in this chapter. The term is understood within a given context. While there have been many attempts to capture the essence of a community, the definition by Frank and Smith (1999) seems to provide a good balance: "Community development is the planned evolution of all aspects of community well-being (economic, social, environmental and cultural). It is a process whereby community members come together to take collective action and generate solutions to common problems" (p. 6). As a 'grassroots' movement, communities become more responsible to organize and plan together and develop healthy options even as they empower themselves. According to Frank and Smith (1999), such an act attempts to reduce ignorance, poverty, and suffering. It not only creates employment and economic opportunities but also achieves social, economic, cultural, and environmental goals (p. 6). Similarly, Singh (1982) defines community development as the "efforts of people of a locality to help themselves, irrespective of caste, creed and socioeconomic differences ... [It] signifies people's joint efforts to develop an arena which is common to all" (p. 20). Taken together these definitions or articulations of the meaning of community development imply 'growth' and this term in itself needs to be seen in its widest sense. As growth may not always be considered 'desirable' or 'better', development may also mean 'change' for the better. Thus, community development usually occurs in response to challenges and opportunities and aims at capacity building.

Most definitions of community development allude to conscious collaboration efforts towards emancipation and amelioration. In fact, the focus of any such initiative differs between an industrialized country and a developing country. For example, traditionally, community development in rural India has attempted to address common concerns surrounding basic human needs including farming, food, worker's rights or equity, literacy, and health (Dore and Mars 1981, pp. 245–334). In Canada and other more industrialized countries, community development has aimed to address issues of access, equity, participation, literacy, adult education, health, and social services.

The role of community development in a nation's growth has been acknowledged by many experts. As Chekki (1979) notes, "community development has been one of the most significant social forces in the process of change" (p. 2). Community development meant many things to different people: economic development, social reformation, housing and education, philosophical and political movements, and organized collective initiatives. The Marxian and neo-Marxian politics – including the Liberation Theology movement – adopted community development within the framework of the organized labor movement. Eventually, community development became a vital component of the volunteer sector.

Within the movement of empowerment pedagogy, Paulo Freire the aforementioned Brazilian educator, occupies an important historical position as a social activist. Having defined the 'literacy-conscientization' movement among the Brazilian farmers, the Freirean 'conscientization' and critical theory addressed adult literacy education toward liberation and empowerment. This in essence, saw a strong relationship between organized political movements and community development. The Freirean process involved dialogue, awareness, mobilization, empowerment, and liberation. Banks (in Campfens, 1977) describes a project at a university and differentiates between applied vs. engaged research (p. 113). In fact, the differentiation is essentially akin to the debate between empirical, positivistic, traditional 'expert' research on community vs. participatory, ethnographic, action research borne out of a phenomenological approach to situational experience that entails research with the community.

So, how can there be a successful transformation of institutional policies and structures? What are some sample initiatives and how have they influenced the institutional culture? The following three points are intended to serve as a brief backdrop to a detailed case study in the Model University (MU).

Inclusivity of the affected: There is no better approach to understanding issues of a given nature than to include the affected in the actual policy-making exercise. This means that individuals from affected or marginalized groups need to be at the table. The leadership needs to reflect the reality in that decision-makers include those who are affected. Institutions with leaders who hail from the affected segments of the population tend to better understand the needs of such marginalized communities and are able to reach out to such groups (Rayner, 2009).

Inclusivity of the neighborhood: Including the surrounding communities. In some sense, downtown universities are privileged to connect with the surrounding communities and engage them by inviting them to use the campus facilities, serve on appropriate committees, offering programming that benefits such communities (Azzopardi, 2011). Beyond the issue of sharing access to facilities, the university is privileged to have experts in the area who can produce original knowledge on various issues relevant to community needs (Morris *et al.*, 2011). Encouraging faculty research to address the needs of the inner city through research involving members in the community can benefit residents of the inner city. As Mendes *et al.* (2014) argue, university researchers have a strong role to play in community development initiatives (p. 173).

Inclusivity through inclusion: One of the most important aspects of a successful initiative entails support from all levels – from the highest official of the institution to the frontline staff. This would mean that students should always serve an integral part of such changes (Carey, 2016).

The Model University[1]

Consider the various initiatives at Model University. The highly capable and qualified head of the institution is a female from a traditionally under-represented group. The Model University (MU) has a dedicated aboriginal educational program to encourage aboriginal, low socioeconomic status (SES) and other marginalized students to earn their degree in Education. These graduates have overcome formidable barriers in their individual trajectories such as crime, addiction, violence, linguistic challenges, poverty, etc.

Many are single, unemployed mothers with dreams and amazing resilience. Some are highly gifted males but from high-risk environments. Schooling is not their strength and many have simply fallen through the cracks. This Education program is not a lower quality, less rigorous, cheaper alternative. As a part of the main campus faculty, programming and instructors are from the regular stream with the same evaluating procedures. The only difference is a better student–teacher ratio along with added support for teaching and learning activities for students who may not be familiar with the usual university challenges. The success rate has been consistently high with 70–80 percent of graduates being hired by the mainstream public school system. Parallel to this program is the MU center for aboriginal students, which provides additional support to ensure that students are not burdened by bureaucratic challenges. This center also allows culturally sensitive and appropriate programming. The MU has a senior Associate Vice-President for aboriginal programming. This affirms that there is a conscious and sincere effort in the leadership to ensure that the initiatives are successful. It also implies designated funds to support these programs. MU also has a model school that caters to high-risk youth, especially from the inner city. Besides the regular support system for students, this unit also offers summer programming to keep the youth engaged in constructive projects. Talent development among special needs and gifted students is also part of the campus programming.

Community programming is a high priority at MU. This includes language classes for newcomers who may not be proficient in English and cultural support for newcomers to acquire the necessary skills for success in a new and foreign environment. Connecting with the immediate community has also been a high priority for MU. Some of the newer infrastructure built in the more recent past includes community groups on the advisory board and a Community Charter has been established to ensure ongoing access to immediate community. As a public institution, MU is now a hosting partner for inner-city groups. This is especially obvious in the area of sports. Inner-city kids from underprivileged backgrounds are now allowed to feel at home on the MU campus. They get access to the sports centre and other MU facilities. MU also has free programming for seniors in the city. These programs allow retired and other seniors to attend sessions of interest. MU also has faculty members presenting lectures at a number of seniors' residences in the city. The participation in these initiatives has been a resounding success. Another seasonal annual enterprise involves the summer camps for inner-city children and youth. This project addresses the issue of many low SES parents not being able to afford daycare or safe and productive activities for their children during the summer.

MU has critical arrangements with the aboriginal elders within the community. Students in specific programs are able to visit various autochthonous bands and learn from aboriginal cultures. Service Learning is another area in which the MU Education program allows students to work with community and non-profit organizations in various parts of the city. Service Learning has the tremendous potential to be both pedagogy and an agent of change. Many studies have explored the benefits of Service Learning (Vickers, Harris, and McCarthy, 2004). In fact, besides the faculty and the university in general, both students and the community have benefited enormously from such joint programs (Chupp and Joseph, 2010). Receiving course credits, student-teachers pick community organizations of their choice and work with experienced mentors. Some students also get to be mentored by instructors working in the government correctional services housing high-risk offenders. This allows students to experience another part of the population within a controlled setting. All these initiatives aim towards inclusivity of diverse populations – either as participants or observers. It also engages various community stakeholders in the life of MU.

MU also has a dedicated department focusing on inner-city/urban housing. This unit also conducts research on rural and other remote housing challenges. The research findings of the unit allow government to make informed and rational decisions in the urban planning of the city.

One of the most exciting major initiatives that has taken on a high-profile national momentum is the mandatory aboriginal course requirement spanning all faculties and departments. Irrespective of the program, all MU students now have a half-credit course requirement that sensitizes them to aboriginal histories and cultures. Just like diversity programming being infused into many courses, the mandatory course requirement is a jumpstart to programming for institutions that are essentially built on indigenous treaty lands. Many Canadian universities have now moved towards requiring all students across programs and faculties to take mandatory courses in aboriginal histories (Macdonald, 2015). As the institutions are built on Aboriginal Treaty lands, the MU President and other university heads now open convocation events with this public acknowledgement. More recently, MU convocations have begun with the traditional bagpipes and concluded with the aboriginal drummers. What a wonderful sea of change that goes beyond the historically perverse theme of a country being founded by two cultures/nations (English and French) – traditionally ignoring the existence of the now displaced indigenous peoples. With continued support and participation of the leadership, higher education institutions are serving as examples for tomorrow.

In common with other educational institutions around the country, MU is a part of the national research ethics initiative that requires research projects to abide by stringent regulations involving human subjects. This is especially useful in guarding research that involves communities. The question to ask is whether universities are mainly required to study communities without giving anything in return or is there a moral responsibility to not only engage, but also involve, the communities toward improving their lives? This may entail conducting 'research with' rather than 'research on' communities. For example, this may also involve more ethnological and phenomenological empowerment research such as action research and oral histories among aboriginal communities.

Education is a public enterprise for the common good. What good is education if the community-at-large does not benefit from public institutions that are mostly funded by taxpayers' dollars? Does the ultimate goal of research enhance the lives of communities in general or is it only a few elite students gaining from such public service? What are the responsibilities of a post-secondary institution? Indeed, they are not set up as community organizations that are required to directly address homelessness or other such issues as various government units are tasked to do this. Unfortunately, some post-secondary institutions have taken on too many community projects at the cost of their core academic programming. This is the other extreme. A good balance is required to address community needs through sound research without sacrificing public responsibility over personal interests.

This discussion does not consider 'community' as the immediate environs of an institution. A community can be the surrounding populations or even beyond. It could even mean international communities. In a global community, we are connected beyond traditional and national boundaries. What affects people in Thailand might, and usually will, affect people in Alaska. Whether it is environment, natural resources, migration, politics, economics, commerce, disasters, or human turmoil: what occurs in one part of the world eventually affects the rest. One cannot ignore the events in any given part of the world. We are intertwined in McLuhan and Lapham's (1994) 'global village' and world communities are linked to each other in one way or another. So, at the global level, how can we be inclusive of international communities?

Not unlike other educational institutions in the country, MU has many international practicum placements for students in the Faculty of Education who would want to be culturally enriched during their teaching practice. These placements in the Far East, Europe, Latin America, South America, Middle East, South Asia, and other parts of the world allow students to spend anywhere between six weeks and ten months living and working with educators and students in these countries. The experiences allow our future educators to become culturally sensitized and enriched global citizens. With increased international migration, many schools in the country are highly multicultural and the classrooms are truly global.

Whether it is a school in Brazil or one down the street, successful educators need to be able to teach within this diversity. Institutions that have forward-thinking leadership will encourage such inclusive education.

One main aspect of successful community engagement projects is the evaluation phase. Many deficiencies can be addressed by being proactive and establishing clear evaluation guidelines. Issues of gaps and other limitations must be considered even before planning such projects (Mbah, 2016).

As to the intervention of universities in community development, back in 1976, Marshall and Miller conducted a pilot extension project involving universities and communities. The report concluded that the project was only partially successful. The exercise involved participation of faculty in research and engagement, an overall revision of the university philosophy, and purposeful participation. This study concluded that university resources and management of community development initiatives required planned coordination and commitment from all levels of the institution. Conversely, unclear power and decision-making structures created impediments resulting in confusion and conflict. Universities have consistently challenged issues surrounding workload and primary responsibilities of academic scholars. As universities have traditionally been seen as centers of excellence in knowledge production and dissemination, academics have contended that the objectives of community development were only corollary to research and teaching. With decreasing resources, academics have argued the case for primary and core functions over social development.

If there was one recurrent theme in this discussion, it would be the crucial and inclusive role of the leadership in the success of any institutional initiative. As Temple and Ylitalo (2009) argue, "The academic leaders and administrators in different roles and positions are the key figures to enable new cultures and community practices to emerge" (p. 278). Thankfully, this is happening on a more frequent basis and, if the current trend continues, the parochial schooling system may give way to a more open and inclusive educational system. Another aspect of this presentation is to emphasize that there exists a desirable symbiotic relationship that is mutually beneficial for both the university and the community (Buys and Bursnall, 2007). Such partnerships empower both partners in the ultimate goal of true and purposeful education.

The university and community relationship spearheaded by inclusive leadership can serve as a powerful agent of change. In turn, such initiatives also strengthen the leadership *per se* in creating those valuable spaces of collaboration that benefit all participants, including the leadership itself.

Overall, some of the challenges faced by university community outreach programs relate to the cultural, political, and economic realities that impinge upon community development. Irrespective of the various concerns, the success of any extensive initiative is dependent on a consolidated effort involving a centralized university level council transcending departments and disciplines. This would ensure stronger support and participation among faculty and staff members. A clearer and predefined relationship between the university and community may alleviate some of the pitfalls and tensions inherent in such complex projects. Clarification of roles and responsibilities among researchers and community participants and the nature of shared resources will facilitate the process. In other words, a common buyout from the President's office down to the various departments is crucial to make the university community venture a success. Thus, a successful community development initiative needs to be an initiative that involves all levels of academics, university administrators, and active community leaders.

This discussion does not purport to provide irrefragable answers; it rather deals with the possibility of initiating a meaningful inquiry into the process entailing structural relationships between institutions and communities – a phenomenon that defies unproblematic or simplistic explanation. We are in a putative state of cultural sensitivity that serves as the precursor to a more inclusive society. We transition towards a system that does not have to apologize for its citizens unable to believe and practice inclusivity; a society that does not stand accused of ignoring its most affected and least-served marginalized peoples. As a community, it is hoped that we no longer need special programming to represent its new-comers, forgotten peoples, and cultures: a country that places no particular group of people or culture above others.

While it may sound utopian, it behoves us well to pause and look at some of the changes that have occurred over the more recent past. Our increasingly multicultural global classrooms with students and teachers from diverse back-grounds no more represent an illusionary monolithic and some misconceived superior culture. It is the product of a natural evolutionary scheme of develop-ment that recognizes and acknowledges diversity and difference – a reality that represents a tapestry of a fair and conscientious society. Within this scheme of development, it should be a privilege for educational institutions to play an important role in bringing this to fruition.

Note

1 To make this more of an academic discussion and less of a promotional material, the focus has been on the initiatives rather than the institution. Hence, the names of the institution and actual projects have been codified.

References

Anchan, J. P., 2010. Emerging technologies, established communities, and evolving uni-versities. Paper presented at the Sixth Commonwealth Forum on Open Learning. November 24, 2010, Le Meridien, Kochi, India.

Azzopardi, A., 2011. Special issue editorial: creating inclusive communities. *International Journal of Inclusive Education*, 5(1), pp. 1–4.

Bernardo, M. A., Butcher, J., and Howard, P., 2014. The leadership of engagement between university and community: Conceptualizing leadership in community engage-ment in higher education. *International Journal of Leadership in Education*, 17(1), pp. 103–122.

Blessinger, P. and Anchan, J. P., eds, 2015. *Democratizing higher education: International com-parative perspectives*. New York: Routledge, Taylor & Francis Group.

Buys, N. and Bursnall, S., 2007. Establishing university–community partnerships: Processes and benefits. *Journal of Higher Education Policy and Management*, 29(1), pp. 73–86.

Campfens, H., 1977. *Community development in Northern Alberta research report*. Presented to the Commission of Northern Affairs, Government of Manitoba, Canada, October 15, 1972.

Carey, P., 2016. The impact of institutional culture, policy and process on student engagement in university decision-making. *Perspectives: Policy and Practice in Higher Education*, pp.1–8.

Chekki, D., ed., 1979. *Community development: Theory and method of planned change.* New Delhi: Vikas Publishing House Pvt. Ltd.

Cherry, D. J. and Shefner, J., 2004. Addressing barriers to university–community collaboration, organizing by experts or organizing the experts? *Journal of Community Practice*, 12(3–4), pp. 219–233.

Chupp, M. G. and Joseph, M. L., 2010. Getting the most out of service learning: Maximizing student, university and community impact. *Journal of Community Practice*, 18(2–3), pp. 190–212.

Coetzee, E., 2012. Community engagement by higher education institutions: A practical model and guidelines. *Africa Education Review*, 9(3), pp. 501–517.

Curcic, C., Gabela, S. L., Zeitlin, V., Cribaro-DiFatta, S., and Glarner, C., 2011. Policy and challenges of building schools as inclusive communities. *International Journal of Inclusive Education*, 15(1), pp. 117–133.

Dore, R. and Mars, Z., eds. 1981. *Community Development.* Paris: UNESCO.

Duke, J. and Moss, C., 2009. Re-visiting scholarly community engagement in the contemporary research assessment environments of Australasian universities. *Contemporary Nurse*, 32(1–2), pp. 30–41.

Frank, F. and Smith, A., 1999. *The community development handbook.* Ottawa: Minister of Public Works and Government Services Canada, Human Resources Development Canada (HRDC).

Freire, P., 1986. *Pedagogy of the oppressed.* Translated from French by Myra Bergman Ramos. New York: Continuum.

Gunasekara, C., 2004. Universities and communities: A case study of change in the management of a university. *Prometheus*, 22(2), pp. 201–211.

Hopson, R., Miller, P., and Lovelace, T. S., 2016. University–school–community partnership as vehicle for leadership, service, and change: A critical brokerage perspective. *Leadership and Policy in Schools*, 15(1), pp. 26–44.

Macdonald, N., 2015. Making history: Two schools make indigenous courses a requirement for graduation. *Maclean's.* Available at: <http://www.macleans.ca/education/ma king-history-2/> [Accessed November 14, 2016].

McLuhan, M. and Lapham, L. H., 1994. *Understanding media: The extensions of man.* Cambridge, MA: MIT Press.

Marshall, H. P. and Miller, R. W., 1976. *The challenges of a community development role for the public university.* West Virginia: West Virginia University, Office of Research and Development.

Martinez, L. S., Perea, F. C., Ursillo, A., Weeks, F. H., Goldstein-Gelb, W., and Brugge, D., 2013. A democratic university–community administrative body dedicated to expanding community-engaged research: the Tufts Community Research Center (TCRC). *Community Development*, 44(1), pp. 97–110.

Mbah, M. F. (2016). Towards the idea of the interconnected university for sustainable community development. *Higher Education Research & Development*, 35(6), pp. 1228–1241.

Mendes, W., Gingras, J., Robinson, P., and Waddell, J., 2014. Community–university research partnerships: A role for university research centers? *Community Development*, 45(2), pp. 165–179.

Morris, M., Schindehutte, M., Edmonds, V., and Watters, C., 2011. Inner city engagement and the university: Mutuality, emergence and transformation. *Entrepreneurship & Regional Development*, 23(5–6), pp. 287–315.

Olowu, D., 2012. University–community engagement in South Africa: Dilemmas in benchmarking. *South African Review of Sociology*, 43(2), pp. 89–103.

Polyzoi, E., Fullan, M., and Anchan, J. P., eds, 2003. *Change forces in post-communist Eastern Europe: Education in transition*. New York: RoutledgeFalmer.

Rayner, S., 2009. Educational diversity and learning leadership: A proposition, some principles and a model of inclusive leadership? *Educational Review*, 61(4), pp. 433–447.

Said, E. W., 1979. *Orientalism*. Toronto, Canada: Random House of Canada.

Schwartz, K., Weaver, L., Pei, N., and Miller, A. K., 2016. Community–campus partnerships, collective impact, and poverty reduction. *Community Development*, 47(2), pp. 167–180.

Shannon, J. and Wang, T. R., 2010. A model for university–community engagement: Continuing education's role as convener. *The Journal of Continuing Higher Education*, 58 (2), pp. 108–112.

Singh, P., 1982. *Community development programme in India*. New Delhi: Deep & Deep Publications.

Temple, J. B. and Ylitalo, J., 2009. Promoting inclusive (and dialogic) leadership in higher education institutions. *Tertiary Education and Management*, 15(3), pp. 277–289.

Vickers, M., Harris, C., and McCarthy, F., 2004. University–community engagement: Exploring service-learning options within the practicum. *Asia-Pacific Journal of Teacher Education*, 32(2), pp. 129–141.

13

A MULTI-LENS VIEW OF INCLUSIVE LEADERSHIP IN HIGHER EDUCATION

Lorraine Stefani

Ma muaka kite a muri
Ma muri ka ora a mua
Those who lead give sight to those who follow
Those who follow give life to those who lead

Pauline Tangiora, Māori Elder

Introduction

The title of this book, *Inclusive Leadership in Higher Education: International Perspectives and Strategies*, in itself represents no less than three contested terms, 'inclusive', 'leadership' and 'higher education'. Asking the meaning of 'inclusive', for example, will draw out differing conceptions from fairly simplistic definitions such as: "Not excluding any section of society or any party involved in something" (Oxford Dictionary, 2016) to more elaborate descriptions of an inclusive organization, such as:

> Inclusive organisations not only have a diversity of individuals involved but more importantly they are learning-centred organisations that value the perspectives and contributions of all people, and they incorporate the needs, assets and perspectives of all into the design and implementation of universal and inclusive programmes. Furthermore inclusive organisations recruit and retain diverse staff to reflect the racial and ethnic communities they serve.
> *(The Denver Foundation, 2016; www.nonprofitinclusiveness.org/ definitions-inclusiveness-and-inclusive-organisations)*

Imagine if we could genuinely assert that our universities live up to the above definition within their leadership ranks! The leadership distribution would look and feel very different from today; all students would feel welcome and included, as opposed to feeling only that they are part of the organizational diversity; the physical environment would not just be accessible but appropriate to accommodate all needs, physical and emotional.

When we consider defining 'leadership' the task is immensely difficult. There are thousands of books written on the subject of leadership, many with a qualifying adjective such as: authentic, transformational, servant, spiritual, essential and exceptional amongst the plethora. Therefore it is problematic to draw a definition from these books and articles each claiming significant differences from each other. The following definitions and descriptions, drawn from business personnel and academics, may actually bring us closer to a definition or definitions that we can apply to higher education without the inevitable claims of unnecessary jargon being used to describe and identify the processes or enactment of leadership:

> Leadership should be the humble, authentic expression of your unique personality in pursuit of bettering whatever environment you are in.
> *(Katie Christy, Founder, Activate Your Talent, 2016)*

> Leadership is being bold enough to have vision and humble enough to recognize that achieving it will take the efforts of many people, people who are most fulfilled when they share their gifts and talents rather than just work. Leaders create that culture, serve that greater good and let others soar.
> *(Kathy Heasley, Founder and President, Heasley and Partners, 2016)*

> Leadership means using one's influence to guide others in successfully achieving a goal without desire for recognition, without worry of what others think and with awareness of issues external or internal that might change the results sought.
> *(Marie Hansen, Dean of College of Business, Husson University, 2016)*

Interestingly, these definitions of leadership all come from women and tend to emphasize authenticity, humility, the importance of growing others and recognizing and embracing diversity of talent. This differs from 'the great man' ideological theory of leadership which emphasizes:

> 'Great' leaders possess characteristics or traits not found in the rest of the population. This concept is based on the belief that great leaders are not made but born with unique characteristics which allow them to rise to the occasion during difficult periods in history to overcome obstacles and lead their nation (organisation) successfully.
> *(Bennis, 2007)*

The latter quote gives rise to the false conception of leadership as command and control. While this may seem to be caricaturing leadership in the 21st century, the chapters in this book reveal the outstanding gender bias in leadership in higher education today, and the views that men in some cultures have of women in general and women in academia in particular. In a recent interview for *University World News*, US journalist and renowned author Gayle Tzemach Lemmon stated that "really talented leaders are always seen as exceptional. Somehow though, when they are female we see them as aberrations. Oftentimes when they are men we see them as leaders and role models" (Marklein, 2016). The idea of the hero leader is not yet dead – and this applies to higher education too!

It may be no surprise to us that the idea of leadership in higher education is problematic. At this moment in time, there is no consensus on the purpose of higher education. Universities today, particularly in the Western world, are stressing their utilitarian nature – get a degree, get a better job – essentially trumpeting their economic impact. And yet, universities can do more than almost any other institution to improve social mobility and social justice. This is one moral purpose of higher education that we can surely all sign up to. Indeed, many of the chapters in this book show just such a moral purpose coming through inclusive leadership. But it is a significant challenge to build, embed and lead an inclusive culture when the entity you are leading is not quite sure of its purpose.

Harlan Cleveland (1985) suggested that outsiders want students trained for their first job out of university, whereas academics want the student educated for 50 years of self-fulfilment. Students want both. Steven Schwartz, writing in *Times Higher Education* in 2003, argued that the goal of university education is to build a fairer, more just society (Schwartz, 2003). Today, in many Western countries, there has been considerable widening of access to university-level education in comparison to the elitism shown three or four decades ago when only the wealthy could afford to send their children to university. The potential for building a fairer, more just society through widening access was, however, relatively short-lived with student tuition fees soon becoming prohibitively high for many potential students. In addition, governments in developed and developing countries are increasingly pushing an agenda that says the primary purpose of higher education is not to 'nourish the soul' (Schwartz, 2003), rather it is to grow the economy. This in itself is not a completely ridiculous agenda, but a consequence of pushing this prime purpose for higher education is that governments are supporting STEM subjects (science, technology, engineering and mathematics) and withdrawing support from, and thereby diminishing, the liberal arts. This is a sad reality at a time of immense global challenges that require the knowledge, the understanding, the critical thinking that students from all academic disciplines can bring to the table. Graduates from the liberal arts subjects including arts and social sciences are perhaps not as constrained in their thinking as scientists and engineers who are often working for national and multinational companies, for example, who have vested interests in the 'solutions' to 21st century problems.

Taking the title of this book as an overall contested concept, it is little wonder that the chapters from diverse authors and researchers from a range of cultural backgrounds provide us with the material to build a rich tapestry from which to begin to theorize the idea of inclusive leadership in higher education. All contexts are different and this book covers many different cultures. What is patently obvious is that, whatever the context and the culture, inclusion and inclusive leadership are not easily achieved—from perception to reality, inclusion for some means exclusion for others, or is perceived as such. This is not always about doggedness or infatuation with the status quo but about the genuine challenges in complex societies and complex institutions to build inclusive learning environments and the need to be nimble enough in our leadership strategies to adapt to rapidly changing circumstances.

The purpose of this chapter is to delve further into the research and draw on the preceding chapters to ask why it is so difficult for universities to recognize, acknowledge and respect difference; why it is that universities are often so impervious to the existence of de facto forms of institutionalized discrimination that they are unable to recognize the threat that some of their accustomed practices pose to their own existence?

Looking at Leadership in Higher Education Through Different Lenses

Higher education in many countries has had significant change imposed over the past two decades. These changes include a massive increase in audit culture and a subsequent increase in compliance measures imposed on staff, as well as the rise of neo-liberalism and the impact of that on the business culture of institutions with a new focus on revenue generation and free-market principles. At a different level, technology has played a role with a demand from new generations of students wanting more flexibility in the way they study or receive tuition. These changes have impacted on the working culture of institutions but they have not resulted in meaningful, sustainable change to the over-riding culture of higher education, which is essentially exclusive, exclusionary and elitist (Shields, 2016). This might once again seem to be contradictory to the huge push for widening access there has been in many countries which has increased the diversity of the student population. However, a mere cursory glance across the widening-access statistics of different types of universities paints an interesting picture. Elitist, research-led universities have very poor statistics for attracting and retaining students from lower socio-economic groups (Havergal, 2016), suggesting we have not moved on much, certainly within the UK, since Stephen Schwartz made his comments on the moral purpose of higher education in 2003 (n.p.):

> If higher education can be made available to students from diverse backgrounds, it can become an instrument for progress toward egalitarian objectives. Although more women and minority-group members have been to

university in recent years, social equity has thus far proved to be an elusive goal. The government is trying to increase the number of people exposed to higher education. Some academics believe that the target will lower standards. Their opponents argue that current university selectivity favours a social elite.

(Schwartz, 2003)

University leaders have not, on the whole, shown the moral courage to look at their organization and the concept of higher education through lenses which focus on inclusion, equity and social justice. There has not been a push for unbiased policy making and implementation, fairer decision making in recruitment and reward systems, the development of programs and courses that are as inclusive as they possibly can be (Shields, 2016). Without doubt it is going to require leaders in higher education to facilitate the transformation from the current tendency to favor hegemonic cultures and traditional paradigms of leadership and instead, strive towards inclusiveness and the removal of barriers to individuals from diverse identity groups being appointed to meaningful leadership roles (Eagly and Chin, 2010).

Achieving this transformation will not be easy and indeed little research actually exists on the question of how race, ethnicity, gender, sexuality and other 'difference' factors (relative to the hegemonic norm) intersect with identity as a leader. There is also, currently, a resounding silence in the literature on the subject of how the diversity of leaders and followers within an organization influences the enactment of leadership (Eagly and Chin, 2010).

The next section further interrogates the intellectual segregation we see in our institutions as a consequence of our failure to leverage the potential of diversity for the sake of striving towards inclusion and inclusive leadership in higher education.

Diversity and Inclusion are Easy Words to Say

If higher education institutions were committed to producing graduates who would promote social justice and social mobility, it would not be unreasonable to see statements indicating this in university mission statements. If we believed that, through interaction with academics and their own peer groups (i.e., within the whole of the student body at their university of choice), students learn about freedom of expression, tolerance of difference and responsible citizenship (Schwartz, 2003), we might reasonably expect to see difference in leadership being role modelled by these same institutions.

However, just as an example of ongoing homogeneity in senior leadership, a close look at the universities in New Zealand, a small country in the Pacific Ocean and the current place of living and working of this chapter author, will show great diversity in the student population but something of a mono-culture if we look at the highest levels of leadership. New Zealand is both a bi-cultural

country deriving its uniqueness from the history of its indigenous Māori population (Stefani, 2015) and, increasingly, a multi-ethnic society as a consequence of
significant immigration of people from many countries.

At the time of writing this chapter, of the eight universities in New Zealand,
one has a woman Vice Chancellor. The senior leadership teams in the universities
comprise predominantly white males (mostly of European origin), with all of the
universities having a Māori Pro Vice Chancellor or Assistant Vice Chancellor or
similarly named position, only one of them being a woman. The Māori senior
academic position exists because of the Treaty of Waitangi (Treaty of Waitangi,
2016), the encapsulation of the relationship between Māori and Pākehā (non-
Māori settlers) drawn up in 1840, which has implications for a number of New
Zealand policy areas, including education (Stefani, 2015). The mission statements
of most of the New Zealand universities contain statements relating to: inclusiveness and transparency in decision making; inclusivity, diversity and equity; and
respect for all. For example the University of Auckland's (n.d.) online statement
on institutional values includes the following:

> The University is committed to creating a diverse, collegial, scholarly com-
> munity in which individuals are valued and respected; academic freedom is
> exercised with intellectual rigour and high ethical standards; and critical
> enquiry is encouraged.

As a long-standing academic at the University of Auckland, I would contend that,
while it does make serious attempts to be inclusive with respect to the student
body, the efforts are nevertheless directed primarily at 'supporting the learning' of
special groups such as Māori students and students from the Pacific Islands known
as Pacifika, the latter being a significant, well established immigrant population in
New Zealand who, like Māori, have suffered huge levels of disadvantage and
discrimination both in education and in employment opportunities (Stefani,
2015).

Like many universities, particularly in Western countries and perhaps more
especially in countries with significant indigenous populations such as New
Zealand, Australia and Canada, what is on offer in our universities is an established institution with its own long-standing, deeply rooted policies, practices,
programs and standards intended to serve the needs of society. Anyone coming
into these universities, whatever their background and intellectual identity, must
simply adapt to the accepted *modus operandi*. There is very often little of what the
'other', meaning anyone of difference, brings in the way of cultural knowledge,
traditions and core values that is recognized, much less respected (Kirkness and
Barnhardt, 2001). This is, in fact, the subject of much debate in New Zealand
tertiary education relating to the different learning approaches and traditions of
Māori students, as is the issue of approaches to leadership that are held sacred in
the Māori population.

The legal frameworks in many countries will disallow discrimination on the basis of race, color, religion, sex and national origin and there are generally equal opportunity statements on websites, but that does not mean there is no discrimination. Today, discrimination is covert and subtle, less blatant. Generous interpretations might suggest it is unconscious bias at play, but as Eagly and Chin (2010) suggest, stereotypes about a social group are, more often than not, incongruent with the attributes that are deemed to be essential to leadership by those who currently hold the most senior leadership positions. Ideas about leadership are influenced by situations and organizational cultures. In research carried out by Chun and Evans (2011) on administrators' experiences of inclusion in higher education institutions in the USA, their findings affirm the issue of subtle forms of discrimination being alive and well within higher education. They found that the contours of discrimination are remarkably similar irrespective of institutional prestige and geographic location. Staff from 'diversity' groups faced micro-inequities; small, repetitive yet difficult-to-prove acts of exclusion and marginalization and people of difference appear to be judged by different standards.

It is so easy to use the words that are considered to be politically correct, to include them in mission and value statements but the reality is that words in themselves do not convince if we look across our institutions and see a predominantly pale, male and stale picture of leadership. There is relatively little research to date on inclusive leadership in higher education. In general terms our models of leadership are derived from traditional paradigms and have little to say about equity, social justice or diversity and yet, to face the challenges of the 21st century, we need much greater flexibility in our thinking in all organizations – but surely higher education institutions should be taking a lead.

In the preceding sections I have attempted to un-package the contested concepts of 'inclusion', 'leadership' and 'higher education' for the purpose of affirming the challenge we must face if a university-level education is to be meaningful and live up to a noble, moral purpose which should not be too much to expect of higher education in the 21st century – to contribute to better, fairer, more equitable and socially just societies.

The next section asks where we are at today in tackling the complexities of researching inclusive leadership in higher education and reviewing what the chapters in this book contribute to our growing understanding of the journey we must take.

Reaching for Inclusive Leadership in Higher Education

As stated earlier, to date there is a curious lack of published research on leadership in higher education. Adding in the critical dimension of 'inclusive' to leadership we find there is even less to draw upon. One reason for this could be the age-old anecdotal message that leadership in higher education is so very different from leadership in any other type of organization, suggesting, therefore, that researching the topic would defy conventional research methodologies. We see this issue of the uniqueness of leadership in higher education coming through in Fiona Denney's chapter (chapter 6) which is based on research funded by the highly respected Leadership Foundation for Higher Education UK (LFHE, 2016). The LFHE was set up in 2004 and delivers its work through programs and events; institutional advice and consultancy, and research on leadership, management and governance for higher education institutions. It may well be the case that higher education is different from other organizations but this does not actually detract from the case for responsible, inclusive leadership. Denney highlights for us many of the contradictions in leadership in higher education, the lack of preparation, the challenges of revolving positions such as Head of Department and the lack of meaningful enactment of leadership.

There has been a tendency to focus on the issue of women in leadership in higher education and this is not surprising given some of the shocking figures relating to women in the professoriate as shown in Kirsten Locke's chapter (chapter 4) for example. Other highly respected researchers including Susan Madsen and Jana Nidiffer give insights into women in leadership in degree-awarding institutions in the USA. Madsen argues that, while there have, without doubt, been advances such as Harvard University appointing its first woman President in 2007, there has been a level of backsliding in the past decade. Madsen (2012) quotes Nidiffer's article in *Gender and Women's Leadership* (Nidiffer, 2010) in which Nidiffer shows that women have made little or no progress in closing the salary gap with their male counterparts and that many women in senior leadership roles are in less prestigious areas such as student affairs for example. Madsen also points out that it is not just about numbers and percentages of women in senior leadership positions, it is also about the future and current female students seeing role models and realizing that they too can strive to be future leaders. She argues that it is also about the different skill sets women bring to the table.

In a heartening chapter from Cathy Sandeen and colleagues (chapter 2) we read of the challenges for female college and university Presidents, but we also read of the characteristics that the women interviewees for their chapter indicate are critical to effective and successful leadership. These characteristics include: taking a democratic approach; being participative and team oriented; relational inclusiveness; seeking multiple perspectives; being ethical; having high emotional intelligence; and being honest and transparent. It is very interesting to compare this list of inclusive leadership attributes with that drawn up by the Employers Network for Equality and Inclusion (ENEI, 2016) detailed in Fiona Denney's chapter and referenced in that of Eqbal Darandari (chapter 7). While there is certainly overlap, the actual words of the interviewees are authentic and give life and meaning to the terms on a list of inclusive leadership characteristics. What we must be careful of is simply drawing up lists of terms that may fit under the umbrella of inclusive leadership and then taking a mechanistic approach to ticking them off. We need to examine how we might enable the development of these skills, how we might use different approaches in recruitment, for example, to determine whether potential leaders actually display these characteristics rather than just repeat the rhetoric. Hearing and reading the narratives of a diverse range of leaders will teach us more and give us different ideas about leadership development interventions.

The other side of the coin from Sandeen's and colleagues' chapter is the issue of women in leadership in different cultural settings. Hayes Tang shares insights into the situation for women in East Asia in chapter 3. These insights have a ring of familiarity. They are very similar to what may have been said about women in leadership in Western higher education institutions a decade or two ago and indeed can still be the case. With the exception perhaps of Taiwan, the culture in East Asian universities is still one in which uninterrupted devotion to work implicitly discriminates against women, who take on most of the family and domestic responsibilities and do not want to give over their lives to academia. Within academia in the East Asian context it appears that the 'old-boys network culture' is alive and well which, of course, excludes women. There is a lack of transparency in promotion criteria and masculine models of communication, mentoring and leadership – providing few role models for the increasing numbers of young women entering higher education study. As Tang outlines, to progress in the academic world, women need to have family support, self-efficacy and determination. Interestingly and, perhaps not surprisingly, given their marginalized positions, women in East Asian countries are stronger advocates of equality, diversity and inclusiveness than their male colleagues.

While there has been a fairly strong focus on women in leadership in the literature pertaining to higher education, the voices and experiences of women who identify as lesbian are noticeable by their absence. There is actually little or no mention of the leadership opportunities or lack of opportunity for the LGBTQI community. There is still a high level of silence around this issue and the chapters in this book maintain that silence with the exception of Lorri Santamaría and Andre Santamaría who are not afraid to say/write the LGBTQI words! In their chapter 11, Santamaría and Santamaría give an example of how universities 'acknowledge' diversity – by setting up centers such as Learning Centers and LGBTQI Centers – but essentially from a deficit mindset, providing what is needed to give students who are lacking, rather than from a position of strength and asking what diverse students bring to the university. Lorri Santamaría and Andre Santamaría outline the grit and the gravitas of leadership and affirm the courage required to be an inclusive leader.

An article in the *Trusteeship Magazine* of the Association of Governing Boards of Universities and Colleges relating to the lack of discourse regarding leadership and the LGBTQI community written by Jeffrey Trammell (2014) tells us this:

I have often observed, while attending various gatherings of board members and presidents, passionate discussions of diversity, inclusion, and the representation of various university or college communities, regardless of the region. But I have heard barely a whisper about LGBT Americans. Is this a blind spot for the leadership of higher education in America?

When Virginia Governor Mark Warner (D) appointed me to the Board of Visitors of the College of William & Mary in 2005, I was not surprised to be the first openly gay trustee in the university's three centuries of existence. But I was most surprised to learn that I could find virtually no other openly gay or lesbian member of the boards of public universities across the nation.

He goes on to say:

It is also instructive to look beyond boards to presidents and top administrators. To what extent have well-qualified LGBT individuals been blocked from institutional leadership?

The author of this chapter can testify to the hostility to difference during interviews for senior positions in universities. No matter how good your curriculum vitae, no matter how persuasive the institution in encouraging one to attend for interviews for senior roles, that interview is over if you do not fit, for whatever reason, with the stereotypical image of a leader in higher education before a single question has been asked. If faced with such hostility, why would members of the LGBTQI community apply for a place in the senior leadership club?

Renowned researchers such as Christine Williams, famous for coining the phrases 'Glass Ceiling', and 'Glass Escalator' (Williams, 1992) and Alice Eagly who has carried out extensive research on gender in higher education (e.g., Eagly and Carli, 2007) are coming to the forefront on this and other issues that denote difference. In a recent publication Williams (2013) has revisited her seminal work on the glass escalator (1992), and recognized that we need to take into consideration factors other than gender when considering leadership. She has written of the problematic issue of the unwarranted universalising of white, middle-class American women's experiences when we examine women in leadership. Likewise Alice Eagly and Jean Lau Chin (Eagly and Chin, 2010) have re-stated the fact that our leadership models are primarily derived from traditional paradigms with little to say on diversity and difference. Eagly and Chin recognize that there is scant research on the shaping of leaders' behaviors by their potentially multi-identities as leaders and members of gender, racial, sexuality, ethnic or other identity groups. These researchers are acknowledging the lack of intersectionality analyses in leadership research to date.

Intersectionality (or intersectional theory) is a term first coined in 1989 by American civil rights advocate and leading scholar of critical race theory, Kimberlé Williams Crenshaw. It is the study of overlapping or *intersecting* social identities and related systems of oppression, domination or discrimination. Kirsten Locke in chapter 4 provides extensive coverage of the concept of intersectionality. Essentially, intersectionality seeks to examine how various bio-logical, social and cultural categories such as gender, race, class, ability, sexual orientation, religion, caste, age, nationality and other axes of identity interact on multiple and often simultaneous levels. Proponents of intersectional theory suggest that the framework can be used to understand how systemic injustice and social inequality occur on a multi-dimensional basis. While intersectionality is not an easy research paradigm, scholars of leadership should, without doubt, consider its relevance in the quest for deeper understandings of inclusive leadership. It would be a powerful means of higher education taking a lead in living up to the previously proposed moral purpose of higher education.

Inclusive Leadership, Social Forces, Cultural Context

Many of the chapter authors in this book write from the perspective of inclusion and inclusive leadership in very different cultural contexts. Brenda Leibowitz (chapter 9) and Mandla Makhanya (chapter 10) for example, very generously provide us with insights into the challenges of inclusive leadership in a charged period in the history of South African universities.

Brenda Leibowitz, in her very first sentence, expresses her bemusement at being invited to write a chapter for this book on the grounds of the relative lack of an inclusive ethos in higher education in South Africa, particularly in the sphere of learning and teaching. She is writing in the space and the place of that critical moment in 2015 when student protests erupted across South Africa. Through her chapter Leibowitz emphasizes that inclusive leadership is highly contextual in relation to space and time and that it is also embedded within social factors in the regional setting.

Mandla Makhanya gives strong recognition to the ongoing challenges post-apartheid of creating environments in which black students and staff feel a sense of belonging in all universities in South Africa. He explains the current social movements and discontent as fitting under a vast umbrella of 'decoloniality' and discusses the role universities play in the continuation of colonial ways of being, with their alien cultures and ongoing 'whiteness'. Mandla explains what it means to him to role model inclusive leadership in his institution in these turbulent times.

The racial tensions in universities in South Africa are a reflection of the ongoing deep divisions in society, the ghosts of the apartheid era still stalk the land. A curriculum still overly influenced by the colonial past fuels the perception and the reality of the lack of racial inclusiveness. The chapters from Leibowitz and Makhanya offer some hope that universities and university leaders can and must engage with the enormous challenge and address the grievances in meaningful and sustainable ways. It will be a long and arduous journey to achieve racial reconciliation and it must be a hope for us that universities and higher education can lead that journey and teach us more about what inclusive leadership means in volatile contexts.

Enakshi Sengupta describes the challenges for higher education leaders in Kyrgystan and Kurdistan to create inclusive learning environments in chapter 8. While scholarships for students with disabilities and orphans are provided, and financial aid for members of families of prisoners of war, these students are seen as getting benefits that other students do not – leading to that sense that what may seem inclusive to one group is seen as unfair to another. Enakshi examines the leadership in three universities, all with special circumstances those of us in the West do not fully understand or appreciate. An interesting and unique point in Enakshi's chapter is the charity discourse relating to students from backgrounds carved out by constant war. Students from certain socio-economic backgrounds are seen as 'victims' suffering incapacity and helplessness – so we can sort that by giving scholarships and reserving places for 'these' students. Inclusion may be the intention, exclusion the outcome.

In the three universities she details, it is interesting to note that there are two male leaders and one female. The two male leaders seem to indicate that context does not make any difference to how you lead. The female leader describes her leadership as adaptive to circumstance, in another example of the different skills women bring to leadership.

Eqbal Darandari from King Saud University details a difficult journey towards inclusion in a university in Saudi Arabia in chapter 7 and describes the journey as 'navigating through tough waves' which is a wonderful metaphor given that a general view of Saudi Arabia is its vast deserts! Eqbal Darandari also emphasizes that the context of inclusion varies among cultures, communities, countries and across time. This is a critical point that she makes and perhaps a sharp reminder that the 'inclusion discourse' cannot be the preserve of Western scholars. Darandari critiques the shift towards empowerment of Saudi nationals (Saudi-ization) through encouraging and promoting leadership. She takes us through the waves of change, one being the shift from non-Saudis essentially running all key businesses and educational organizations, to a period of creating inclusion and inclusive leadership for Saudis using her institution as a role model. She presents some very interesting demographics in Saudi Arabian universities, which some readers may find surprising. Eqbal also offers a range of inclusive leadership models and frameworks which could be used for measuring the level of inclusivity shown by organizations.

The University as Role Model for Society?

Universities, particularly those that receive public funding, have responsibilities not just within the corridors and lofty towers of academia but also to society at large. In New Zealand it is actually written into the 1989 Education Act that universities will act as the 'conscience and critic of society'. This privilege may not be articulated so clearly globally but at some level it is surely part of the moral purpose of higher education.

In chapter 12 John Anchan asserts that the degree of success of an institution's inclusivity and community depends on leadership and leaderful behaviors being promoted, valued and modelled across the entire enterprise. He evidences this through a case study detailing the university/community partnerships in a context not often opened up for scrutiny – that of working with the indigenous people of the land and community. Anchan's chapter makes one feel proud of what a university/community partnership can achieve, raises awareness of the challenge of recognising and 'permitting' culturally different approaches to leading and leadership and re-affirms the wider responsibility of universities to be role models within their communities.

In chapter 5 on distributed/distributive leadership, Cathy Gunn considers this paradigm to have a number of aims: to grow leadership capacity and future leaders, to support emergent leaders, and that more inclusive cultures and environments in higher education are a positive consequence of distributed leadership. The point she is subtly making is that this positive outcome is not highlighted in higher education as a key objective of distributed leadership. Through her case studies, key themes emerge including that distributed leadership acknowledges leaders and leadership irrespective of an individual's hierarchical positioning, that the leadership and concomitant responsibilities are negotiated not delegated and, importantly, a wider range of individuals can gain experience of what it means to be a leader and engage in leaderful practice. As Gunn explains, inclusion in the context of distributed leadership 'moves beyond the more commonly acknowledged aspects of diversity such as gender, sexuality, religion, ethnicity, or indigeneity. It also includes extrinsic aspects such as diversity of role, experience, level of appointment, and assignment of formal authority'.

Where To From Here?

What comes through strongly from the chapters in this book and the existing literature on inclusive leadership in higher education is that universities in the 21st century must acknowledge, value and promote diversity of leaders and leadership in all their different forms to reap the potential advantages. This is one of the most important challenges facing modern organizations, and the university as an entity is no exception to this. The traditional pale, male, stale hero leadership paradigm has no place in modern society with all its complexity. Likewise, regarding gender, we need to move beyond the narrow conception of white middle-class women's experiences in leadership. For scholars of leadership, intersectionality is a paradigm that needs to be brought to the foreground as a means of theorizing inclusive leadership. Those involved in designing leadership development programs need to move out of the comfort zone of examining and re-examining the traditional parameters of leadership which ignore equity and social justice. Culture, context, time, place and space are critical contours of inclusion and cannot be sidelined. The world is a global village and we should be preparing students for the multi-cultural, multi-dimensional future.

The chapter authors in this book have shown great courage in detailing their research, their observations and their experiences. We need to see more of that moral courage coming from those currently at the top, holding the most prestigious leadership positions in higher education. We need to see current leaders in higher education display the moral courage required to shift their collective capacity to preserve their own esteemed status and instead use that collective capacity to influence the future; to stop applying double and triple standards to anyone of difference, and show the humility we expect and want from leaders to reflect the diversity of the academic community, by opening the doors to leadership to those they have hitherto marginalized and sidelined.

References

Bennis, W., 2007. The challenges of leadership in the modern world: Introduction to the special issue. *American Psychologist*, 62(1), pp. 2–5.

Christy, K., 2016. 33 ways to define leadership. *Business News Daily*, [online] 5 April 2016. Available at: <http://www.businessnewsdaily.com/3647-leadership-definition.html> [Accessed 19 September 2016].

Chun, E. and Evans, A., 2011. Creating an inclusive leadership environment in higher education. *The Higher Education Workplace*, 3(2), pp. 21–24.

Cleveland, H., 1985. *The knowledge executive: Leadership in an information society*. New York: Dutton/Plume.

Crenshaw, K. W., 1989. Demarginalizing the intersection of race and sex: A black feminist critique of antidiscrimination doctrine, feminist theory and antiracist politics. *The University of Chicago Legal Forum*, 140, pp. 139–167.

Denver Foundation, 2016. Available at: <www.nonprofitinclusiveness.org/definitions-inclusiveness-and-inclusive-organisations> [Accessed 15 September 2016].

Eagly, A. H. and Carli, L. L., 2007. *Through the labyrinth: The truth about how women become leaders*. Boston, MA: Harvard Business School Press.

Eagly, A. H. and Chin, J. L., 2010. Diversity and leadership in a changing world. *American Psychologist*, 65(3), pp. 216–224.

Employers Network for Equality and Inclusion (ENEI), 2016. Available at: <http://www.enei.org.uk> [Accessed 19 September 2016].

Hansen, M., 2016. 33 ways to define leadership. *Business News Daily*, [online] 5 April 2016. Available at: <http://www.businessnewsdaily.com/3647-leadership-definition.html> [Accessed 19 September 2016].

Havergal, C., 2016. Elite universities 'going backwards' on widening access. *Times Higher Education*, [online] 18 February 2016. Available at: <http://www.timeshighereducation.com> [Accessed 20 September 2016].

Heasley, K., 2016. 33 ways to define leadership. *Business News Daily*, 5 April 2016. Available at: <http://www.businessnewsdaily.com/3647-leadership-definition.html> [Accessed 19 September 2016].

Kirkness, V. J. and Barnhardt, R., 2001. First nations and higher education: The four r's – respect, relevance, reciprocity, responsibility. Available at: <http://www.anjn.uaf.edu/IEW/winhec/FourRs2ndEd.html> [Accessed 19 September 2016].

Leadership Foundation for Higher Education (LFHE), 2016. Available at: <http://www.lfhe.ac.uk/> [Accessed 19 September 2016].

Madsen, S., 2012. Women and leadership in higher education: Current realities, challenges and future directions. *Advances in Developing Human Resources*, 14(2), pp. 131–139.

Marklein, M. B., 2016. There are so many leaders we don't see: Transformative leadership. *University World News*, 26 June, 2016. Available at: <http://www.universityworldnews.com/publications/archives.php?mode=archives.php?mode=archive*pub=1&issueno=419&format=html> [Accessed 20 September 2016].

New Zealand Education Act, 1989. Available at: <http://www.legislation.govt.nz/act/public/1989/latest/DLM175959> [Accessed 12 September 2016].

Nidiffer, J., 2010. Overview: Women as leaders in academia. In: O'Connor, K., ed. *Gender and women's leadership: A handbook,* Vol 11. Thousand Oaks, CA: Sage, pp. 555–564.

Oxford Dictionary, 2016. Inclusive definition. Available at: <https://en.oxforddictionaries.com/definition/inclusive> [Accessed 19 September 2016].

Schwartz, S., 2003. The higher purpose. *Times Higher Education*, 16 May 2003. Available at: <https://www.timeshighereducation.com/comment/columnists/the-higher-purpose/176727.article> [Accessed 19 September 2016].

Shields, C. M., 2016. The promise of transformative leadership. *University World News*, 6 May 2016. Available at: <http://www.universityworldnews.com/article.php?story=20160503141549626> [Accessed 10 September 2016].

Stefani, L., 2015. Democratizing higher education: The land of the long white cloud. In: Blessinger, P. and Anchan, J., eds. *Democratizing higher education: International comparative perspectives*. New York and Oxfordshire, UK: Routledge, pp. 111–124.

Trammell, J. B., 2014. LGBT challenges in higher education today: 5 core principles for success. *Trusteeship Magazine*, May/June 2014. Available at: <http://agb.org/trusteeship/2014/5/lgbt-challenges-higher-education-today-5-core-principles-success> [Accessed 10 September 2016].

Treaty of Waitangi – Te Ara Encyclopaedia of New Zealand. 2016. Available at: <http://teara.govt.nz/en/treaty-of-waitangi> [Accessed 12 June 2017].

University of Auckland, n.d. Mission and values. Available at: <https://www.auckland.ac.nz/en/about/the-university/mission-and-values.html> [Accessed 19 September 2016].

Williams, C. L., 1992. The glass escalator: Hidden advantages for men in the 'female' professions. *Social Problems*, 39(3), pp. 253–267.

Williams, C. L., 2013. The glass escalator, revisited: Gender inequality in neoliberal times. *Gender and Society*, 27(5), pp. 609–629.

CONTRIBUTORS

John P. Anchan is Professor of Education and Associate Dean of the Faculty of Education, University of Winnipeg, Canada. He has served as Director of Education, Executive Director of the University's Centre for Teaching, Learning & Technology, Acting Dean of the Faculty and past-President of HETL. Besides journal articles, his books include *Exploring the Role of the Internet in Global Education* (primary author and co-authored with S. Halli; NY: Edwin Mellen Press); *Change Forces in Post-Communist Central Europe: Education in Transition* (co-edited with M. Fullan and E. Polyzoi; Toronto: RoutledgeFalmer Press); and *Democratizing Higher Education: International Comparative Perspectives* (co-edited with P. Blessinger; NY: Routledge).

Patrick Blessinger is adjunct Professor of Education at St. John's University, a STEM educator with the New York State Education Department, and founder and chief research scientist of the International Higher Education Teaching and Learning Association (in consultative status with the United Nations). Dr. Blessinger is the editor and author of many books and articles and he is a contributing writer and analyst for several global educational news outlets such as The Hechinger Report and University World News. He teaches courses in education, leadership, and research methods. Dr. Blessinger has received several educational awards such as Fulbright Senior Scholar to Denmark (U.S. Department of State) and Governor's Teaching Fellow for the State of Georgia, USA.

Christine K. Cavanaugh teaches human resource management and leadership for the University of Maryland University College, and higher education leadership and ethics for Immaculata University. Her scholarly work focuses on women's leadership and she co-edited *Aging in America* (2010). Chris received her

Bachelor of Science degree in management from the University of Maryland, and her MBA and EdD from the University of West Florida. Dr. Cavanaugh is also President and Certified Executive Coach for Pathseekers II, Inc., a consulting company focused on coaching and executive, board, and senior management development; conducting assessments and evaluations; improving human performance technology; conducting workshops/retreats; and facilitating strategic planning. Her certifications include Senior Professional in Human Resources (SPHR), Curricular Practical Training (CPT) and ACC.

Eqbal Z. Darandari is a consultant in the field of measurement, statistics, program evaluation, and quality assurance for public and higher education in Saudi Arabia. Eqbal currently works as a consultant with the National Commission for Academic Accreditation and Assessment (NCAAA). She has held numerous positions at King Saud University and particularly specializes in the area of quality assurance and enhancement. She presents numerous workshops and training in the field of quality and evaluation in Saudi Arabia and abroad. She has also directed several quality and development projects for Saudi universities and offered consultations. She is a member of several professional bodies globally and locally, such as board member of the Measurement and Evaluation Association and of the Public Education Evaluation Commission in Saudi Arabia.

Fiona Denney is currently Director of the Brunel Educational Excellence Centre – a centre launched in 2014 at Brunel University London to enhance learning and teaching support for both staff and students. She is a member of the Executive Committee of the UK Council for Graduate Education and a Principal Fellow of the Higher Education Academy. Fiona has worked in UK universities for 20 years. Her primary interest is academic leadership and how universities can support their academic and research staff better to deal with the many challenges they encounter. In 2015, Fiona led a group funded by the Leadership Foundation for Higher Education to carry out research into the experiences of academic leaders in order to provide an experiential insight into leadership development.

Deborah Ford serves as Chancellor of the University of Wisconsin-Parkside. Prior to 2009, when she joined UW-Parkside, Dr. Ford served as Vice President for Student Affairs at the University of West Florida, and Vice President for Student Affairs and Dean of Students at Spalding University (Kentucky). Dr. Ford holds her Bachelor of Science from the University of Louisville, her Master of Education from Indiana University, and her Doctor of Education from the University of Louisville.

Corey Gin is the Founding Director for the Leadership and Employee Enrichment Program (LEEP) at California State University, East Bay. The LEEP

Program is a presidential initiative to address the needs of all staff at CSU East Bay. As a talent management consultant, Corey seeks to address the unique leadership challenges that public higher education organizations currently face. His experience as an educational technology leader is central to helping create new opportunities for others throughout the organization. Prior to his work at CSU East Bay, Corey was the director for California Technology Assistance Project (CTAP) – Region V, a regional branch of a statewide organization responsible for integrating technology into K12 schools/districts. Corey was responsible for leading his organization to create and maintain professional development and support for three focus areas: online/hybrid learning; 21st century classrooms; and local, state, and federal grants. His passion is to promote and support diversity and inclusion, beyond the rhetoric to meaningful action.

Cathy Gunn is Deputy Director of the Centre for Learning and Research in Higher Education (CLeaR) at the University of Auckland. Cathy was the Head of e-Learning within CLeaR from 2007–2015. Cathy has developed a portfolio of more than 100 scholarly publications in 25 years working in the tertiary education sector. She is an active member of international learning technology networks including ACODE (Australasian Council on Open, Distance and e-Learning) and ASCILITE (Australasian Society for Computers in Learning and Tertiary Education). In 2009 ASCILITE presented Cathy with a Life Member Award after she had served two terms as President.

Hei-hang Hayes Tang is Assistant Professor of Education Policy at the Education University of Hong Kong. A sociologist, he is interested in the fields of education policy, the academic profession, and youth studies. The notions of democratization in education, scholarship of application, and academic entrepreneurialism inform his current research projects. A hard problem in social science that Hayes has been engaging in is possible solutions to educating a meaningful citizenship for Hong Kong's young generation. Upon invitation, he delivered a Fulbright-Hays seminar entitled "Seeing China's Governance from Hong Kong Youth Perspective" for a delegation of American school teachers during their visit to the University of Hong Kong in August 2015.

Brenda Leibowitz is Chair: Teaching and Learning, in the Faculty of Education at the University of Johannesburg. Her key role in the university is to support the scholarship of teaching and learning amongst academics. She is presently convenor of the Teaching Advancement at University (TAU) Fellowships Programme and convenor of the South African Universities Learning and Teaching (SAULT) Forum. She holds a PhD in Education from the University of Sheffield. Her research interests include the scholarship of teaching and learning, social justice, practice-based approaches to learning, and professional learning.

Kirsten Locke is Senior Lecturer in the School of Critical Studies of Education, Faculty of Education and Social Work at the University of Auckland. Her research explores educational issues through philosophical lenses. Kirsten was a 2016 recipient of the Early Career Research Excellence Awards at the University of Auckland. She was also the recipient of the Philosophy of Education Society of Australasia (PESA) Doctoral award in 2009, the Faculty of Education Early Career Excellence in Teaching award in 2012, the 2016 School of Critical Studies awardee for innovation in teaching, and her doctoral thesis was placed on the Dean's List for excellence in research in 2011. Kirsten is currently Associate Dean Teaching and Learning at the Faculty of Education and Social Work. She leads a comparative research project exploring gendered career trajectories in Danish and New Zealand universities with co-researchers at Aarhus University.

Mandla Makhanya was appointed Principal and Vice Chancellor of the University of South Africa on 1 January 2011 and is a prominent scholar in higher education leadership and advocacy. Professor Makhanya is Treasurer of the African Council for Distance Education (ACDE) and has recently been appointed President of the International Council for Distance Education (ICDE). He is Deputy Chairperson of the South African National Commission for UNESCO and Chairperson of the Culture Sector of the South African National Commission for UNESCO. In 2007 the University of Athabasca in Canada conferred upon him a PhD (Honoris Causa) in recognition of his outstanding leadership at Unisa and his contribution as a distinguished scholar in distance education. Professor Makhanya is currently Vice President of the Higher Education Teaching and Learning Association (HETL).

Cathy Sandeen is Chancellor of the University of Wisconsin Colleges and University of Wisconsin-Extension. She oversees 13 two-year liberal arts transfer institutions and UW Colleges Online as well as UW-Extension, which includes continuing and professional education, cooperative extension, public broadcasting, and business and entrepreneurship programs. Cathy's remit encompasses 2,400 faculty and staff, 13,000 students, and 1.5 million public contacts per year. An educational innovator, Dr. Sandeen previously served as Vice President for Education Attainment and Innovation at the American Council on Education in Washington, DC. She has also held several positions within the University of California System, including Dean at UCLA.

Andrés P. Santamaría is Lecturer in Educational Leadership at the School of Education, Auckland University of Technology, New Zealand. Dr. Santamaría's area of expertise is leadership for diversity and his research interests range from leadership for social justice and educational equity to principal efficacy in underperforming schools. Andrés currently serves on an interdisciplinary, cross-cultural team of scholars in partnership with the Maori Achievement Collaborative

(MAC), a network of approximately 60 Maori and non-Maori mainstream school principals throughout Aotearoa, New Zealand. The focus of this research project is to support, engage, improve, and promote culturally responsive leadership practices for improving 'Maori student success as Maori'. He is Co-editor of *Culturally Responsive Leadership in Higher Education: Promoting Access, Equity and Improvement* published by Routledge in 2016.

Lorri J. Santamaría is Associate Professor of Educational Leadership at the Faculty of Education and Social Work, University of Auckland. Dr. Santamaría engages scholarly writing and research in the areas of Pre-K–HE leadership for social justice and educational equity including diversity for educational improvement. In her research she interrogates the roles and intersectionalities of race, sexuality, language, gender, and exceptionality in leadership and learning. Lorri's collaborative cross-cultural research platform addresses the needs of systemically underserved peoples in the USA, as well as Maori and Pacifika communities in the Auckland Metro area. She is lead editor of *Culturally Responsive Leadership in Higher Education: Promoting Access, Equity and Improvement* published by Routledge in 2016.

Enakshi Sengupta is working as Assistant Professor at the American University of Kurdistan. Enakshi obtained a PhD from the University of Nottingham (UK) on the topic of Research in Higher Education. Prior to this she obtained the qualification of MBA (with merit) from the University of Nottingham and a master's level degree in English Literature from Calcutta University, India. Her research focuses primarily on the topic of inclusion. Her specific interests include: integration of racially diverse student communities; curricular changes to incorporate integration in the classroom situation; strategizing and creating scorecards to measure levels of integration; refugee education; in-group and out-group integration in higher education as an aftermath of racial hatred and genocide.

Lorraine Stefani is Professor of Higher Education Strategic Engagement at the University of Auckland. At the time of writing she holds the position of President of HETL, the Higher Education Teaching and Learning Association. She is a Senior Fellow of both the Staff and Educational Development Association (UK) and the Higher Education Academy (UK). She is also an accredited leadership coach. Professor Stefani is a member of the Senior Women in Leadership Group at the University of Auckland. She has published widely on topical issues including leadership in higher education and evaluation of academic development in addition to a range of issues pertinent to the 21st century learning organization.

APPENDIX 1

Full list of scholarships and grants provided at the American University of Central Asia

Financial Aid for Students with Disabilities: Amount: up to 90 percent tuition – Available to applicants who are accepted into one of AUCA's programs as full-time students, maintain an overall GPA of at least 2.7 (as an existing student), can demonstrate financial need, and have a disability category of 1 or 2.

Orphan Awards: Amount: up to 90 percent tuition – Available to applicants who are accepted into one of AUCA's programs as full-time students, maintain an overall GPA of at least 2.7 (as an existing student), and can demonstrate financial need.

Open Society Institute (OSI) Scholarships: These scholarships are awarded to Commonwealth of Independent States (CIS) applicants admitted to AUCA with competitive entrance exam scores and who have a demonstrated financial need. The number of scholarships is based on the pool of applicants and the availability of funds.

Full Scholarships: Full scholarships ($500 of the tuition is to be paid by the student, housing allowance and stipend are provided). The number of full scholarships depends on the availability of funds. Scholarship eligibility review is performed annually before a new academic year.

Partial Scholarships: Partial Scholarships ($2,000 of tuition is to be paid by the student). The number of partial scholarships depends on the availability of funds. A partial scholarship may include housing allowance and stipend, if the grant allows. Recipients of partial scholarships with housing allowance and stipend are selected on the basis of demonstrated financial need. This award is automatically renewable as long as the student maintains an overall GPA of at least 2.7.

Higher Education Support Program (HESP) Scholarships: (three cohorts, ten female students each). These are awarded to female applicants from Afghanistan. The grant supports one academic year in the AUCA Preparatory Program. If the student is admitted and is enrolled in one of the AUCA bachelor's degree programs she will be provided with a full scholarship (free tuition, housing allowance and stipend) covering a full undergraduate study program. Applications should be made directly to AUCA.

Scholarships from the US: Central Asian Educational Foundation (CAEF): Amount: 100 percent – These scholarships are granted for eight semesters to first-year students of the Business Administration program and Economics program. This aid is provided to Central Asian students who have excelled at the entrance examinations and come from disadvantaged families. Applications should be made directly to CAEF.

Aga Khan Foundation Scholarships: These scholarships are administered directly by the donor organization.

US Embassy Scholarships for applicants from Tajikistan: The US Embassy awards scholarships (full tuition, housing allowance and stipend) for Tajik students for eight semesters at AUCA. Two full and one partial scholarship for undergraduate study and two scholarships for the Preparatory Program are offered. (<https://www.auca.kg/en/need-based/>)

President's Scholarship: Up to five students from the President's list are eligible for the President's Scholarship. Each student receives a cash prize up to $500. (The President's list is only for fourth-year students. To win a place on the President's list, a student must have earned at least 108 credits with a cumulative GPA of at least 3.8 and have received no Fs or Xs.) (<https://www.auca.kg/en/p7713290/>)

Scholarships from donors

Hersh Chadha Journalism Scholarship – 40 percent tuition scholarship for students pursuing degrees in journalism and mass communications.

Mary Schweitzer Scholarship – $1,500–$2,000 tuition scholarship for students pursuing degrees in Anthropology.

Bank of Asia Scholarship – $1,000 tuition scholarship and internship at Bank of Asia. Available to students from the Kyrgyz Republic (outside Bishkek). (<https://www.auca.kg/en/merit-based/>)

INDEX

When the text is within a table, the number span is in italic.
When the text is within a note, this is indicated by page number, 'n', note number.

Taylor & Francis eBooks

Helping you to choose the right eBooks for your Library

Add Routledge titles to your library's digital collection today. Taylor and Francis ebooks contains over 50,000 titles in the Humanities, Social Sciences, Behavioural Sciences, Built Environment and Law.

Choose from a range of subject packages or create your own!

Benefits for you

» Free MARC records
» COUNTER-compliant usage statistics
» Flexible purchase and pricing options
» All titles DRM-free.

Benefits for your user

» Off-site, anytime access via Athens or referring URL
» Print or copy pages or chapters
» Full content search
» Bookmark, highlight and annotate text
» Access to thousands of pages of quality research at the click of a button.

REQUEST YOUR **FREE** INSTITUTIONAL TRIAL TODAY

Free Trials Available
We offer free trials to qualifying academic, corporate and government customers.

eCollections – Choose from over 30 subject eCollections, including:

Archaeology	Language Learning
Architecture	Law
Asian Studies	Literature
Business & Management	Media & Communication
Classical Studies	Middle East Studies
Construction	Music
Creative & Media Arts	Philosophy
Criminology & Criminal Justice	Planning
Economics	Politics
Education	Psychology & Mental Health
Energy	Religion
Engineering	Security
English Language & Linguistics	Social Work
Environment & Sustainability	Sociology
Geography	Sport
Health Studies	Theatre & Performance
History	Tourism, Hospitality & Events

For more information, pricing enquiries or to order a free trial, please contact your local sales team: www.tandfebooks.com/page/sales

 Routledge Taylor & Francis Group | The home of Routledge books

www.tandfebooks.com